Especially for

....

From

....

Date

....

DAILY WISDOM

WISDOM

FOR MEN

— 2022 —

DEVOTIONAL COLLECTION

BARBOUR
PUBLISHING

Print ISBN 978-1-63609-002-3; 978-1-63609-263-8

eBook Editions:
Adobe Digital Edition (.epub) 978-1-63609-221-8
Kindle and MobiPocket Edition (.prc) 978-1-63609-222-5

Cover Design 978-1-63609-002-3: Greg Jackson, Thinkpen Design

Published by Barbour Publishing, Inc., 1810 Barbour Drive, Uhrichsville, Ohio 44683, www.barbourbooks.com

Our mission is to inspire the world with the life-changing message of the Bible.

Member of the
Evangelical Christian
Publishers Association

Printed in China.

INTRODUCTION

Happy New Year! And welcome to the 2022 edition of *Daily Wisdom for Men*!

The key word for this year's *Daily Wisdom for Men* is *unshakable*. One of the Bible's important themes is the unshakable nature of God. He is steadfast, unwavering, and immovable in all His ways—in other words, a God on whom you can fully depend!

In Ephesians 5:1 (NIV), the apostle Paul encourages his readers to "follow God's example." That means a lot of things, one of which is that we Christian men are to live our lives of faith unshakably. Even though the world around us is being shaken in many ways, seemingly every day, God wants us to remain unshaken and unshakable.

The inspiration for this year's daily devotionals is taken from each day's scripture readings in our popular "Read Thru the Bible in a Year Plan," which you can find at the end of this book. The plan will help you read the daily Bible passages and then spend a few minutes reading that day's devotional writing.

God wants to grow you into a man of unshakable faith, unshakable love, and unshakable obedience. It is the hope of the men who wrote this year's *Daily Wisdom for Men* devotion, as well as the people at Barbour Publishing, that God will use your daily Bible reading, as well as the writings in this book, to help make you the unshakable man the Lord wants you to be.

The Editors

HOW WILL YOU
BEGIN THE NEW YEAR?

*Blessed is the one who does not walk in step with the wicked or stand
in the way that sinners take or sit in the company of mockers, but whose
delight is in the law of the LORD, and who meditates on his law day
and night. That person is like a tree planted by streams of water.*

PSALM 1:1–3 NIV*

◆──────◆──────◆

What if you were to begin this new year with this simple question:
What do I delight in? According to Psalm 1, your delight plays a
major part in determining your destiny for this coming year.

If you keep company with those who mock what is good, who indulge
their every craving, or who live their lives in opposition to God's goodness,
then you will find yourself far from God and from God's blessing. Such
company is unstable and blows along with the latest winds of desire. There
is no root or depth, as life is consumed with the moment, leaving tomorrow
hanging in the uncertainty of the wind.

Conversely, if you delight in the teachings of the Lord and keep them on
your mind, you have firm roots that offer stability and the blessing of God.
You'll find a secure place to face the highs and lows of life as they unfold in
the coming year.

---

*Lord, help me to see the wisdom of delighting in Your Word
at the beginning and end of each day.*

*A Read through the Bible in a Year plan that follows each devotion can be found at the back of this book.

GOD SEEKS THE DISOBEDIENT

*When the cool evening breezes were blowing, the man and
his wife heard the LORD God walking about in the garden.
So they hid from the LORD God among the trees. Then the
LORD God called to the man, "Where are you?"*

GENESIS 3:8–9 NLT

◆ ◆ ◆

As Adam and Eve hid from God in the cool of the evening, they feared
that all had been lost in paradise. How could they face God knowing
they had disobeyed a clear, direct command? The good news is that God
sought them out, restoring their relationship despite their disobedience and
their own sense of shame that sent them into hiding.

Throughout this new year, you will surely have highs and lows, and you will
even face moments of shame and disappointment over your actions—whether
from the present moment or from your past. Shame can give way to guilt
and fear, leaving you hiding from a loving God who desires to restore you.

Standing out in the open before God in a spirit of repentance and
hopefulness may feel like the last thing you want to do when bearing such a
burden of guilt. Yet God is seeking you, even today, wanting nothing more
than to restore you.

*Father, I confess that I have failed and disobeyed Your commands.
But I look to You in hope that You can restore me to a relationship with You.*

REPENTANCE SHOULD BE VISIBLE AND CURRENT

"Bear fruit in keeping with repentance. And do not presume to say to yourselves, 'We have Abraham as our father,' for I tell you, God is able from these stones to raise up children for Abraham."

MATTHEW 3:8–9 ESV

◆———◆———◆

John the Baptist wanted his listeners to know that past faithfulness and accomplishments were not a guarantee of future obedience or blessing. The religious leaders in particular were especially confident in their position based on their past recognition and status as religious guides. Yet God was more concerned with their hearts and the actions they took in the present.

This is a trap you can fall into all too easily—assuming your past faithfulness or position within a religious group is a sign of your security in the future. These external markings are meaningless when it comes to God's blessings. How you live today will be far more important.

John the Baptist was more interested in questions like these: Have you repented of your failures? Are you aware of your weaknesses? Are you willing to change how you live?

If you choose to live in obedience to God, the visible fruit of that choice will be a changed life, not just a title or a position within a group.

Father, I repent of my poor choices and self-serving actions, and I ask that You would change my heart and desires so that I live according to Your direction.

WHAT SUSTAINS YOU?

*The tempter came to him and said, "If you are the Son of
God, tell these stones to become bread." Jesus answered,
"It is written: 'Man shall not live on bread alone, but on
every word that comes from the mouth of God.' "*
MATTHEW 4:3–4 NIV

I n Jesus' moment of physical weakness, the tempter tried to instill doubt in
His mind. How would Jesus respond to a challenge to prove that He was
God's beloved Son? The trick linked both His physical and spiritual hunger
as He longed both for food and for God's support in His time of trial.

How do you handle moments of discouragement, doubt, or even weakness?
It's certainly a temptation to demand some kind of proof from God. At the very
least, you surely want a solution to your problem—a concrete fix for the short
term that also assures you of God's presence and care. Yet your relationship
with God amounts to more than answers to prayer or proof of His care.
Seeing the short-term fix won't really lead to abundant life in the long run.

Jesus promised that you can rest in the promises of God, the scriptures,
and even the ways God may be revealed through your situation. This is where
long-term perseverance and hope come from.

*Father, I trust You to guide and support me,
even when I pass through times of want.*

WHEN IS THE *BEST* TIME TO PRAY?

*Listen to my cry for help, my King and my God, for I pray
to no one but you. Listen to my voice in the morning, LORD.
Each morning I bring my requests to you and wait expectantly.*
PSALM 5:2–3 NLT

◆———◆———◆

There technically isn't a "best" time to pray. Anytime you seek God is a good time. Yet the writers of scripture often mention one time for prayer as a choice that is far more common than any other: the morning. Why would the morning come up so often as an ideal time for prayer?

Consider how each day begins with the typically quiet moments at dawn. Then televisions chatter, cars fill the roads, smartphones buzz, and calendars fill up. Responsibilities increase, ideas flood your mind, and you end up moving from one task to another. It may feel like the list of things to do will never end—until you crash on the couch or in your bed at the end of the day.

It's no mistake that the psalmist seeks God early in the morning, making requests of Him in a moment of quiet and focus. Nothing else is pressing at that moment except attention to God. This quiet time of prayer in the morning is a moment of waiting, a patient expectation for a loving and present God.

*Jesus, help me to wait patiently and expectantly
as I trust You with the requests on my mind.*

JESUS ASKS FOR MORE THAN THE BARE MINIMUM

*"For if you love those who love you, what reward do you
have? Do not even the tax collectors do the same? And if
you greet only your brothers, what more are you doing
than others? Do not even the Gentiles do the same?"*

MATTHEW 5:46–47 ESV

◆───────◆───────◆

J esus asked His followers to learn from His example and to rely on God's presence in their lives to help them love people who are offensive, mean, and even hostile. This call to love enemies recognizes that the source of love is beyond what they can see or think on their own.

Consider the source of love for people who love you, take care of you, and support you. The relationship itself helps to generate the love. It is reciprocated between two people. Even the most corrupt or self-serving people find people around them to share their love and affection. They recognize the need for relationships and a support network. There is nothing wrong with love on these terms, but it doesn't amount to the higher calling that Jesus modeled.

As you encounter people who are hostile or offensive toward you, Jesus asks you to rely on His love and mercy to get by. You can't rely on a reciprocal relationship here. Without God's support, love will be all but impossible.

*Jesus, help me to love others with the grace
and mercy You have showed to all.*

ARE YOU TOO BUSY FOR GOD?

*The LORD said to Abraham, "Why did Sarah laugh and say,
'Shall I indeed bear a child, now that I am old?' Is anything too
hard for the LORD? At the appointed time I will return to you,
about this time next year, and Sarah shall have a son."*

GENESIS 18:13–14 ESV

This important exchange between God and Abraham only happened because Abraham made time for God. When Abraham saw the travelers walking in the heat of the day, he dropped everything and humbled himself to care for their needs. Can you imagine how this story would have played out if Abraham and Sarah had decided they already had enough on their plates?

This story of God's promise is an invitation to consider how you can make space to notice Him, to listen, and to be aware of what's around you. Would Abraham and Sarah have had a chance to hear this message from the Lord if they had focused only on their own concerns for the day?

You may feel like your life is full of important tasks and priorities, but taking time to listen to God is essential. Is it possible to be so focused on the good things in front of you that you miss the message of God or the answer to your prayers?

*Lord, help me to stop and listen,
waiting patiently for Your response to my prayers.*

WHAT ARE YOU STORING UP FOR YOURSELF?

"But store up for yourselves treasures in heaven, where moths and vermin do not destroy, and where thieves do not break in and steal."
MATTHEW 6:20 NIV

Jesus knew that every person is trying to store something or hold on to something for the future. In His day, the religious leaders tried to hold on to the praise and admiration of the public. Even His own disciples argued over who was the greatest and who would sit at the right hand of Jesus.

What are you holding on to today? What are you trying to store up for the future? There's a good chance that you want to be regarded well by others, to have some financial security, and to have a measure of certainty about the future. Yet these goals and desires can get in the way of the treasure God wants to give you.

There is a different kind of treasure you can store up and hold on to, trusting that God will reward your obedience and the grace you show toward others. The certainty you seek can be converted into faith in God, and this faith is what He promises to reward. Yet these rewards remain unseen and even unknown. You don't know exactly what your reward will be, but if you look to Jesus in faith, God has promised to reward you.

Jesus, help me to live my life in faith,
trusting in the rewards You have stored up in heaven.

DOES PRAYER ACTUALLY WORK?

*"So if you sinful people know how to give good gifts
to your children, how much more will your heavenly
Father give good gifts to those who ask him."*
MATTHEW 7:11 NLT

◆――――◆――――◆

Parents care deeply for their children and give them good gifts, but that doesn't necessarily mean they can or will give their kids everything they ask for each day. Even when the answer isn't "no," it very often may be "wait."

Although not a perfect or comprehensive image of prayer, the concept of parents and children helped Jesus convey to His listeners both the concern of God for His people and the more complex dynamics at work in prayer that go beyond telling Him, "Give me what I want!"

Do you even know whether you're asking for something that is good for you? Jesus is inviting you to think of prayer as a relationship with a caring God who wants to give you good things, much like a parent would give a child good things. Consequently, this means God sometimes gives you what you didn't ask for and not what you think you need. That simple explanation hardly captures all of your disappointments or struggles in prayer, but it does offer you encouragement to pray with greater hope and expectation.

*Father, I trust that You are a loving parent
who wants me to pray in faith and hope.*

WHERE DO YOU TURN?

The LORD is a refuge for the oppressed, a stronghold in
times of trouble. Those who know your name trust in you,
for you, LORD, have never forsaken those who seek you.
PSALM 9:9–10 NIV

W hy are some people oppressed and others aren't? Do they have less money? Do they look different?

People who are oppressed and marginalized are forgotten by the powerful, who are only aware of their own advancement, wealth, and power. Injustice and oppression go hand in hand, as any means to keep undesirable people out of the way is considered acceptable.

While some people may forget or even oppress others for the sake of their own gain, the Lord won't forget the people who suffer the most. While everyone else in society may turn away from the most unwanted people, the Lord offers them the refuge of His immediate presence. Those seeking the presence of the Lord may find Him closest to the people most likely to be forgotten.

Even more importantly, the Lord is attentive to people who seek Him. No one is forgotten or marginalized before God. All people have equal access to Him. Trusting in God's name is all that is required.

Lord, help me to see people who are
forgotten and care for them the way You do.

WHO WILL BE BLESSED BECAUSE OF YOU?

"I will multiply your offspring as the stars of heaven and will give to your offspring all these lands. And in your offspring all the nations of the earth shall be blessed, because Abraham obeyed my voice and kept my charge, my commandments, my statutes, and my laws."

GENESIS 26:4–5 ESV

◆───◆───◆

Abraham and his family made a number of difficult moves at a time of extreme danger and uncertainty—with threats of famine and attack by nearby rulers and kings looming each year. After leaving his family of origin far behind, Abraham chose to depend fully on the Lord, keep His commands, and seek His direction throughout his life. He had an opportunity to more fully experience God's presence and blessing because of his choices. Yet Abraham wasn't the only one who benefited. Generations to come enjoyed his blessings as well.

There are many reasons for you to obey the Lord today and to seek Him for your own benefit and blessing. Of course, those benefits and blessings are not a guarantee. You can just as easily choose to go your own way and try to achieve your desired outcomes on your own. But the truth is faith and obedience really do matter—day in, day out. The result will come down to whether you live by faith or only by what you can see.

Jesus, help me to live by faith so that everyone around me can enjoy Your blessings.

WILL GOD NOTICE WHAT'S WRONG?

*Why does the wicked man revile God? Why does he say to himself,
"He won't call me to account"? But you, God, see the trouble of the
afflicted; you consider their grief and take it in hand. The victims
commit themselves to you; you are the helper of the fatherless.*

PSALM 10:13–14 NIV

G od's attention to the misdeeds of the wicked and the suffering of the afflicted is a common theme throughout the psalms. It's assumed that you will live differently if you believe that God takes notice of your misdeeds. Meanwhile, suffering and affliction will be made bearable if you expect God to notice and bring relief, or at least reward your perseverance.

Of the many reasons someone sins, one is surely the belief that God isn't watching and won't call anyone to account for his conduct. Yet today's psalm can assure you that God will hold the wicked to account for their actions and that He will also take notice of those who are suffering affliction and loss.

God sees those who suffer and who don't have advocates. This should serve as a reminder for you to notice them as well. If God is the helper of the fatherless, God's people surely should do the same.

*Father, help me to see and to support the
people who are afflicted and forgotten.*

IF YOUR SOUL IS SICK, JESUS CAME FOR YOU

When Jesus heard this, he said, "Healthy people don't need a doctor—sick people do." Then he added, "Now go and learn the meaning of this Scripture: 'I want you to show mercy, not offer sacrifices.' For I have come to call not those who think they are righteous, but those who know they are sinners."

MATTHEW 9:12–13 NLT

◆————◆————◆

At a time when the majority of the people of Israel longed for a powerful king and a righteous judge to banish sinners from the land, Jesus offered a different path toward holiness and healing. Rather than presenting Himself as a judge or as a ruler who would separate the sinners from the holy, He showed up as a doctor who actively sought out the "sick" who had been infected with sin. He desired to heal people and restore them to spiritual health so that they could live in God's kingdom.

When you sin, you may want to hide from God in shame. Sin can hang over your head like a guilty sentence in court, where a righteous judge threatens to send you away. Such a mindset is far removed from what Jesus embodied and spoke of when He met sinners. Jesus' only requirement of people was confession—a humble realization that they were sinful people who needed God's healing power in their lives.

Jesus, I confess my faults and failures,
trusting that You can heal and restore me today.

WHAT PROMPTS THE LORD TO TAKE ACTION?

"Because the poor are plundered and the needy groan, I will now arise," says the LORD. "I will protect them from those who malign them." And the words of the LORD are flawless, like silver purified in a crucible, like gold refined seven times.

PSALM 12:5–6 NIV

What does the Lord notice? What prompts Him to arise and take action? Today's psalm says that the plight of the poor is among God's top priorities. When the poor are slandered, plundered, and calling out in their grief, He takes notice and even takes action to protect them. Those who mistreat the poor or slander them place themselves against God and against the pure words of the Lord that promise deliverance one day.

You have surely heard accusations and slander against the poor, the second-guessing of their ability, motivation, or education. What do you make of such statements? If you hope to imitate the Lord, then your first instinct should be to protect the poor, to speak up for them, and to offer help whenever possible. Such a pledge from the Lord to help the poor isn't a statement to take lightly. The word of the Lord is pure and refined, calling you to the highest ideals of love and service.

Father, help me to see the suffering of the poor and to take action in accordance with Your holy Word.

GOD TREASURES HIS PEOPLE

"What is the price of two sparrows—one copper coin? But not a single sparrow can fall to the ground without your Father knowing it. And the very hairs on your head are all numbered."
MATTHEW 10:29–30 NLT

I t's impossible to keep track of how many birds fly past you in a given day. They appear to be beyond counting. And even if you could keep track of the birds in your location, you have things to do and responsibilities. If a bird dies, that's hardly your concern. Life must go on.

When describing God's love and concern for you, Jesus adopted an expansive image of God's deep love and concern for all of creation. Just as God the Father knows when a single bird falls to the ground, He also knows the smallest details about you and your well-being.

Such an assurance can give you an unshakable confidence in God the Father's deep love for you. He is attentive to the slightest losses and moments of grief in your life. You won't be overlooked. There's no such thing as God the Father being too busy to notice you or forgetting what your needs are. If even the hairs on your head are numbered, then surely He knows exactly what you need in each moment.

Father, I will rest today in Your present love that is fully aware of the highs and lows of my life.

HOW BADLY DO YOU WANT GOD'S BLESSING?

Then he said, "Let me go, for the day has broken." But Jacob said, "I will not let you go unless you bless me." And he said to him, "What is your name?" And he said, "Jacob." Then he said, "Your name shall no longer be called Jacob, but Israel, for you have striven with God and with men, and have prevailed."

GENESIS 32:26–28 ESV

◆ ◆ ◆

It may be odd to think of Jacob actually wrestling with God and even demanding a blessing. Whether or not Jacob actually knew who he was wrestling against, there is no doubt that he considered his opponent holy and righteous enough to bestow a blessing. Even if such a physical struggle for a blessing appears unusual, Jacob's tenacity and determination are worthy of consideration.

What are you willing to endure for the sake of a blessing? It's safe to rule out an all-night wrestling match for most of us, but are you willing to wait on God, to struggle through your doubts, or even to ask someone else to pray for you? There's a good chance you will need the help of others in order for your spiritual health to thrive. In fact, you can count on it.

If you hope to stand firm in your faith, take some time to seek a blessing from someone else.

Lord, I ask for Your blessing of perseverance and hope today.

THE MARKS OF GOD'S PEOPLE

Lord, who may dwell in your sacred tent? Who may live on your
holy mountain? The one whose walk is blameless, who does what is
righteous, who speaks the truth from their heart. . .who lends money
to the poor without interest; who does not accept a bribe against
the innocent. Whoever does these things will never be shaken.
PSALM 15:1–2, 5 NIV

Today's psalm notes that those who are unshakable are also those who are just in their actions toward God and toward their neighbors. Justice and righteousness mean they are blameless in what they say and in their economic practices. In the psalmist's time, interest could be especially crippling and predatory for the poor, who lacked sufficient means to back up loans and who could be devastated with a few bad breaks. Leaders were especially susceptible to bribes because they lacked accountability and oversight, leaving the poor to fend for themselves.

As we remember the legacy of Martin Luther King Jr. today, this psalm helps us remember the complexity of his message, which extended beyond treating those of a different race as fellow equals before God. King also advocated for fair wages for workers, better labor laws to protect workers, and justice system reforms so that black men and women were treated the same as white men and women in the courts.

Lord, help me to live justly with my words and actions.

WHERE WILL YOU FIND REST?

*Then Jesus said, "Come to me, all of you who are weary
and carry heavy burdens, and I will give you rest. Take my
yoke upon you. Let me teach you, because I am humble and
gentle at heart, and you will find rest for your souls."*
MATTHEW 11:28–29 NLT

◆━━━●━━━◆

Where do you go to find rest? The answer may not be as obvious as you think. At the time of Jesus, people took comfort in their religious heritage, obedience to certain laws, and the guidance of their teachers. Over time, this turned into a system of self-reliance for many, and religious leaders even exploited the goodwill of the people. What should have freed the people to love and serve God became a burden.

Jesus offers another path to freedom. While He still has expectations and responsibilities for His path forward, this "yoke" of commitment is easy to bear and will lead to a place of rest. If you feel like you can't get to a place of spiritual health or like you're always struggling to keep up, now is the perfect time to tell Jesus that you need Him to show you the path forward. If you struggle and stumble, He won't leave you behind or give you more than you can bear. His gentleness will carry you forward.

Jesus, I gladly pick up Your yoke today and will listen as You speak into my life.

GOD'S FAVOR, EVEN IN TIMES OF SUFFERING

But the LORD was with Joseph and showed him steadfast love and gave him favor in the sight of the keeper of the prison. And the keeper of the prison put Joseph in charge of all the prisoners who were in the prison. Whatever was done there, he was the one who did it.

GENESIS 39:21–22 ESV

◆━━━━◆━━━━◆

The worst possible losses and suffering hit Joseph. Even when life seemed to be working out as well as it could under the circumstances, he soon found himself the victim of yet another major injustice. Locked away in prison, Joseph remained faithful to the Lord and served well among his fellow inmates. Even though he'd been slandered and mistreated, he continued to be honorable and just. He carried out his responsibilities with skill and dedication, even if he couldn't see how things would work out in the future.

Your circumstances don't tell the whole story of God's presence and faithfulness. Even a time of affliction and injustice can become an opportunity for God to work in your favor. Your faithfulness today will go a long way toward preparing you for the future, where circumstances may change and God's power will be on full display.

Lord, I trust that even in times of suffering and loss, I can rely on Your favor and deliverance.

YOUR WORDS WILL LAST

*"And I tell you this, you must give an account on
judgment day for every idle word you speak. The words
you say will either acquit you or condemn you."*
MATTHEW 12:36–37 NLT

◆────◆────◆

J esus often heard His followers say some troubling and irresponsible things. From James and John asking Jesus to call down thunder on people, to Peter trying to persuade Jesus to avoid the cross, their words carried the potential to cause some really big problems. Jesus wanted His listeners to know that God noticed what they said and would one day acquit or condemn them based even on their words.

Your words have power to give life, encouragement, and freedom to others. They also have the power to condemn, discourage, and bind others. Basic everyday statements can have eternal consequences that extend beyond what we can imagine. The stakes are high, and you can't afford to speak carelessly without considering how someone will either benefit or suffer from what you say. It is far better to carefully weigh what you say today than to worry about how you'll give an account for your careless words before God. That day is coming, even if it seems far off at this particular moment.

*Jesus, help me to speak with wisdom and care so that I bring
blessings to others and avoid judgment for idle words.*

ARE YOU AWARE OF GOD'S REWARDS?

The LORD has dealt with me according to my righteousness; according to the cleanness of my hands he has rewarded me. For I have kept the ways of the LORD; I am not guilty of turning from my God.
PSALM 18:20–21 NIV

The writers of the psalms often mention the tendency of the wicked to sin as if God will never punish them. In fact, they seem to thrive, not reaping the consequences of their actions for years but instead enjoying prosperity, while those who fear God struggle and find themselves on the outside looking in. Will the disparities between these two groups ever be evened out so that justice reigns and the righteous are rewarded for their faithfulness?

While you can count on some difficult times and even injustices happening, the Lord promises to reward you according to your righteous actions. If your hands are "clean," then God will treat you accordingly. In the heat of the moments of temptation, consider that God's reward will come to you if you call on Him and prevail.

You don't necessarily know the details of the Lord's reward. Will it come to you in this life or in the next? The details aren't clear. Yet you can rest assured that God sees your goodness, and perhaps that can help you persevere in difficult times.

Holy Spirit, help me to remember the rewards that await me if I live righteously.

SEEING THE BIG PICTURE

So Joseph said to his brothers, "Come near to me, please." And they came near. And he said, "I am your brother, Joseph, whom you sold into Egypt. And now do not be distressed or angry with yourselves because you sold me here, for God sent me before you to preserve life."
GENESIS 45:4–5 ESV

Joseph didn't hold his suffering against his brothers. He resolved to look at the ways God had worked throughout his life's circumstances to lead him to a place of blessing. While Joseph's brothers surely felt a mix of emotions, ranging from fear to regret, they had an opportunity to be completely forgiven and to move on despite their grievous treatment of Joseph.

At the lowest points of loss or conflict, you may struggle to see the big picture and to forgive those who have hurt or offended you. How can you move on after someone has mistreated you? Although Joseph's story is quite extraordinary, it offers a helpful approach you can apply in your own life: reviewing the outcome of suffering and looking for God's hand at work.

You may even see how God has been at work through your misfortunes, and that will move you toward greater mercy. With this big-picture view, you may even become more concerned about the anger and shame that your offenders bear.

Father, help me to see Your hand at work so that I can forgive others readily.

WHAT SHOULD YOU REQUEST FROM GOD?

But who can discern their own errors? Forgive my hidden faults.
Keep your servant also from willful sins; may they not rule over me.
Then I will be blameless, innocent of great transgression.

PSALM 19:12–13 NIV

◆———————◆———————◆

The psalmist writes that errors can be difficult to discern without God's guidance and mercy. Surely everyone can come up with an explanation or justification for sinful behavior, whether or not such explanations are sincere and honest. In addition, the psalmist notes that even the truly obvious willful sins can be challenging to avoid. Even for the obvious sins, he asks God for help and deliverance from the sins that could rule over him.

What is your position today when it comes to sin? Do you fear God and hope to remain blameless and pure before Him? Or do you hope to escape God's notice for now, eventually taking advantage of His mercy and patience?

The struggle for today is to ask God for discernment and protection to help you avoid sin. Temptation will always be a part of your life, and you could stumble into sinful acts when you least expect it. Today's prayer from Psalms can help you remain close to God and in His good favor.

Father, help me to see the impact of sin in my life and to remain vigilant
and humble as I seek to remain obedient to Your commands.

WHAT IS KEEPING YOU FROM GOD?

"The Kingdom of Heaven is like a treasure that a man discovered hidden in a field. In his excitement, he hid it again and sold everything he owned to get enough money to buy the field."

MATTHEW 13:44 NLT

Speaking to people who generally had limited resources and few possessions of value, Jesus drove home the immense worth of God's kingdom. Selling all of his possessions, possibly even his home, could leave a man destitute and unable to provide for himself or his family. Yet the treasure he sacrificed everything to find would prove more valuable many times over.

Jesus is asking you to consider your commitments and priorities today. What is keeping you from pursuing God and the priorities of His kingdom? It may be a jam-packed schedule or professional priorities or a leisure activity that has consumed hours of your time. Then again, your possessions may serve as a weight holding you back from drawing near to God.

The treasure of God's kingdom is worth more than these things that will one day pass away. Your security in His kingdom is the only unshakable thing you can count on, and that's why it's worth giving up everything else to obtain it.

Father, help me to see what holds me back from seeking first Your kingdom and Your righteousness so that I can let go and pursue Your kingdom first.

FEAR IS A POISON

*But the more they were oppressed, the more they multiplied and the more
they spread abroad. And the Egyptians were in dread of the people
of Israel. So they ruthlessly made the people of Israel work as slaves.*
EXODUS 1:12–13 ESV

The prosperity of the Israelites became their undoing in the eyes of the Egyptians. Since the Israelites were a foreign people living as refugees in Egypt, they were viewed as a potential threat. The Israelites could have overthrown the supremacy of the Egyptians, so the pharaoh ordered them to work as slaves. This oppressive approach paid off for a while, but it ultimately led to significant tragedy and suffering for the Egyptian people.

It's likely that you view certain people or groups of people as either a threat or, at the very least, a group you want to keep an eye on. That seed of fear may have been planted by family or friends, and it may not be something you notice easily. Yet so much sin and suffering come about in our world because of misplaced fear.

Once you fear someone, praying for that person becomes difficult. If you can attack the root of your fears of others, you'll be free to pray for them, and you'll be saved from the consequences of fear in your life and in the lives of others.

*Father, help me to identify the ways fear divides
and harms people so that I can love others freely.*

MERCY IS THE BEST SOLUTION

*But Jesus gave her no reply, not even a word. Then his
disciples urged him to send her away. "Tell her to go away,"
they said. "She is bothering us with all her begging."*
MATTHEW 15:23 NLT

◆———◆———◆

I t can be a shock to read that Jesus and His disciples ignored the Canaanite
woman's pleas for mercy for her daughter, who was tormented by a demon.
They surely knew Jesus could simply say the word to cast out the evil spirit.
Instead, they pled with Jesus to use His words of life to send this woman
away, not the demon. The fix to their problem should have been obvious.
Send the demon away, and the begging for mercy they found "so annoying"
would end too.

Although Jesus eventually relented and healed the daughter of the woman
in today's reading, it's difficult to understand how the disciples couldn't see
the woman's need for mercy and healing. It's possible that you may encounter
or know someone who is carrying a deep need right now. You may not notice
this need, or you may not be aware of it, or you may simply want to avoid it.
Whatever the details, you can play a part in the healing of others if you take
the time to notice and show mercy for their deepest needs. Perhaps the things
you find most "annoying" are what you need to pray about today.

*Jesus, help me to see those suffering around
me, and spur me to show them mercy.*

HOW CAN YOU DISQUALIFY YOURSELF?

Then the Lord said to him, "Who has made man's mouth? Who makes him mute, or deaf, or seeing, or blind? Is it not I, the Lord? Now therefore go, and I will be with your mouth and teach you what you shall speak."

Exodus 4:11–12 ESV

◆———◆———◆

Moses had plenty of persuasive and sensible reasons why he should be disqualified from the work God set before him. Having spent a large portion of his life isolated as a shepherd, he wasn't qualified to speak to the ruler of Egypt. He feared that he would struggle to speak clearly. His only problem was that God's arguments and God's power were far superior and significantly more persuasive. The Lord promised to show him what to speak and to guide him as he confronted Pharaoh.

In what ways have you tried to disqualify yourself from serving others? Do you have excuses ready-made for God when the call to help others comes your way?

There's no doubt that you may feel unqualified—or maybe extremely busy. Yet if God has truly called you to serve, then you have an opportunity to obey His clear call. God wants you to depend on the Holy Spirit working in your life, not on the talent or ability you bring.

Holy Spirit, I trust that You can prepare me for every good work You've called me to do.

GOD IS PRESENT IN THE DARKNESS

Even though I walk through the darkest valley, I will fear no evil,
for you are with me; your rod and your staff, they comfort me.
You prepare a table before me in the presence of my enemies.
You anoint my head with oil; my cup overflows.

Psalm 23:4–5 niv

The psalmist takes comfort in the Lord's direction in his life, remembering that he is only a sheep being led by God. Yet guidance doesn't guarantee quiet days by streams of water. In fact, there may be moments of loss and struggle, uncertainty and suffering. While God provides for His people, He also walks with them through the darkest valleys, providing what they need even while their enemies loom.

Going through the darkest valley may not sound like a great option to you, but there undoubtedly will be hard times ahead. Loss and suffering will come your way eventually, and the question isn't how you can avoid such challenges but whether you are willing to depend on God to guide you through them. Are you waiting on God to set a table before you and care for your needs? Are you willing to hope in Him alone, even if His solution isn't what you're hoping it will be?

Lord, I trust that You are my Shepherd who
can guide me through the dark valleys of life.

WHO'S IN CHARGE?

Peter exclaimed, "Lord, it's wonderful for us to be here! If you want, I'll make three shelters as memorials—one for you, one for Moses, and one for Elijah." But even as he spoke, a bright cloud overshadowed them, and a voice from the cloud said, "This is my dearly loved Son, who brings me great joy. Listen to him."

MATTHEW 17:4–5 NLT

Peter thought he had a great plan for capitalizing on the fantastic revelation of Jesus' divinity. If only he could properly promote it with three shelters so that people could show up and worship Jesus, he could ensure that everyone knew about this vision. Yet God the Father said from a cloud that Peter wasn't in charge here. It was his job to listen to God's dearly loved Son—full stop.

Perhaps you have some plans in mind that you need to place before God in prayer. It's possible that you may even need to put everything on hold for a time of listening. Even if you've meant well in setting up your plans and even if you've started out with good motives, the most important matter is whether you've listened to God's beloved Son. It's possible that Jesus may have very different plans from your own—plans that could end up being for your great benefit and for the blessing of many.

Jesus, help me to wait and listen, even when my own plans appear perfect.

IT'S TIME TO LET GO OF SHAME

Remember, LORD, your great mercy and love, for they are from of old.
Do not remember the sins of my youth and my rebellious ways;
according to your love remember me, for you, LORD, are good.
PSALM 25:6–7 NIV

Guilt and shame can become great burdens to bear, preventing people from seeking God or asking for His forgiveness. The psalms are filled with confessions of guilt and requests for God's mercy, but the good news is that shame and guilt never have the last word. The writers of the psalms always returned to God's mercy, patience, and forgiveness as their sources of hope. Even the failures of the past didn't disqualify them from God's love.

You may have memories of your past weighing you down today. Perhaps you carry a sense of shame over a personal failure, such as speaking harshly or irresponsibly, that left someone hurt and wounded. Even if you see these mistakes for what they are, they can take on an oversized role in your identity. Are your failures really defining events for who you are?

God's mercy and forgiveness are so much larger than your shame. When you have confessed your sins, you can take comfort in God's love covering anything that would have weighed you down in the past.

Father, help me to accept Your mercy and forgiveness as I let go of shame.

WHAT CAN YOU LEARN FROM CHILDREN?

Then he said, "I tell you the truth, unless you turn from your sins and become like little children, you will never get into the Kingdom of Heaven. So anyone who becomes as humble as this little child is the greatest in the Kingdom of Heaven."

MATTHEW 18:3–4 NLT

J esus frequently addressed His disciples' delusions and misplaced priorities when they imagined themselves sitting on thrones next to Jesus the King. They believed they would have places of honor where important people would notice and admire them. When they traveled with Jesus, they dismissed the very people Jesus came to save, such as a corrupt tax collector, a promiscuous woman, and children who sought the blessing of God. Yet the humility and trust of the children before them showed the clearest picture of greatness in God's kingdom.

What if today's passage became a daily assignment, an invitation to observe the way children trust their parents or humbly rely on others? How have you seen children model the type of faith that Jesus desires?

You also have an opportunity to consider who you are most likely to notice. Are you paying attention to the people Jesus welcomed? Such priorities may help you figure out what you value and where you have placed your faith.

Jesus, help me to notice and imitate the people who humble themselves and who place their faith and trust wholly in You.

THE RESENTMENT RETREAT

*Then Peter came up to Him and said, Lord, how many times
may my brother sin against me and I forgive him and let it go?
[As many as] up to seven times? Jesus answered him,
I tell you, not up to seven times, but seventy times seven!*
MATTHEW 18:21–22 AMPC

◆ ◆ ◆

People will sometimes say or do things you don't like or find offensive, and hurt will be the outcome. If you want to be a slave, then be a victim. Withhold forgiveness and demand a repayment no one will ever be able to make. But when you do, understand that you aren't standing your ground but slipping backward.

You could celebrate National Freedom Day today by offering forgiveness to those who need it—even if they don't deserve it. That's standing firm, holding your ground, and fixing your feet in a forward direction. Don't retreat to bitterness, anger, and resentment. It's a harsh condition that leaves you indecisive.

You want freedom but keep returning to your prison cell. Stop counting how often you forgive. Just trust God, forgive those who hurt you, and be set free.

*Father, I want to do what You do. Because You forgive me, help me be
brave enough to forgive others. Help me set my feelings aside and obey
You while I trust Your outcome. I want to remember that my rebellion
left You on the cross. It was Your forgiveness that invited me home.*

A COMMITMENT TO LEARN

*"The LORD is my strength and my song, and he has
become my salvation; this is my God, and I will
praise him, my father's God, and I will exalt him."*
EXODUS 15:2 ESV

Moses was in the mood to praise. He recognized God's power in saving the people of Israel. He had learned to trade fear for faith. The people struggled to follow his example and kept making poor choices. God gave them forty years to learn that He was worth following. Some failed to learn. Maybe this lesson is a struggle for you too.

Moses was on sturdy footing with God. Most of the Israelites were not. Moses followed while the people walked away. Moses praised God while the people grumbled. As each day passed, they were no closer to possessing the land God had promised.

As you celebrate Groundhog Day, remember a nation of people who seemed to see their shadow every day and then faced more time in the wilderness.

When God wants to teach you something, make a commitment to learn. Make the change so tomorrow will be better than today.

*God, the idea of never seeing progress makes me fearful. I
don't want to stay where I am, but I'm afraid of what will be
required to get me to the place You want for me. When You lead
and I follow, I'm never alone in this new life with You.*

UNSHAKABLE–INCOMPARABLE

The LORD will give strength unto his people;
the LORD will bless his people with peace.
PSALM 29:11 KJV

U*nshakable*. If this word could describe anyone completely, it would be God. You can stand unshakable in His protection, but God doesn't need to rely on anyone or anything to exist without doubt, fear, and anxiety.

From His place of unshakable glory, God offers His family peace, strength, and blessing. A weak and disturbable god could not do that. He wouldn't be at peace, so He couldn't offer peace. His strength would be in question, so few would attempt to rely on it. His blessings would be meaningless.

If you've ever wondered why God needs to be incomparable in every category, look at it this way: It has everything to do with His ability to meet your needs. If you want to live an unshakable life, you must connect with an unshakable God. You will need to trust in a powerful God who loves you and has a future for you. Only then can you live fearlessly, unmoved by circumstances that challenge your willingness to stand strong.

Father, when You are challenged, You win. When bad
things happen, You aren't surprised and never run away.
You know what happens next, so the mess that may seem
to be my present doesn't look like Your future for me.
Help me stay close to You—God unshakable.

NO EASY TRANSITION

*When the people saw the thunder and lightning and heard the
trumpet and saw the mountain in smoke, they trembled with fear.
They stayed at a distance and said to Moses, "Speak to us yourself and
we will listen. But do not have God speak to us or we will die."*

EXODUS 20:18–19 NIV

The Israelites were in the wilderness and at the beginning of a new journey with God. But they weren't far enough away from their life of slavery in Egypt. The idea of coming to God boldly wasn't an easy transition for those with the mind of a slave and the heart of a sinner.

It's possible you've read of God's power. You know He created the world and everything in it. He sets up kingdoms and removes kings from power. The thought of coming to Him can leave you looking up the definition for the word *timid*. It could send you running to find a dark corner in which to hide. It could bring you to the place where you understand God's holiness and your impurity. But it's in this place of personal instability that you can meet the unshakable God. He strengthens your spiritual spine and invites you to walk with Him and never hide.

*God, may I seek to hear from You and not run when
You speak. Help me be unshakable in Your presence
and fearless in the mission You have for me.*

UNSHAKABLE ANSWERS

[Jesus said to the mother of James and John,] "What is it you want?" . . .
She said, "Grant that one of these two sons of mine may sit at
your right and the other at your left in your kingdom."
MATTHEW 20:21 NIV

Your prayer never leaves God wondering if He is wrong about something. If the answer is no, then there's nothing you can say or do to cause God to think He has made a mistake. His yes is a full-throttle *yes*, and His no should stop you in your tracks.

Read God's Word enough and you'll learn what He will say no to. It might keep you from asking for things He has already rejected.

You might conclude that doing the wrong thing is right because it makes you feel better, but your feelings don't outrank a rule-making God. You should be shaken when the unshakable God says no. You should be unshaken when that same God moves you in the direction that He knows is best and will be a blessing to you.

No one can know the chain of events inspired by an answered prayer. Likewise, no one can know the chain of events inspired by doing something God has said no to. One scenario is good. The other? Not so much. God gives unshakable answers.

Father, there's safety in knowing there's a reason You
decline my requests. You're the unshakable God and You know
all the things that are for my good and Your glory.

A FUTURE WITH GOD

*I am trusting you, O LORD, saying, "You are
my God!" My future is in your hands.*
PSALM 31:14–15 NLT

◆━━━◆━━━◆

Being unshakable, immovable, and steadfast is connected to a trust in what God says about your future. If you really understand that there is a future with God that exists beyond your life on earth, then it's easier to trust Him with each moment of the temporary existence you're living now.

Your future should never stay in your hands. You aren't in a contest to be the most self-reliant among men. You trust a God you pledge allegiance to. You are in His hands because He holds you there. He offers protection, comfort, and closeness.

It's hard to conjure an image of the word *immovable* in an environment where God would not be a refuge, could not offer help, or would not stand with His family.

You get to see God work in your life and in the lives of others. You get to hear words that praise Him for an outcome that no one saw coming but that could be described as amazing.

Leave this page saying, "I trust You. You are my God. My future is in Your hands."

*God, when I doubt, help me trust. When I forget, remind me that You are
God. When I am uncertain, remind me I have a future—with You.*

EVERY HOUR A SUNRISE

"Now, order the Israelites to bring you pure, clear olive oil for light so that the lamps can be kept burning. In the Tent of Meeting, the area outside the curtain that veils The Testimony, Aaron and his sons will keep this light burning from evening until morning before GOD."
EXODUS 27:20–21 MSG

E verywhere you go, make God famous. Let your mouth speak words that describe His wonder. Let your mind spend time thinking about His goodness. When you do, you shouldn't be surprised that your stance is firm, your heart undivided in your opinion of God, and your trust in Him sure.

Consider this: Every hour the sun is rising on a new place on this big blue marble. And with every sunrise, God is creating a new day to be enjoyed, cherished, and used wisely. He never sleeps, naps, or daydreams. God is on the job, and people who love Him share His good news every hour of every day—just like the priests who were ordered to maintain a physical light in the tabernacle to point to God's light, even when most people slept. God is famous—declare it.

Father, is it okay to tell You that talking about You can be hard? Well, it is— or at least can be. Help me be boldly identified with You and wise enough to follow what I know. Be my stability in an unstable world.

AN OPPOSITE OUTCOME

*No one was able to answer Him a word, nor from that
day did anyone venture or dare to question Him.*
MATTHEW 22:46 AMPC

◆   ◆   ◆

The religious leaders in Jesus' day asked Him questions that typically caused the interrogated to wither. They had seen false messiahs come and go and their followers disperse in a cloud of delusion. They must have been certain that this day would be no different. But they were talking to Jesus, and He actually *was* the Messiah. He had come to rescue humanity and He was unflinching. He answered them in ways they hadn't expected. Each interaction was a surprise, and they were losing ground. They were seeking to publicly humiliate Jesus, but the outcome was the opposite.

You can follow Jesus, learn from His Word, and find answers that leave you just as unflinching. You don't need to be unkind in your answers to others. In your kindness, point back to the truth you're learning. And even if no one listens or believes, you're speaking truth—and truth is an invitation to freedom. And freedom is what we all need.

*God, You bring truth and ask me to believe it. You show up with
power and bring healing to the broken, strength to the weak, and
kindness to the stepped on. Everyone needs what only You can bring.*

PRAISE JUST FITS

Shout for joy in the LORD, O you righteous!
Praise befits the upright.
PSALM 33:1 ESV

◆———◆———◆

When was the last time you shouted because you were excited about something you were engaged in? Likely the most common response would have to do with *sports*. Your team scores and you cheer. The opponent does something underhanded and you boo. You wear the jersey, talk about the game's outcome with friends, and memorize the stats. You have a favorite team and you want people to know and appreciate your team's players. . .and maybe even become fans.

When you are unwavering in your thoughts about God, you have the freedom to shout for joy. Other people might hear it, and that's a good thing. They need to know Jesus. Who better to share Him than you? What better time than now? How better than to speak words from your mouth?

Praise is like a well-tailored shirt. It just fits. Use it to honor God, and if others hear you, they might want to know more. The unwavering are unashamed. They share the truth because the truth has changed their perspective. The idea of people-pleasing has to make room for remembering God's goodness and sharing it.

Father, You are a blessing and I'm the blessed. You give and I receive.
You are overwhelming and I'm overwhelmed. May my praise make
the trip from my mind and heart to my mouth and actions.

PREPARED FOR A PURPOSE

In the hearts of all that are wise hearted I have put wisdom.
Exodus 31:6 KJV

God told Moses what needed to be done to construct and maintain His tabernacle. God chose men who would manage the artistic design, metalwork, and everything else that needed to be made. Today's verse indicates that God made these men wise. He provided the stability they needed to do a big job for a big God.

This verse also suggests that before these men knew they were chosen, God had given them wisdom. They would need it for the work they would do.

It's reasonable to conclude that God sometimes uses the lessons you've learned to help you do what He needs you to do, but He can also call you first and equip you on the job. Why isn't there just one way to prepare people for their purpose? Each person is unique—and God isn't limited in the ways He works.

Gain courage in knowing that God's good work in your life will not be a copy of someone else's story. Let God unfold your purpose. Then add it to your story and share it.

God, sometimes I wonder if I'll ever be useful to You. Thanks for the encouragement in Your Word. I know You can work in me to help others in a way that's personal. Help me stand strong and wait for You.

FOUND FAITHFUL

"It will be good for that servant whose master
finds him doing so when he returns."
MATTHEW 24:46 NIV

I imagine following Jesus when He walked the dusty roads in the land of Israel. You would have a personal perspective on everything He did and everything He said. But when Jesus was no longer physically with the disciples, did their memories of their time with Him fade with the passing of time? Did people find strength only when He was with them?

Being in Jesus' presence changed most of the disciples for life. But today it can be a little harder to stay enthused about walking with a God you've never seen. God wants you to walk with Him, and that's why He sent His Spirit to help you stay faithful, available, and unshakable.

Jesus didn't come so His followers could live with a collection of fond memories. Jesus came to change their world. Today, He prepares people like you to tell His story to everyone and to every generation.

You've been given a job to do. Be found faithful when Jesus returns.

Father, I've never seen You face-to-face, but I've met You
through faith in Your Son. Your Spirit helps me. I'm made
strong because of You. Help me make the choice today to follow
You. May that be my choice until I take my last breath.

AN UNSHAKABLE LIFE

The LORD will rescue his servants; no one who
takes refuge in him will be condemned.
PSALM 34:22 NIV

D o you want to live an unshakable life? Pay attention to God's promises and be encouraged.

You are redeemed, bought back from a life that could never really be described as *life*. You traded a death sentence for eternal life. You traded a guilty verdict for no condemnation. What's the downside of *that* trade? How are you disadvantaged by gaining God's help?

Every day you have a choice to make. You can try to figure everything out with your own limited strength, knowledge, and ability—or you can access God's unlimited *everything*. He doesn't need additional resources or a second opinion. What He knows will answer any of your questions.

When you understand that God views you as *not guilty*, when you grasp the idea that you no longer have to obey the urge to make bad choices, and when God's new life for you feels like home, then uncertainty becomes an unwelcome neighbor.

The family connection God made possible is the very thing that makes believers bold and brave.

God, I should never look at what I can't do as a reason for insecurity. I should look at what You can do and ask for help. You've given me a home and declared me innocent. That's nothing I've done, but everything You've given. I'm grateful.

STRUGGLE VERSUS VICTORY

[O LORD,] let me hear you say, "I will give you victory!"
PSALM 35:3 NLT

———————◆———————◆———————

David was being pursued by people who didn't have his best interests in mind. He was certain he would be destroyed if he didn't receive help. He wanted to be unshakable, but he was shaken and felt alone.

You've been there, right? But the shaken can be transformed when they understand that God will give them victory. They understand that little things mean big things in the hands of a good God. It's okay to pray, "God, I'm asking You to declare victory in my struggle."

Your faith in God's ability is the source of victory. It's the belief that God never disowns you, leaves you behind, or decides you're not worth the effort.

Today's verse demonstrates that God was approachable in Old Testament times and involved in the affairs of humanity.

God fully understands the struggles you're going through. He has a specific way to deal with each one of your crises and can help you eliminate your unsettled feelings. Worry will always leave you shaken, and anxiety will leave you with unanswered questions. But being unshakable means you trust God's ability to answer in a way that satisfies your deepest longings.

Father, I want victory that comes from Your plan book. I don't want to settle for my own answer to a problem I don't completely understand. Let me hear You say, "I will give you victory!"

WHEN DID YOU DO THAT?

*"I was hungry and you fed me, I was thirsty and you
gave me a drink, I was homeless and you gave me a room,
I was shivering and you gave me clothes, I was sick and you
stopped to visit, I was in prison and you came to me."*
MATTHEW 25:35–36 MSG

It's easy to think of romantic love on February 14. But Valentine was not the originator of love, and romantic love is not the same love that God gives you. In His commitment to you, He looks at how you respond to other people.

Could God say to you the words Jesus spoke in the verses above? They were spoken as part of a story He told of a future time. Jesus told His disciples that whenever His family did any of these things for any other person, it was as if they were doing it for Him. He placed a high premium on loving others enough to help them.

Being unshakable means you're decisive. You don't have to guess if you should love people enough to help them. When you model God for people who *need* to meet Him, they might *want* to meet Him.

*God, You want me to show love and compassion to the
people around me. You help me and You want me to
help others. Give me a heart to do just that.*

CLOUD AND FIRE

*Throughout all their journeys the cloud of the Lord
was upon the tabernacle by day, and fire was in it by
night, in the sight of all the house of Israel.*
EXODUS 40:38 AMPC

Good leaders inspire strong followers. It's true for the soldier who follows a general into battle. It's true for an employee who follows the vision of his company leader. Every memorable movement has had a strong leader. That doesn't always mean the leader was worth following, but it makes the point that if a leader is indecisive, he will never lead effectively.

God had to give Moses a spiritual spine. Only then could he lead the people. God delivered a visible reminder of His unshakable glory by providing a cloud by day and a pillar of fire by night to lead the people. He supplied food and water in what looked like impossible circumstances. He was unswerving in His commitment. *He led.*

God leads today. His commitment hasn't diminished. His love hasn't failed. Unshakable leadership can lead to unshakable followers, but it's always your decision. Do you trust God enough to follow? Or will you insist on trying your own way? Will you be unshaken, or will you be fearful?

*Father, I can follow because You lead. You always have my best in
mind, so when I follow You, I don't have to fear where You lead.
Give me courage to see Your path and take the next step.*

UNNERVED AND HUMBLED

[Jesus] came to the disciples and found them sleeping.
And he said to Peter, "So, could you not watch with me one
hour? Watch and pray that you may not enter into temptation.
The spirit indeed is willing, but the flesh is weak."
MATTHEW 26:40–41 ESV

◆──────◆──────◆

Why share a story that features people who were shakable? Perhaps because every man who has ever lived has endured a personal shaking that left him unnerved, embarrassed, and humbled. It's good to know your experience is mirrored in the Bible. You may have a unique personality, but your life experience is probably not as unusual as you may think.

It's important to understand that everyone starts this life journey shaken. For every story of a man being bold, there is a beginning defined by timidity. For every instance of unwavering determination to move forward, there is a story of indecision.

There is no condemnation here, just an encouraging voice inviting you to stand in the place of the unshaken, to leave indecision behind, to make the decision to follow—*and then follow.*

The disciples weren't always unshaken. They just learned to follow the One who will stand firm forever. That's a great example to follow.

God, lead me away from this place of uncertainty. On my
own, I am unnerved, embarrassed, and humbled. Lead me to
the place where I begin to follow You, the Unshakable One.
Help me remember that boldness comes from You.

AN UNSHAKABLE COVENANT

When Pilate saw that he was getting nowhere,
but that instead an uproar was starting, he took water
and washed his hands in front of the crowd. "I am innocent
of this man's blood," he said. "It is your responsibility!"
MATTHEW 27:24 NIV

When Jesus died, the earth physically shook. Before that, Peter's heart shook when he lied repeatedly about knowing Jesus. Sandwiched between those two events, a Roman governor named Pilate saw the potential for a riot over Jesus, and he too was shaken.

Shaken people make poor decisions. Shaken people make bad leaders. *Shaken people would agree.* But God can take human insecurity and still get His work done. In Peter's case, the lesson he learned from his time of being shaken led him to become a strong leader in the early church.

All of the unnerving events you read about in Matthew 27 led to the death, burial, and resurrection of Jesus. The shaking led to an unshakable covenant between God and mankind. You can be unshakable because the very bad day that was Jesus' crucifixion means there is nothing that can keep you from God.

Father, this walk I'm on finds me confronting things that make
me nervous. It seems like anger might be a good response—
or sadness, or maybe fear. Strengthen my spiritual knees and
ankles, because I want to stand with—and for—You.

DESCRIBING GOD

Trust in the LORD and do good;
dwell in the land and enjoy safe pasture.
PSALM 37:3 NIV

◆━━━━◆━━━━◆

Do you ever move your heart to self-preservation mode? It's a decision that says you will *not* be hurt again—you'll make sure of it. This decision rejects trust as worthwhile. It stiff-arms friendship. It's sarcastic in the presence of compassion. It leaves you a distorted caricature of what you once were, and you bear little resemblance to the man God created you to be.

You've assumed responsibility for protecting your heart, and the acidic juices of bitterness are doing their best to destroy you. It's almost as if you've agreed to allow life to set your teeth on edge, shake you up, and set you up with a lifetime contract for daily deliveries of scar-inducing pain.

Faithfulness describes God. *Trust that.* Where He leads, He also feeds. Everything you need to follow, He provides. If you receive good, it's because God sent it. Settle in, settle down, and never settle for less than the adventure of the unshaken with God as your guide.

God, why is it that when I'm faced with the choice of embracing pain or Your healing, I often choose the path of pain? Help me remember that You don't ask me to work harder—You invite me to come to You for help. You don't ask me to worry—You take care of everything.

FORWARD PROGRESS

Be still in the presence of the LORD, and wait patiently
for him to act. Don't worry about evil people who
prosper or fret about their wicked schemes.
PSALM 37:7 NLT

◆———————◆———————◆

Unshakable people are patient people. They know it's uncommon for prayers to be answered immediately.

You need to trust that God answers prayers and that "yes" answers can take time. While you wait, you'll be tempted to consider the forward progress of people who don't care about God. You can't make them live by the same beliefs you have. They have different ideas about trust, love, and life. If they don't know Jesus, they won't see the significance of trusting Him. Sadly, when they are shaken, they may not think to turn to the only One who can keep their feet from stumbling.

Don't get in a rush. Don't entertain worry. Don't wring your hands over things you can't control. The patience you express by waiting for what you can't yet see speaks volumes about the trust you have in God. This is a snapshot of the unshakable life God desires for you.

Rest. God is with you. Wait. He will act. Be unshakable.

Father, I have been guilty of acting like people who don't trust
You—and of expecting those same people to act like people
who follow You. I should stand unshakable because those who
don't follow You need to see what that looks like.

THE DUBIOUS,
DOUBTING DISCIPLES

*Meanwhile, the eleven disciples were on their way to Galilee,
headed for the mountain Jesus had set for their reunion. The moment
they saw him they worshiped him. Some, though, held back,
not sure about worship, about risking themselves totally.*
MATTHEW 28:16–17 MSG

◆ ◆ ◆

You've probably been to the funeral of someone you love. You were sad. You wished that person was still with you. But you don't expect someone to say they came back to life. Jesus' disciples experienced this. Some held back. Some were unwilling to take the risk to be unshakable—even though Jesus had said not only that He would die but also that He would rise again.

It's easy to ignore the unbelievable. Saying, "God said it, so I believe it," can be difficult—even though that's the right response.

Once the dubious, doubting disciples saw Jesus, they experienced an internal shift that caused their doubt to evaporate.

When you find yourself doubting what you said you believed, read Matthew 28 again. Jesus did what you can't—so when He asks you to do something He knows you can't do, He's telling you that there's no reason to doubt the outcome. Stand unshaken. God is with you.

*God, the Bible is filled with real people, and the only difference
between some of their choices and mine is You. I can't think
of a good story in Your Word that doesn't include You.*

NO MATCH FOR MY GOD

For in You, O Lord, do I hope; You will answer, O Lord my God.
PSALM 38:15 AMPC

◆

When you read Psalm 38, verse 15 might seem out of place. David admitted to being foolish and living with wounds. He sinned and struggled with burdens. Friends left him; enemies found him. People were happy to see him flounder. Opposition was his nemesis.

Then a verse of unshakable faith shows up. David declared that God would answer his cry for help. He said his hope was not misplaced. He said that God was also Lord. This damaged man knew where to turn. God would make this man king.

This isn't a rags-to-riches story. It's the story of a man who knew that everything bad that could ever happen to him was temporary. All the pain would come to an end. There would be relief, and his hope was in trusting the God who answers. His story exemplifies the life of the unshaken.

David wasn't the only one. He wasn't the first. He wasn't the last. He is just one more bright example of purpose meeting trouble and saying, "You're no match for my God."

Father, I need to be careful whom I trust. Experience says that not everyone will do the right thing. Not everyone will care. But You will, have, and do. Answer me in my struggle and remind me that a better day is coming.

DELIBERATE PRAYER

And rising very early in the morning, while it was still dark,
he departed and went out to a desolate place, and there he prayed.
MARK 1:35 ESV

◆———◆———◆

It's possible you could argue that Jesus was shaken when you read the first chapter of Mark. But you'd be wrong. Yes, Jesus prayed, but praying isn't the act of a shaken man. It's the mark of the courageous. Prayer is admitting you want something better. It's being willing to ask God for something you know He wants you to have.

Jesus wasn't worried or anxious. He rose early in the morning. He didn't want distractions, so He sought a private place for a very personal conversation with God.

Unshaken people pray deliberately, seriously, and determinedly. Prayer is not a last resort, a little-used option, or a personal obligation. It is a powerful moment when someone God created takes the opportunity to talk to the Creator.

Shaken people are afraid of God. They will try to wish Him away, push Him aside, or act as if He has never been real. So they don't rise with the intention of praying. They are frightened at the idea of being alone with God. They run away.

Pray. Be intentional. Live unshaken.

God, help me come to You intentionally, knowing that
You listen, You care, and You're the only real help I'll
ever need. Faith always demonstrates strength.

THE PRAISE TIMELINE

*Many, O Lord my God, are thy wonderful works which
thou hast done, and thy thoughts which are to us-ward: they
cannot be reckoned up in order unto thee: if I would declare
and speak of them, they are more than can be numbered.*

Psalm 40:5 KJV

◆━━━◆━━━◆

Grab a notebook or journal and your favorite pen. Write down all the
wonderful things God has done for you and in the lives of others. This
trip down memory lane will inspire praise—and praise looks good on you. It
improves your ability to live unshaken.

Think about what God has done, what He's said, and where He's taking
you. Be detailed and don't settle for quick answers that sound correct. Dig
deep and get specific, and you might find it leads you to remember even more
praiseworthy events lodged strategically along your journey timeline. Praise
Him for these too.

The unshaken get even bolder. They share parts of their story with the
shaken. This isn't an "I'm better than you" move. It's a notice that says, "Hey,
have you heard about my God?"

Let praise strengthen your courage and let God inspire praise.

*Father, I've never given You much to work with, but You
take the very little I have and re-create me and make me so
new that there are days I don't recognize myself compared
with who I once was. Thank You for this new life that keeps
giving me reasons to stand—stand tall and stand strong.*

UNTRUSTWORTHY CONCLUSIONS

. . .and Judas Iscariot, who betrayed him.
MARK 3:19 NIV

◆——————◆——————◆

Y ou read through Mark and find a list of names. These names belonged to men who followed Jesus. Disciples. And at the very end of that list? "Judas Iscariot, who betrayed him."

Judas was *that guy*—the one who broke rank and forsook the One who does not forsake. Judas did something he would be remembered for, but not in a good way. His life choices left him shaken and he never got over it.

This disciple not only abandoned Jesus—he betrayed Him. He pretended to follow and then walked away. He encountered love, but he didn't think it was enough.

A six-word verse makes it clear that some people will struggle with certainty. They can encounter God the Rock yet conclude that He is an unstable foundation. They trust only their own conclusions, which leaves them shaken, uncertain, and weak.

Judas did not endure, persevere, or hold on. He trusted money, himself, and his vision of the future. He lived upside down—*shaken*. He had the proof of three years with Jesus, but that didn't lead him to real, abundant, forever life.

Don't be *that guy*.

God, I want to make a fresh commitment to follow You today.
Help me do it again tomorrow. It's easy to sit on the sidelines
and dream dreams that don't include You. But I want to live
unshaken, to endure without second thoughts, and to persevere
in my walk with You—because You give me strength.

A BOLD REQUEST

*[David] said, "Have mercy on me, L*ORD*;*
heal me, for I have sinned against you."
PSALM 41:4 NIV

◆ ◆ ◆

God loves to be merciful. He can heal emotional, spiritual, and physical wounds. He may not heal every wound, because some serve as reminders of what you don't want to experience again. God loves to welcome the unshaken and hear their bold requests.

King David didn't make perfect choices, because no man is perfect. To break God's law means to immediately receive a guilty verdict and a death sentence. The unshaken respectfully approach God with a request for mercy—*not getting a judgment they actually deserve*. David's soul was disjointed because sin caused him to fall out of step with God. The closeness he needed was slipping away. David didn't wait. He pursued the bold choice of restoration. He admitted he was wrong.

You have the same choice and can find similar mercy. You can run, but hiding does you no good. God knows where everyone is at all times, what's on their hearts, and what's inflicting pain on their souls. Stand strong. Admit your guilt. Be restored.

Father, You know everything I think, say, and do. I might
hide my choices from others for a while, but I can never hide
anything from You. Help me be brave enough to admit You're
right, strong enough to accept help, and unshaken enough to
talk to You before I step to the sidelines in shame.

STOP DOING THAT

"Do not stand idly by when your neighbor's life is threatened."
LEVITICUS 19:16 NLT

◆——————◆——————◆

God's lawbook was lengthy, but it boiled down to two primary rules for unshakable living: Love God, and love everyone else. The laws provided examples of what love looked like. You could get hung up on the restricting conditions found in the two words "Do not." That's a key to the *example* part. This verse, stated positively, could read, "Love helps when neighbors need help."

Love helps when there's nothing in it for you. It helps others because God helped you. It even helps when that person would never help you. Love gives what someone needs, even when they don't deserve it. God called it mercy and added grace. You need to be unshakable to live that way. Remember that God loved you before you gave Him a thought. He sent Jesus to rescue you when there was no guarantee you even wanted His help.

Maybe many people don't like the "Do not" kind of verses because they point out the things they probably do and say, "Stop doing that." Maybe that's just what you need to hear.

God, I don't always like being told what to do or not do. It makes me feel as if I have no choice. But You may be reminding me that as a Christian, I'm supposed to choose love before anything else. Help me to choose love.

TURN TO JESUS

After Jesus crossed over by boat, a large crowd met him at the
seaside. One of the meeting-place leaders named Jairus came.
When he saw Jesus, he fell to his knees, beside himself as he begged,
"My dear daughter is at death's door. Come and lay hands on her
so she will get well and live." Jesus went with him, the whole
crowd tagging along, pushing and jostling him.
MARK 5:21–24 MSG

❖

Most religious or "meeting-place" leaders did not like Jesus. They thought He was trying to make them irrelevant. They had power, and they believed Jesus was trying to take it from them. But when sickness came to the home of one of these leaders, he turned to Jesus.

Jairus was one of the few religious leaders who discovered unshakable faith in the One who came to heal.

You don't have to exist in the place of spiritual maturity to know that Jesus is the right source for your needs. In desperate times, people who need help turn to Jesus. It's the best decision you can make.

Father, help me talk to You even before I think I need help.
I don't want to make a habit of coming to You only when I have
nowhere else to turn. I'd like for my conversations with You to
be the best place to share my concerns. Help me be bold enough
to share my status updates with You first—and always.

UNSHAKABLE CERTAINTY

*I will not trust in and lean on my bow, neither shall my sword
save me. But You have saved us from our foes and have put
them to shame who hate us. In God we have made our boast all
the day long, and we will give thanks to Your name forever.*

Psalm 44:6–8 ampc

W eapons won't always rescue you, and your skills will often let you
down. But God rescues in the ways that really matter. You'll never
need to be ashamed of God, even when others are ashamed that they lost. Let
people know what God has done for you, and show Him appreciation every day.

If that sounds a lot like the passage you just read, it's because it was
supposed to. It's a summary of those who choose an unshakable response.

The more you trust in anything other than Christ, the more shaken
you will become. Lean on your bow, trust in your sword, and see people as
enemies—and you'll find those things can't replicate the certainty found in
a deep trust in God.

*God, my lips might sound more courageous than my heart really is.
I can get caught up in the idea of developing a personal strategy for
dealing with things I can't control. Help me to ask for help, to trust You
to help me, and to know that these will always be my best choices.*

THE ORIGINAL HERO

*In your majesty ride forth victoriously in the cause of truth, humility
and justice; let your right hand achieve awesome deeds.*

PSALM 45:4 NIV

❖

Think of a hero who fights for truth and justice. If your first thought is of a man in a skintight blue outfit with a red cape and underwear, you need to get your head out of the comic books. The concept of heroism is much older than the "Man of Steel."

The origin of the word *hero* is likely related to pre-Greek words for "protector." In Psalm 45, the psalmist paints a portrait of God as the ultimate hero who fights against evil, wins the loyalty of His beloved, and is remembered by the nations for His awesome deeds.

In a world where flaws are embraced, truth is treated as subjective, humility is seen as weakness, and justice is an unattainable ideal, a hero like this may seem outdated. Yet it is God's flawless nature that makes Him the hero we need. It is His truth that makes it possible for us to trust Him. God's humility makes Him approachable. And His justice makes His sacrifice worth laying hold of.

How can you praise God as the hero He is? By reflecting His priorities in the world He came to save.

Lord, have victory in my life against lies, pride, and injustice.

SECOND CHANCES

"If one of your fellow Israelites falls into poverty and is forced to sell himself to you, do not treat him as a slave. Treat him instead as a hired worker or as a temporary resident who lives with you, and he will serve you only until the Year of Jubilee."

LEVITICUS 25:39–40 NLT

The Sabbath is a weekly day of rest for God's people. The Sabbath Year—celebrated every seventh year—is a year of rest for God's land. The Year of Jubilee is a special Sabbath Year, celebrated every fifty years, and is beneficial to both God's people and His land.

The Year of Jubilee was a kind of economic and agricultural reset button. Land sold by one generation reverted back to the original owner's family. People who had indentured themselves to others were set free.

In the agrarian society of the Old Testament, the Year of Jubilee prevented individuals from amassing large estates and made it possible for poor families to have the means to try again. It reminded people that God is the One who owns all things. All land, wealth, and physical bodies are temporary, but He endures forever.

Today is Ash Wednesday, the day believers begin counting down to Easter, when Jesus' sacrifice and resurrection gave believers a second chance in God's eyes. Like the Year of Jubilee, Ash Wednesday is a reminder of God's permanence and His love of second chances.

Father God, thank You for giving second chances.

HUMBLE PERSISTENCE

But she answered him, "Yes, Lord; yet even the
dogs under the table eat the children's crumbs."
MARK 7:28 ESV

◆━━━━◆━━━━◆

J esus healed people in a lot of different ways. It didn't matter if they were nearby or far away—if they had faith in Jesus, He worked miracles for them. That's why the episode of Jesus and the Syrophoenician woman is such a surprise. She obviously had faith, but Jesus seemed hesitant to help her.

Mark 7:25–27 (ESV) says, "A woman whose little daughter had an unclean spirit heard of him and came and fell down at his feet. Now the woman was a Gentile, a Syrophoenician by birth. And she begged him to cast the demon out of her daughter. And he said to her, 'Let the children be fed first, for it is not right to take the children's bread and throw it to the dogs.' "

This mother poured out her heart to Jesus and He compared her to a dog? She could have turned away, but she pled her case again, humbly asking for the same treatment a dog would get at the master's table. This woman's faith in Jesus was tested and found true. Jesus healed the woman's daughter.

When your faith is tested, humbly persist. Jesus isn't being mean; He knows what's best. If you have faith, He may not always grant your request, but He will always give you what you need.

Lord, strengthen my faith in You.

MISUNDERSTANDINGS

" 'You have eyes—can't you see? You have ears—can't you hear?' Don't you remember anything at all?"
MARK 8:18 NLT

◆ ◆ ◆

A married couple was packing for a trip when the wife noticed that her husband was unusually quiet. She asked, "What are you thinking?"

"Later," the husband replied and continued packing.

A half hour into their trip, the wife nervously asked her husband, "Are you upset about something? What's wrong?"

The husband looked confused. "Nothing's wrong," he said.

"Earlier, you told me to wait when I asked what you were thinking," she said.

"No," he replied. "You asked what I was thinking. I was thinking about our trip, which was happening later in the day."

Misunderstandings are unfortunately as common today as they were in biblical times. Mark 8:14–21 relates one such misunderstanding.

After the disciples forgot to bring bread with them, Jesus warned them to be wary of the leaven—the yeast that makes bread dough rise—of the Pharisees. The disciples thought Jesus was talking about their lack of bread, forgetting His miraculous ability to multiply food.

The disciples should have known Jesus was warning them against the self-centered "leaven" of the religious authorities. They should have listened better.

If you've been a believer for a while, it may be tempting to tune out and assume you understand what God wants. But what He wants is for you to keep listening so you understand Him perfectly.

Lord, help me listen to understand You perfectly.

THE BIG PICTURE

God reigns over the nations; God sits upon His holy throne.
PSALM 47:8 AMPC

Warehouse workers for nationwide retail chains don't often think about their company's CEO. They have more immediate concerns—getting their jobs done, trying not to get sick, making sure they get to work on time and home on time to take care of their kids. They may see photos of the CEO or get company-wide communications from the CEO occasionally, but for the most part they're caught up in smaller-picture matters.

God's people can be the same way. You might know God rules over everything, but you aren't as concerned with that as with keeping your job, feeding your family, and paying your bills. The tendency is to treat God like an immediate supervisor rather than the owner of the company.

But God is the owner of everything, and His people are subject to Him before anything else.

As Derek Webb sang in his 2005 song "A King and a Kingdom," "My first allegiance is not to a flag, a country, or a man. My first allegiance is not to democracy or blood. It's to a King and a Kingdom."

Don't get lost in the small picture. Are you treating God like an immediate supervisor, or are you serving Him as the King over everything?

Sovereign God, keep me from thinking of You as either too removed to care or too powerless to change things. You are my King.

THE GREATEST

Sitting down, Jesus called the Twelve and said, "Anyone who wants to be first must be the very last, and the servant of all."

MARK 9:35 NIV

◆━━━◆━━━◆

Released in August 1963, *I Am the Greatest* by Cassius Clay—better known in later years as Muhammad Ali—was a Grammy-nominated trash-talking album of spoken word poetry. The title track on the album proclaims, "This brash, young boxer is something to see. And the heavyweight championship is his destiny. This kid fights great. He's got speed and endurance. But if you sign to fight him, increase your insurance."

The boxing legend didn't lack confidence.

Throughout history, many guys have tried to portray themselves as the most talented, most interesting, and most extraordinary men in the universe, but this isn't the way to greatness.

Jesus' disciples learned this lesson in Mark 9:33–35 (NIV): "They came to Capernaum. When he was in the house, he asked them, 'What were you arguing about on the road?' But they kept quiet because on the way they had argued about who was the greatest. Sitting down, Jesus called the Twelve and said, 'Anyone who wants to be first must be the very last, and the servant of all.' "

The world may pay attention to men who call themselves great. Some men, like Ali, are actually great at what they do. But true greatness comes not from a man's abilities or popularity; it comes from his service for God.

Lord, keep me humble and help me serve well.

ONE THING

*As Jesus was starting out on his way to Jerusalem, a man
came running up to him, knelt down, and asked, "Good
Teacher, what must I do to inherit eternal life?"*

MARK 10:17 NLT

Jesus was a fan of the seemingly impossible. He performed amazing miracles. He told His disciples they could move mountains with a tiny amount of faith. But the best seemingly impossible thing Jesus did was clear the path to eternal life.

Unfortunately, for some it's seemingly impossible to find it.

When the rich young ruler asked Jesus what he had to do to inherit eternal life, Jesus told him to follow the Old Testament law.

" 'Teacher,' the man replied, 'I've obeyed all these commandments since I was young.' Looking at the man, Jesus felt genuine love for him. 'There is still one thing you haven't done,' he told him. 'Go and sell all your possessions and give the money to the poor, and you will have treasure in heaven. Then come, follow me.' At this the man's face fell, and he went away sad, for he had many possessions" (Mark 10:20–22 NLT).

Jesus doesn't want or need your possessions. He wasn't saying the young man could buy his way into eternal life. He was pointing to the one thing the man didn't want to give up.

What is the one thing holding you back from God?

Lord, take everything I have so I can have everything You want to give me.

SET APART

"All the days of his vow of separation, no razor shall touch his head.
Until the time is completed for which he separates himself to the LORD,
he shall be holy. He shall let the locks of hair of his head grow long."
NUMBERS 6:5 ESV

A Nazirite was someone who consecrated himself to the Lord to be used for a special purpose. Most Nazirite vows were temporary. The only lifelong Nazirites recorded in the Bible were Samson, Samuel, and John the Baptist.

Nazirites couldn't cut their hair, couldn't eat any products made from grapes, and had to avoid contact with dead bodies. For Nazirites, long hair was a public display of their dedication to God.

In a similar way, Jesus has set you as a believer aside for a special purpose.

First Peter 1:14–16 (ESV) says, "As obedient children, do not be conformed to the passions of your former ignorance, but as he who called you is holy, you also be holy in all your conduct, since it is written, 'You shall be holy, for I am holy.' "

Regardless of your hair length, can others see how the Lord has set you apart? Does your conduct display your dedication to God? Are you avoiding contact with the sins Jesus put to death on the cross?

God is calling you to be holy so others will see the difference and praise Him for His works.

Lord, may my consecration be obvious.

WRITTEN ON OUR HEARTS

*"So shall they put my name upon the people
of Israel, and I will bless them."*
NUMBERS 6:27 ESV

In 1979, archaeologist Gabriel Barkay uncovered two small silver scrolls at a burial site at Ketef Hinnom, just south of Jerusalem. The scrolls were worn as amulets and inscribed with a shortened version of the priestly blessing found in Numbers 6:24–26 (ESV): "The LORD bless you and keep you; the LORD make his face to shine upon you and be gracious to you; the LORD lift up his countenance upon you and give you peace."

These scroll amulets date back to the seventh century BC, putting them among the earliest written evidence of the covenantal name of God—*Yahweh*. This blessing has survived to modern times and can now be found as decorative art in Christian bookstores.

The intention of the priestly blessing was for God's people to carry His name with them as evidence of the old covenant. But we have been given a new covenant. We don't need to wear amulets with God's name and blessing because we have them written on our hearts.

Second Corinthians 3:3 (ESV) says, "And you show that you are a letter from Christ delivered by us, written not with ink but with the Spirit of the living God, not on tablets of stone but on tablets of human hearts."

Are you living as a testament to the Lord?

Jesus, thank You for writing Your name on my heart!

THE SACRIFICE OF THANKSGIVING

"Offer to God a sacrifice of thanksgiving, and perform your vows to the Most High, and call upon me in the day of trouble; I will deliver you, and you shall glorify me."

PSALM 50:14–15 ESV

❖

The sacrifice of thanksgiving isn't when someone forces you to say "Thank you" even when you don't feel like it. It's actually an Old Testament sacrifice akin to the Thanksgiving holiday celebrated in modern times.

Leviticus 7:11–18 outlines how a sacrifice of thanksgiving was to be performed. Basically, the sacrifice was a kind of feast shared by God, the priest who facilitated the offering, and the individual providing the sacrifice. Individuals were even allowed to bring along friends or family members to share in the sacrificial feast.

This kind of sacrifice was different from one offered to cover over sins. It was a celebration of God's goodness because of—or in spite of—the circumstances of the giver's life.

Psalm 50:15 (ESV) gives this reason for performing such a sacrifice: "Call upon me in the day of trouble; I will deliver you, and you shall glorify me."

Whether today is the best day ever or a day of trouble, right now is always the right time to celebrate God's unshakable goodness. You don't give God praise so He will help you, but as recognition that no matter what happens, He is good.

God, help me give thanks at all times.

NOT FAR

When Jesus saw that he had answered wisely, he said to him, "You are not far from the kingdom of God." And from then on no one dared ask him any more questions.

MARK 12:34 NIV

◆ ◆ ◆

The distance between hitting a golf ball onto the green and scoring a hole-in-one may be only a few inches, but the difference is substantial. When a scribe asked Jesus about the most important commandment, their dialogue was like a golf game:

" 'The most important one,' answered Jesus, 'is this: "Hear, O Israel: The Lord our God, the Lord is one. Love the Lord your God with all your heart and with all your soul and with all your mind and with all your strength." The second is this: "Love your neighbor as yourself." There is no commandment greater than these.'

" 'Well said, teacher,' the man replied. 'You are right in saying that God is one and there is no other but him. To love him with all your heart, with all your understanding and with all your strength, and to love your neighbor as yourself is more important than all burnt offerings and sacrifices' " (Mark 12:29–33 NIV).

The scribe hit his ball onto the green. He knew the answers but lacked a relationship with Jesus. If you know the answers too, but aren't spending time with Jesus, "not far" might as well be a million miles from the hole.

Lord, please close the gap between "not far" and safely home.

THE HOLE OF SIN

Behold, I was brought forth in [a state of] iniquity; my mother
was sinful who conceived me [and I too am sinful].
PSALM 51:5 AMPC

H ave you ever tried to dig half a hole? It can't be done. As soon as you start digging, you have a whole hole, no matter how it's shaped. By its nature, there is no such thing as half a hole.

There's also no such thing as kinda sinful. As soon as you sin, you are sinful. And since everyone is born a sinner, no one stands a chance at being righteous. Ecclesiastes 7:20 (AMPC) says, "Surely there is not a righteous man upon earth who does good and never sins."

Fortunately, God knew humans couldn't climb out of the hole of sin by themselves, so He filled in the hole with His own righteousness.

Romans 3:22–23 (AMPC) says, "Namely, the righteousness of God which comes by believing with personal trust and confident reliance on Jesus Christ (the Messiah). [And it is meant] for all who believe. For there is no distinction, since all have sinned and are falling short of the honor and glory which God bestows and receives."

There's no digging your own way out of sin. You need God's help to fill in the hole. He's willing to give you the righteousness you lack so that you can live sin-free in His grace.

Lord, keep me from trying to fix my own sin problems.

HOWEVER

And they told him, "We came to the land to which you sent us.
It flows with milk and honey, and this is its fruit. However, the
people who dwell in the land are strong, and the cities are fortified
and very large. And besides, we saw the descendants of Anak there."
NUMBERS 13:27–28 ESV

Upon the Israelites' arrival at the Promised Land, Moses sent spies from each tribe to explore the land. For forty days, the spies searched out the condition of the land, the fortifications of the cities, the stature of the residents, and the food growing there.

Numbers 13:23 (ESV) says, "And they came to the Valley of Eshcol and cut down from there a branch with a single cluster of grapes, and they carried it on a pole between two of them; they also brought some pomegranates and figs."

Food wasn't going to be a problem. However, the cities were well fortified and the residents were huge. The majority of the spies looked at the challenges and spread fear among their tribes.

The residents of the Promised Land were definitely bigger and stronger than the Israelites, but God was bigger and stronger still.

When you take on a new challenge, don't ignore the problems you'll face, but trust God's ability to help you face them. If God's promises are overshadowed by a "however," your confidence in God is too low.

God, replace my fears of inadequacy with trust in Your ability to help me.

MOVE FORWARD

Peter said to him, "Even if everyone else deserts you, I never will."
MARK 14:29 NLT

◆——————◆——————◆

Scholars believe Peter was Mark's primary source for his account of Jesus' life and work—the Gospel of Mark. This may surprise you, given how many times Mark paints Peter in a negative light.

Following His final Passover meal, Jesus foretold Peter's denial. Mark 14:27–30 (NLT) says, "On the way, Jesus told them, 'All of you will desert me. For the Scriptures say, "God will strike the Shepherd, and the sheep will be scattered." But after I am raised from the dead, I will go ahead of you to Galilee and meet you there.' Peter said to him, 'Even if everyone else deserts you, I never will.' Jesus replied, 'I tell you the truth, Peter—this very night, before the rooster crows twice, you will deny three times that you even know me.' "

Peter promised, but Mark 14:66–72 tells how he failed. God is never surprised by the failures of His people. He knows the best of intentions often go unfulfilled.

When your good intentions turn into bad actions, you have to do what Peter did. Own your mistakes, then move forward in God's grace. Peter didn't let his momentary denial of Christ stop him from becoming the rock on which the church was founded.

Don't let mistakes stop you from being the man God wants you to be.

Lord, forgive my mistakes and help me move forward in grace.

IGNORANCE VERSUS FORGIVENESS

The fool says in his heart, "There is no God." They are corrupt,
and their ways are vile; there is no one who does good.

PSALM 53:1 NIV

L ook at any elementary class when the teacher is absent and you can see the relationship between authority and behavior. In the absence of authority, kids do what they want, fearless of any consequences for their actions.

This is the picture David paints in Psalm 53—a classroom in chaos, the students unaware of the teacher watching from outside the door.

Psalm 53:2–3 (NIV) says, "God looks down from heaven on all mankind to see if there are any who understand, any who seek God. Everyone has turned away, all have become corrupt; there is no one who does good, not even one."

Since other Bible passages say *everyone* is corrupt—see Ecclesiastes 7:20 and Romans 3:10–12—what makes an atheist different from one who believes in God?

The difference isn't one of internal righteousness, but of accepted forgiveness.

David calls atheists "fools," not because they are ignorant of God's existence, but because they deny it in the face of strong evidence. If they deny God's authority, they think they'll avoid sin's repercussions.

Believers, knowing their actions are corrupt, seek forgiveness for sins instead of pretending there are no consequences for them.

If someone you know denies God's existence, don't act holier than them. Show them that forgiveness is better than willful ignorance.

Lord, may Your forgiveness be evident in me.

KORAH'S REBELLION

And as soon as he had finished speaking all these words,
the ground under them split apart. And the earth opened its
mouth and swallowed them up, with their households and all
the people who belonged to Korah and all their goods.
NUMBERS 16:31–32 ESV

❖

Ever get jealous of how God is using someone else? Maybe you wouldn't put it like that. Maybe you just feel like if you were in someone's role, you could do the job better. Or maybe you think some see themselves as superior because they're in charge.

This was what Korah felt toward Moses. As a Levite, Korah served in the tabernacle, but he wasn't a priest and he didn't have the same connection to God. So Korah gathered men to his cause and complained.

Numbers 16:3 (ESV) says, "They assembled themselves together against Moses and against Aaron and said to them, 'You have gone too far! For all in the congregation are holy, every one of them, and the LORD is among them. Why then do you exalt yourselves above the assembly of the LORD?' "

Korah allowed his jealousy to consume him. As a result, he was consumed by the earth at God's command (see Numbers 16:31–32).

If God has given you a task, do it to the best of your ability. Don't look at how He's using someone else. You are responsible for you.

Lord, help me be satisfied with the tasks that are mine to do.

THE BUDDING STAFF

When he went into the Tabernacle of the Covenant the next day,
he found that Aaron's staff, representing the tribe of Levi, had
sprouted, budded, blossomed, and produced ripe almonds!
NUMBERS 17:8 NLT

✦

The civil parish of Aspatria in Cumberland, England, is named for the ash walking stick carried by St. Patrick. Legend tells how St. Patrick, as he traveled back to Ireland from his parents' home, stuck his staff in the ground while he preached. Apparently, it took so long for the people of Aspatria to understand his message that the staff took root and grew into a tree.

The miracle of a staff coming back to life is not unique to St. Patrick. It was also the sign to the Israelites of Aaron's priestly authority before God.

After the rebellion of Korah, God spoke to Moses and had each tribe submit a staff with the tribe's name on it. Aaron added his staff to the others, and they were all placed before the ark of the covenant in the tabernacle for the night. The next day, Aaron's staff had sprouted, flowered, and borne ripe almonds. For the tribes of Israel, the sign was clear: God worked through priests, not directly with individuals—not yet.

Today, the priesthood's ability to come before God is open to everyone because of Jesus' enduring sacrifice. Like St. Patrick's walking stick and Aaron's staff, God breathes His life into previously dead things.

Father, I praise You for breathing life into me!

SEEKING JESUS

"Don't be alarmed," he said. "You are looking for Jesus the Nazarene, who was crucified. He has risen! He is not here. See the place where they laid him. But go, tell his disciples and Peter, 'He is going ahead of you into Galilee. There you will see him, just as he told you.'"

MARK 16:6–7 NIV

The women had a plan. It wasn't a fully formed plan—they had no idea how they were going to roll the stone away from the tomb's entrance—but the women knew they had to see Jesus again. So early in the morning, they gathered spices to anoint His body and went to the tomb where He was buried. But things didn't go as planned.

You probably have a plan for your life. It may not be a fully formed plan. Maybe it only covers eating, working, and sleeping, but it's a plan. Then the unexpected happens and the plan goes out the window.

Like the women at the tomb found out, when you plan to seek Jesus, you will find Him, even if it's not where you thought He'd be.

Matthew 7:7–8 (NIV) says, "Ask and it will be given to you; seek and you will find; knock and the door will be opened to you. For everyone who asks receives; the one who seeks finds; and to the one who knocks, the door will be opened."

Lord, help me find You where You are, not where I'd expect You to be.

FEAR

*In God have I put my trust: I will not be
afraid what man can do unto me.*
PSALM 56:11 KJV

❖ ❖ ❖

Fear is a powerful motivator. When fear hits, the brain gets hijacked by the amygdala and releases chemicals to prompt the fight-or-flight response. Your heart rate increases. Your blood pressure goes up, directing blood away from the intestines and toward skeletal muscles. Your breathing speeds up to supply oxygen to the blood. You are ready for action!

While you may not have control over your body's response to a scary stimulus, you do have the rationality to master your fight-or-flight instinct. When you get back control of your brain, ask yourself, "Is this thing worth being afraid of?"

The best antidote to fear is trust. You may be afraid to jump out of an airplane, but if you trust the parachute, you can overcome your fear. You may be afraid of evil, but if you trust God, your soul is safe from harm.

Matthew 10:28 (ESV) says, "Do not fear those who kill the body but cannot kill the soul. Rather fear him who can destroy both soul and body in hell."

The point isn't to be afraid of God but rather to recognize His power over all situations. Let this holy fear make you ready for action—then trust God with the results of that action.

Lord, help me trust You more than I fear the things of this world.

BALAAM'S LESSON

And the Lord opened the mouth of the donkey, and she said to Balaam,
What have I done to you that you should strike me these three times?
NUMBERS 22:28 AMPC

◆━━━━━◆━━━━━◆

The story of Balaam and his donkey (found in Numbers 22) is pretty funny. Balaam, the world-renowned seer-for-hire (or for-profit prophet) cannot see the angel blocking him on his way to deliver a curse upon Israel. He has been blinded by greed, but his donkey can see reality clearly. When God enables the donkey to speak, Balaam converses with her as though this were a normal, everyday thing. Then God opens Balaam's eyes to see what the donkey sees, and he reacts just as the donkey did—he bows down, falling on his face. When the angel calls out Balaam's cruel treatment of his donkey, Balaam recognizes his sin but is sorrier for getting caught than for committing the sin.

Numbers 22:34 (AMPC) says, "Balaam said to the Angel of the Lord, I have sinned, for I did not know You stood in the way against me. But now, if my going displeases You, I will return."

It would probably be a funnier episode if it didn't sound so familiar. Talking donkeys aren't prevalent, but people are still blinded by sin, treat miracles as commonplace events, and feel worse about getting caught than committing sin. Sound familiar? Pray about it!

Lord, open my eyes and heart to Your truth.

OVERWHELMING GOOD NEWS

And the angel said unto them, Fear not: for, behold, I bring
you good tidings of great joy, which shall be to all people.
LUKE 2:10 KJV

P icture shepherds in a field. It's nighttime. Most are dozing, but a couple stand watch against threats to their flock. Everything is peaceful. . .until it isn't.

Luke 2:9 (ESV) says, "And an angel of the Lord appeared to them, and the glory of the Lord shone around them, and they were filled with great fear."

If you were relaxing in a field and an angel appeared out of seemingly nowhere, you'd be filled with great fear too! Then after the one angel gives the news, a whole host of them appear and proclaim, "Glory to God in the highest, and on earth peace among those with whom he is pleased!" (Luke 2:14 ESV).

It would be an overwhelming experience for anyone. But the most overwhelming part of the angelic visit wasn't the sound or the surprising appearance. It was how Christ's birth was good news for all people. Every person from every nation for all time would be blessed by Jesus' arrival.

Yes, Christmas is nine months and four days away, but it's never too early to celebrate Jesus. The shepherds couldn't keep quiet about the good news they were told (see Luke 2:15–17). You shouldn't either, regardless of the season.

Jesus, help me share the good news of Your arrival with everyone I know.

GOD'S DELIVERANCE

Deliver me from my enemies, O God; be my fortress
against those who are attacking me.
PSALM 59:1 NIV

◆──────◆──────◆

A man's home may be his castle, but it isn't much of a fortress against men intent on violence. Psalm 59 is David's prayer for protection, inspired by events that occurred while King Saul still held Israel's throne.

The scene may be familiar if you've ever seen a comedy about a kid avoiding school. First Samuel 19:11–14 (NIV) says, "Saul sent men to David's house to watch it and to kill him in the morning. But Michal, David's wife, warned him, 'If you don't run for your life tonight, tomorrow you'll be killed.' So Michal let David down through a window, and he fled and escaped. Then Michal took an idol and laid it on the bed, covering it with a garment and putting some goats' hair at the head. When Saul sent the men to capture David, Michal said, 'He is ill.' "

By the time the men searched the home and found the decoy, David was praying and writing psalms in the next county over.

While Saul lived, David knew his life was in danger, but instead of eliminating the threat, David prayed for deliverance. He did what he could by listening to the life-saving advice of others, but he knew God was his fortress above all else.

When you need deliverance, use common sense and trust God—like David did.

God, You are my fortress.

JESUS' GROWTH MONTAGE

*And Jesus increased in wisdom and in stature
and in favor with God and man.*
LUKE 2:52 ESV

◆——————◆——————◆

A "montage" is a film technique where a series of clips are edited together, usually set to music, and used to show the passage of time or repetitive events in a digestible form. If the book of Luke were a film, Luke 2:52 would be shown as a montage.

Sandwiched between Jesus as a boy teaching his elders and John the Baptist preparing the way for Jesus' adult ministry, this verse might get lost in a daily reading, but it communicates a mind-boggling truth about Jesus.

As God in the flesh, Jesus had all of God's abilities and powers at His disposal. Yet Luke 2:52 shows Him as fully human. Jesus grew up, gaining wisdom and stature and favor—like a normal guy.

If it was possible for Jesus—God incarnate—to grow in wisdom, you have no right to act like a know-it-all. If Jesus went through puberty and grew up physically like the rest of us, He understands humanity at its most awkward level. And if Jesus could grow in favor with God, being God Himself, you must never portray yourself to the world as having arrived spiritually.

Luke 2:52 shows how Jesus became more than He was, and He came to make you more too.

---

*Lord, help me grow in wisdom and favor by
reading Your Word and becoming like You.*

GENEALOGY

"Produce fruit in keeping with repentance. And do not begin to say to yourselves, 'We have Abraham as our father.' For I tell you that out of these stones God can raise up children for Abraham."
LUKE 3:8 NIV

◆   ◆   ◆

Interest in genealogy research has skyrocketed with the advent of the internet and DNA analysis. Sites like Ancestry.com and services like 23andMe make it possible to identify previously unknown family members across the globe. The idea of belonging to a specific family is an important aspect of someone's identity as a person.

This was especially true in New Testament times. Paul, a former Pharisee, cited his ancestry as a potential source of pride. In Philippians 3:4–5 (NIV), he says, "If someone else thinks they have reasons to put confidence in the flesh, I have more: circumcised on the eighth day, of the people of Israel, of the tribe of Benjamin, a Hebrew of Hebrews; in regard to the law, a Pharisee."

Family is important, but if your identity is caught up more in your genealogy than in being a child of God, your priorities are off. God wants the world to see your resemblance to Him more than your resemblance to your parents or grandparents.

Want to look like your heavenly Father? Bear fruit in keeping with repentance. Show the Spirit's work in your life. Humbly love others as God loves you.

God, may I look like You.

SHORTCUTS

"I will give you the glory of these kingdoms and authority over them," the devil said, "because they are mine to give to anyone I please. I will give it all to you if you will worship me."
LUKE 4:6–7 NLT

———◆———◆———◆———

What if there was an easier way? It's an innocent question that can open the door to wicked possibilities.

Jesus came to save the world for our good and for the glory of God. He went to the cross to pay for our sins, and God was glorified by His sacrifice. But what if there was an easier way? Before you condemn this as heretical thinking, remember that Jesus Himself asked the Father whether there was another way (see Matthew 26:39).

Satan had a shortcut. In exchange for a little worship, Satan would give Jesus the glory of all the kingdoms of the world (see Luke 4:6–7).

Did Satan really have the authority to make this offer to Jesus? John 12:31 (NLT) refers to Satan as "the ruler of this world." Whether or not he had the authority, Satan's offer came with a catch. Jesus had to disobey the first commandment by worshipping Satan instead of God.

Whenever a shortcut comes with a commandment-breaking catch, do what Jesus did. Answer Satan's temptation with scripture and submit yourself to God. Say, "Not my will, but Yours be done."

Lord, help me take the hard way when a shortcut would dishonor You.

SIN HAS CONSEQUENCES

*But if you will not do so, behold, you have sinned against
the Lord; and be sure your sin will find you out.*
NUMBERS 32:23 AMPC

A s they approached Canaan, the Israelite tribes of Reuben and Gad saw an opportunity for themselves in the area south of the Sea of Galilee, outside the Promised Land. The land was good for livestock and for raising families, so they came to Moses with an offer. The men of Reuben and Gad would lead the Israelites in conquering the Promised Land in exchange for the area south of it.

Moses accepted the offer but gave this warning: If they didn't help the rest of the Israelites conquer the Promised Land, they would have sinned against the Lord and they would suffer the consequences. Even if Moses wasn't around to make sure they followed through, the Lord would know and their sin would find them out.

Sin always has consequences. Whether a broken promise—the sin in question in today's verse—or adultery or a lie or simple selfishness, sin *always* has consequences. Whether anyone else discovers your sin, God knows about it, and the presence of sin in your life breaks the relationship between you and Him.

Fortunately, Jesus' sacrifice has paid for your sins. His forgiveness is available to all who repent. Turn from your sin and accept God's grace, and your relationship with Him will be restored.

God, thank You for offering restoration when my sin breaks our relationship.

UNSHAKABLE FORTRESS

For God alone my soul waits in silence; from him
comes my salvation. He alone is my rock and my
salvation, my fortress; I shall not be greatly shaken.
PSALM 62:1–2 ESV

Included in the classic film *Raiders of the Lost Ark* is a scene where Indiana Jones faces an accomplished swordfighter. The swordsman has obviously spent years honing his craft because he flourishes his blade with impressive skill. The script for the film originally called for Indy to have a long sword fight with this guy, but the filming process was running behind and the set was incredibly hot. Finally, someone suggested Indy use the gun on his belt to take down the swordsman, and the iconic scene was born.

You may think you have great defenses built up around you. You may take comfort in your bank account. Maybe your house is an underground nuclear bunker. Or possibly you've spent your life learning martial arts. When it comes to God, your protective measures are as useful as a sword in a gunfight.

Learning to defend yourself isn't a bad thing, but no one can defend himself from God's will. Fortunately, He's on your side. He is the fortress that cannot be shaken, and prayer is your key into His safety. God doesn't promise you won't face trouble, but no matter what troubles you face, your soul is safe with Him.

God, may the safety of my soul give me peace beyond understanding.

UNPOPULAR OPINION

"Not one of you from this wicked generation will live to see the good land I swore to give your ancestors, except Caleb son of Jephunneh. He will see this land because he has followed the Lord completely. I will give to him and his descendants some of the very land he explored during his scouting mission."

DEUTERONOMY 1:35–36 NLT

Caleb was one of the twelve spies who searched out the Promised Land prior to the Israelites' forty-year sojourn in the wilderness. He was one of the only ones to advocate for Israel's immediate possession of the land. As such, he was one of the only ones from his generation who survived the wilderness to see the Israelites enter the Promised Land.

When he spied out the land, did Caleb not see the giants who lived there? Did he miss the fortified cities? No. He saw everything the other spies saw, but his vision didn't stop at the difficulties they'd face. Caleb saw a powerful God who led His people out of slavery with miracle after miracle. Caleb's faith in God was stronger than his fear of the enemy.

There will be times when your faith in God will put you in the minority. Your opinions won't be popular with the leaders of this world. When you face such a time, remember that Caleb's faith was rewarded while the other spies were allowed to die in the wilderness.

Lord, may my faith be stronger than my fear.

FOUR WOES

"But woe to you who are rich, for you have received your consolation. Woe to you who are full now, for you shall be hungry. Woe to you who laugh now, for you shall mourn and weep. Woe to you, when all people speak well of you, for so their fathers did to the false prophets."

LUKE 6:24–26 ESV

T he American dream is sometimes described as an American's inalienable rights to life, liberty, and the pursuit of happiness. It's found in the Declaration of Independence and has pervaded the American ethos since this country was founded.

Life and liberty are easy enough to understand, but the pursuit of happiness can mean just about anything. Many Americans think money will make them happy, so they see America as a place to get rich. Some Americans see food as the answer to happiness, which might be why the US is among the most obese countries in the world. Some seek happiness by pushing bad feelings away through entertainment. Some think happiness is having the most "likes" on social media.

If riches, food, laughter, and popularity are the things you pursue to be happy, Jesus says, "Woe to you."

America is a great place, but it is not a believer's final destination. This existence is not the reward. It is the battleground. If you are satisfied with the American dream, you're settling for less than God's best.

Lord, please reorder my priorities.

A JEALOUS GOD

For the Lord your God is a consuming fire, a jealous God.
Deuteronomy 4:24 niv

J ealousy is usually seen as a bad thing, but there are times when it is the essence of love. The word *jealous* has the same origin as the word *zeal*. The idea is one of exclusive commitment to and fervor for a person or thing. When God made a covenant with the Israelites, He was looking for an exclusive commitment in the same way married couples take vows to be exclusive to each other.

God doesn't want to share your affections with lesser gods. You might be thinking, *No problem. I don't have any idols lying around.* But idols are sneaky things. You may not have a statue of a cow you bow down to, but you might have a flat-screen TV that demands more attention than your Bible gets.

God isn't jealous because He's worried or has low self-esteem. He knows no idol man could worship is able to take care of his needs. He wants to be your exclusive God because He alone can take care of you. Why waste time on anything less?

Lord God, forgive me for the times I turn to idols to get my needs met instead of coming to You. Make me exclusively Yours. Close my ears to the voices that offer to take care of me, when really I am Yours alone to take care of as You please.

HELPING THE POWERLESS

Then he went up and touched the bier they were carrying him on, and the bearers stood still. He said, "Young man, I say to you, get up!" The dead man sat up and began to talk, and Jesus gave him back to his mother.

LUKE 7:14–15 NIV

Jesus had compassion for everyone, but He specifically sought opportunities to help the powerless—and few people in society were more powerless than childless widows. In Jesus' day, a woman's rights were bound up in her husband or male children. If a woman didn't have a man in her life to speak for her and protect her, she might well be cast out of society to become a beggar.

So when Jesus saw the widow of Nain walking alongside her only son's coffin, He used the opportunity. In a scene reminiscent of the Old Testament prophet Elijah—see 1 Kings 17:17–24—Jesus brought the widow's son back to life.

The widow now had a protector again. The people who witnessed the miracle believed Jesus was the prophet they were waiting for. Modern readers can see an example of Christ's heart and priorities.

As Jesus sought out opportunities to help the powerless, so should you. The widows of Jesus' society were practically voiceless, but Jesus heard their cries. In what position of society has God placed you to hear the voiceless? How can you lend them your power?

Lord, help me to see and act on opportunities to help the powerless.

YOUR REFUGE

The righteous will rejoice in the LORD and take refuge in him.
PSALM 64:10 NIV

◆————◆————◆

When God says you can rejoice in Him and take refuge in Him, that's exactly what He means. No matter how you feel today, God loves you and always will. He is always near enough that you can run to Him whenever you need shelter from life's storms.

The enemy likes to confuse you by telling you that God isn't really there for you, that He has left you alone to fend for yourself. The devil likes to slip close to you and tell you that God is too far away to hear you or comfort you. But the Bible says otherwise.

Believe that God's love for you doesn't change. Take refuge in Him and stay connected to His Word. See the Bible as His letter to you. God's written Word says that He takes care of His people when they are going through difficult times. In the middle of life's storms, God always stands up for His children and protects them.

So rejoice in the Lord—and always remember that you can run to Him, your place of refuge, when life is tough and you don't know what to do.

Lord, sometimes it's hard to believe that You really care about what I'm going through. Help me remember that You love me. Thank You for this new day. Stay close to me and be my refuge and strength.

WHAT'S YOUR MOTIVATION?

Love the LORD your God and keep his requirements,
his decrees, his laws and his commands always.
DEUTERONOMY 11:1 NIV

Today's scripture verse tells us much about the kind of relationship God wants with His people—one based on mutual love.

God wants you to love Him, and He wants that love to motivate you to live in a way that pleases Him. It really is that simple!

The fact that God *commanded* Israel to love Him says something about the nature of the Christian man's love for the Lord—namely, that loving God isn't a matter of feelings or emotions but of choice. You can't always trust your feelings, but you can choose to hold fast to your commitment to God.

You can do all kinds of things that God says to do in the Bible, but it doesn't mean anything if love isn't your primary motivation. God loves you, and He wants everything you do to come as a result of your love for Him.

When you try to obey God's commands just because you think it's the right thing to do or because you're afraid of the consequences of disobedience, then you're headed for failure. But when you choose first to love God, you'll find that obedience becomes your second nature.

Father, thank You that I can have a relationship with You based on love. Help me to live the life You want me to live because I love You.

OBEY AND SERVE

It is the LORD your God you must follow, and him you must revere.
Keep his commands and obey him; serve him and hold fast to him.
DEUTERONOMY 13:4 NIV

Sometimes life can feel overwhelming, but those who trust and obey God can have overwhelming joy in their hearts. This was true for people in the Bible, and it's true now. God made sure His word to His children is constant. Jesus said there would be trials but that He would overcome the world.

It's easy to forget that God always sees and hears you. But God does hear you because He thinks about you and loves you so very much. He calls you His child, and that makes you worthy of His love.

When you remember your true identity in Christ, life's problems won't seem so ominous. When you recall that Jesus knew you while you were still in your mother's womb and that He died for you, you will spend more of your time praising Him and holding fast to Him. You will never go wrong when you keep God's Word in your heart and obey and serve Him!

Father, some days it feels like the world is closing in around
me and I'm trapped. Even though I know You love me, I let
doubt creep in. Take over and give me rest. Remind me how
important it is for me to hold fast to You and obey You.

GOD'S CONSISTENT LOVE

Come and see what God has done,
his awesome deeds for mankind!
PSALM 66:5 NIV

G od is not a human, and that means He doesn't change His mind. God won't tell you He loves you one day and then turn His back on you the next. That's not who He is. He wants you to know that His character and love are consistent. He wants you to depend on Him, especially on days when your life seems to be falling apart.

When you feel like God is distant and nothing makes sense, let His love for you be the anchor that keeps you stable in the storm. Only then can you see each day as a gift to be enjoyed with your heavenly Father.

As you study God's Word, let it fill your heart with truth. Let it be your spiritual food that keeps you satisfied all day long. Tell God everything that's on your heart. He wants to listen to you because He loves you and wants you to spend time with Him every day.

Lord, thank You for listening to me when I come to You.
Help me remember that You are always with me and that
You love me. Thank You for giving me this new day to spend
in Your presence. Help me to bring You glory today.

HE CARES

For the LORD your God will bless you in all your harvest and
in all the work of your hands, and your joy will be complete.
DEUTERONOMY 16:15 NIV

You are God's precious child. He knows you like no one else knows you and cares for you more than anyone else will ever care for you. God loves you with a love that knows no equal and that will never end.

The enemy will tell you lies about God's love, hoping to make you doubt. He wants you to doubt that what God says is true. The attacks sound like, *You're not really as important to God as you think.* Or *God is tired of you doing the same wrong thing over and over.* Or *You are one out of billions of people. There's no way God can love you like you think He does.*

Nothing is strong enough to pull you away from God's love. Let your heart be rooted in who He is and in His love for you. Keep your eyes on Him and His goodness—and never forget how much He cares for you. When you do, your feet will remain on solid ground.

Lord, thank You for being at the beginning of my day and staying with me all the way through it. There are days when I feel like You're far away, taking care of other people and forgetting about me. Remind me daily how much You care about me.

LIFE'S DISTRACTIONS

"Take nothing for the journey—no staff, no bag,
no bread, no money, no extra shirt."
LUKE 9:3 NIV

◆━━━━◆━━━━◆

Distractions everywhere! Phones. TVs. Books. Games. Then there's shopping, sports, errands, chores—an endless list of activities tempting you to neglect spending time with your heavenly Father. These things are not necessarily wrong, but they can become idols if you're not careful.

God can deliver you from harm and keep you from becoming distracted. That doesn't mean you won't have trouble in this life—remember, Jesus said there would be trouble. But the good news is that He has overcome the world. The enemy knows he cannot beat you, so he tries to get your mind off God and on life's issues. Don't let him succeed!

God is your source of spiritual strength, so you need to keep your focus on Him above anything else. Don't let the cares, burdens, and distractions of life pull you away from that wonderful place of real faith in God. Believe that He is with you and for you always.

God, thank You for caring about me. Some days I can tell that
the devil is trying to take my eyes off You. He tries to keep me
looking down at the distractions of the world and not up at
Your glorious throne. Help me see You in everything today.

GOD IS GOOD TO YOU

The land yields its harvest; God, our God, blesses us.
PSALM 67:6 NIV

◆━━━━━◆━━━━━◆

Think about all the ways God has been good to you. Keep a record of the harvest He has provided for you. When you do that, you'll be surprised at the true riches you've received from Him. Consider this new day an opportunity to rejoice at the goodness the Lord has shown you. Take some time to marvel at the different ways His love has brightened your days.

The devil is lurking around the corner, hoping you won't recognize God's goodness and provisions. He's always there, tempting you on those long days when your patience is like a frayed rope. He wants you to leave thoughts of God's blessings on the ground as you walk through life untethered to heaven's bounty.

But remember God's mercy—when Jesus saved you, when He made a way from the desert to the fertile field of forgiveness. The gift of new life welled up within your heart and freed you from the chains of sin. God chose to show you compassion instead of wrath, love instead of fury. Recall just how good God has been—and continues to be—to you.

Lord, each day seems to have a way of taking my eyes off You
and Your goodness. Open my eyes to all the ways You bless me.
Thank You for everything You do for me.

TRUE GREATNESS

"For it is the one who is least among you all who is the greatest."
LUKE 9:48 NIV

When the disciples asked Jesus who was the greatest of their group, His reply showed them the importance of being humble, serving from a heart of love, and knowing that God is in charge.

Your life in Christ is not about trying to be the most important or the greatest. It's about humbly serving God and others first. It's about seeing others as more important than yourself. It's about following the example of Jesus, who came to earth not to be served but to serve and to give you His very best.

Humility before Jesus will give you all the confidence you need to serve Him and to treat others as more important than yourself. Set down your pride and embrace humility. When you do, you'll see His greatness at work in your life. When you put Jesus first in every way, He will show you true greatness.

Jesus, sometimes I feel tempted to serve myself before I serve others, to try to make myself great in other people's eyes. You told Your closest followers they shouldn't act that way. Please keep me humble and willing to be the "least" of Your followers.

NEVER STOP

You gave abundant showers, O God;
you refreshed your weary inheritance.
PSALM 68:9 NIV

Sometimes waiting on God can be a difficult test of patience. But realizing that God has you right where you are for a reason can help you hold on. Don't let unanswered prayers distract you from seeking Him and asking Him for what you need. Never stop pursuing Him, and never stop asking Him for what you know He wants you to have.

God doesn't get tired of hearing from you, and He doesn't roll His eyes when you ask for the same things over and over. So spend more time with Him and focus on His character as you bring your requests to Him. He wants you to keep seeking and asking, knowing that He wants to bless you.

God is in the business of taking care of what's precious to Him. That includes you! Stop worrying about why certain things happen (or don't happen) the way they do and start getting to know your Maker with everything that's in you. When you devote time to your heavenly Father, life will begin to make sense. Don't keep getting caught up in all the distractions. Never stop getting caught up in Jesus and following after Him with all your heart.

Father, help me to stay focused on You and Your goodness as I
wait for You to answer me when I bring my requests to You.

THE DONKEY AND THE KING

"Love the Lord your God with all your heart and with all your soul and with all your strength and with all your mind."

LUKE 10:27 NIV

Members of the Roman army rode on horses to show their military power. Jesus rode into the city of Jerusalem on a donkey, an animal that symbolized peace. Many people lined the streets to see the man they thought would save them from Roman rule. But Jesus was there to save people from themselves. He was there to show them and the world what true love looks like.

Jesus was about to lay down His life for the world. He loved humanity so much that He left His home in heaven to come to earth to die so that lost people could be saved. But many in the crowd left that day missing the point. They walked away from Jesus, not receiving His love.

Rejoice that you are called a child of the King! Spend the rest of your days loving Him with everything within you and resting in the peace His love brings. Thank Jesus for loving you enough to ride that donkey into the city where He would eventually give up His life so that you can live forever with Him in heaven.

Jesus, thank You for being my example of real love. Please help me live my life like I was there that glorious day You entered Jerusalem on a donkey's colt. Help me love You with everything I have.

WHEN HE SPEAKS

For I command you today to love the LORD your God, to walk in obedience to him, and to keep his commands, decrees and laws.
DEUTERONOMY 30:16 NIV

◆――――◆――――◆

Sometimes it's easy to forget that God *wants* to do good things for you. He is in the business of blessing His people—as long as they obey Him from a heart of love. This is what faith is all about. It's knowing that God wants to have a loving relationship with you so that He can give you great things. Love always gives, and God's perfect love gives perfectly.

The enemy's number one goal is to keep you from loving God with your whole heart—to keep you from following Him and spending time with Him in prayer. If he can do that, he can more easily tempt you into disobedience, which robs you of God's very best.

Seeing God's blessings in your life comes down to one thing: obeying what God tells you to do in His written Word, the Bible. Yes, it really is that simple! The more you do life God's way, the quicker your eyes will be open to the glorious riches He has for you.

Lord, thank You for Your love. Help me to obey You from a heart of true love—not because I'm afraid You'll stop loving me. Remind me that I am loved and that You have good things for me when I do the things You've told me to do.

GOD'S PROTECTION

Summon your power, God; show us your strength,
our God, as you have done before.
Psalm 68:28 niv

God's love and protection are all around you. The Bible says that God goes before you and behind you, keeping you safe from the enemy's and the world's attacks. Nothing can sneak up and snatch you away from Him. Even though you may not be aware of it, God powerfully protects you at all times.

God's power made the universe, and it also made your heart. His power formed the mountains, and it also sustains your life. God's power is mighty enough to carry you through your current struggles and place you gently down in peaceful places.

The enemy is most effective when he can get you to question God's promises. He tries to attack your hope during those times when you are waiting for God. In those times, recall what God's power looks like. Read your Bible and see how God protected and cared for His servants, even in the most perilous circumstances.

God did that for His people in ages past—and He does it for you today!

Lord, help me to remember the truth that You protect me and preserve me, even when I'm not aware of it. Help me remember that You hear and see everything. Thank You for having everything under control!

CLEANING UP

"Be generous to the poor, and everything will be clean for you."
LUKE 11:41 NIV

◆━━━━━◆━━━━━◆

J esus was invited to the home of a Pharisee for dinner. This Jewish religious leader was surprised that Jesus didn't wash before sitting down for the meal. But Jesus knew what He was doing. In fact, He pronounced a handful of "woes" as He explained to the man that his focus was on the wrong things and on the wrong place. Jesus told him that it doesn't matter how clean the outside looks. The inside is what matters.

It was the same all the way back in the Garden of Eden, when the devil tempted Adam and Eve with the things they could see. On the outside, what was wrong with eating a little fruit? On the inside, the first couple would deliberately disobey their Creator and open the door for sin to contaminate their hearts.

Jesus told the Pharisee to be generous to the poor. To live an unselfish life. To live more like Jesus did and less like he had been living.

Think about the ways your life has changed since Jesus "washed" you. Having your heart washed clean opened your eyes to see more of God's blessings—and to see how you can bless others.

Lord, I need to confess that I'm often just worried about me. Please clean up what's on the inside. I know that when You do that, I'll be changed— changed in my thinking and in the way I treat others.

NOTHING TO FEAR

*"Be strong and courageous. Do not be afraid; do not be discouraged,
for the LORD your God will be with you wherever you go."*
JOSHUA 1:9 NIV

When you feel anxious or lacking in confidence, think about how Joshua might have felt when God put him in charge of leading the Israelites into the Promised Land. He had to follow Moses as leader of a whole nation. Talk about feeling inadequate! If anyone had opportunity to feel unworthy, it was Joshua.

God knows exactly what you're going through. He knows your feelings of inadequacy. But He has called you to be a light in a dark world. Hear Him tell you to be strong because He is your strength and to be courageous because He is your source of courage. God is on your side, and He is infinitely bigger than any struggle you will ever face.

God promised to be with Joshua wherever he went—and He promises you the very same thing. The enemy will try to make you feel isolated and unworthy, but God always encourages you and strengthens you with His presence. That's because He wants you to succeed in doing the things He has called you to do.

*Heavenly Father, thank You for being my source of
strength and encouragement. Help me to keep my eyes from
focusing too much on the size of my problems here on earth.
Keep my mind and heart focused on You every day.*

AT THE CROSS

"For where your treasure is, there your heart will be also."
LUKE 12:34 NIV

A beautiful treasure is left in plain sight amid the darkness of Golgotha. Right there, where all the pain and sadness came together, is a heart of love that beats for you. It was strong enough to handle the mocking soldiers and their whips, and it was humble enough to be spit on and not spit back. Your Savior's heart was giving enough to make sure you had a way home, back to the loving arms of your Creator.

Good Friday, when we commemorate the day our Lord was made to carry His cross through crowds of onlookers, doesn't necessarily feel like a day of celebration. At first glance, it feels more like a somber moment when evil won and all that was good perished. But don't lose sight of the cross. It was there that the King of kings said, "It is finished."

Where is your treasure? Is it in something made by human hands? Jesus, your perfect and wonderful treasure, said your heart is where your treasure is. Let your heart be found in Him.

Lord, I can't imagine what You went through the day You gave Your all on the cross. Before the pain and anguish tore at Your heart and body, You prayed for me. Please help my heart stay connected to You.

JESUS IS ALIVE!

May your salvation, God, protect me.
PSALM 69:29 NIV

◆————————◆————————◆

The cross holds great worth for you. The Romans intended it to bring death, but God used it to bring salvation and eternal life. The crowds gathered and witnessed the ultimate sacrifice for you and countless others who have called on the Name above all names. Jesus gave His life so you could have life eternally.

Once Jesus was placed inside the grave, a massive stone was rolled in front of the opening and guards were ordered to keep watch. The enemy employs a similar tactic in your daily life. He will throw one obstacle after another in your path to try to keep you distracted and feeling trapped. He wants all your attention on the problems so you might forget that the grave wasn't the end for Jesus.

Jesus is alive! And because He lives, the power of sin and death is broken. Because He lives, you can have unbroken fellowship with the God who loved you enough to send His only Son to earth. Because He lives, you get to live forever with Him in heaven.

Lord, thank You for showing me that the sadness of the grave didn't last long. You died, but You rose again! Thank You for always being with me and for reminding me of the love You demonstrated for me when You conquered sin and death by fulfilling Your promise to rise from the dead.

ALIVE AND WELL

May those who long for your saving help always say, "The LORD is great!"
PSALM 70:4 NIV

◆   ◆   ◆

God is so much bigger than your burdens. He is the Almighty One who parted seas and caused high city walls to crumble. He fed His people in the desert when they were hungry and calmed the stormy seas. And He is the One who brought Jesus back from the dead.

But just think about this for a moment: that same power that raised Jesus from death to life is in you through God's Holy Spirit! Nothing on earth compares. Nothing this world has to offer will ever be able to give you the power that comes from God.

This is who your God is—and what He does for you. He is powerful enough to do all the things listed above—and loving enough to care for you and every one of your needs.

Today is Easter, the day Christians around the world commemorate Jesus' resurrection. Make time to listen to Him today. Praise Him for His love—a love so strong that He came to earth so that you can live with Him forever in heaven.

Lord Jesus, thank You for giving Yourself for me. On this day, I want to reflect on the fact that even though You died a terrible death for me on a cross made of wood, You didn't stay in the grave for long. You're alive!

SUNLIGHT AND STORM

Be my rock of safety where I can always hide.
PSALM 71:3 NLT

———◆———◆———◆———

God is not some faraway entity who won't answer when you call on Him. He loves you and wants you to call on Him and ask Him to keep you safe. He will answer you every time you call on Him. In fact, He blesses you and protects you even before you ask Him.

The enemy wants you to feel alone and isolated. If he can get you to focus on your situation and your feelings, then he has you right where he wants you. He hopes you'll grow weary waiting for God to answer and give up.

But there's hope, so you don't have to give up. That hope's name is Jesus, and He understands everything about you and wants you to find peace and safety in Him. He wants you to hide in the shadow of His wings and give Him all your worries and cares.

Whether the sun is shining or the rain is pouring, let Jesus be your constant. He will never let you down!

Lord, help me remember that You will never leave me and that You are my place of safety. Remind me every day that You love me and have good things for me. Remind me that You are always with me and will give me victory.

PRAISE HIM MORE AND MORE

As for me, I will always have hope; I will praise you more and more.
PSALM 71:14 NIV

C linging to hope no matter what kind of day you're having is the best way to walk with Jesus. Having hope in Him doesn't mean simple wishful thinking. It's knowing that Jesus has a perfect will for your life. It's knowing that no matter your present situation, He's always with you, always blessing you.

Praise God today for every single thing He has given you and done for you. Praise Him for giving you a hope that will never disappoint—even through those times when you're faced with so many unknowns. Praise Him and thank Him for saving you, and cultivate a heart of thanksgiving for the ways He will continue to bless you and keep you until the day you enter His eternal kingdom.

Maintaining a grateful spirit means praising and thanking God more and more each day. So use His special gift of "today" to make yourself a living song of praise for the God who gives you His very best every day.

Lord, I want to praise You more and more each day. Remind me daily to express my gratitude for all You have done for me— and for all You continue to do for me each and every day.

SELFLESS SERVICE

*"When you give a banquet, invite the poor, the crippled,
the lame, the blind, and you will be blessed."*

LUKE 14:13–14 NIV

◆ ◆ ◆

A Christian man shouldn't do things for others so he can receive something in return in this life. Jesus calls His followers to serve "the least of these" (Matthew 25:40) and said that people who serve those who cannot repay them here on earth will receive their reward in heaven.

If you're like most men, you are often tempted to worry about yourself, even as you do all you can to serve others. Sometimes you might be tempted to spend your time building your own kingdom here on earth instead of working for God's eternal kingdom. But that's not how God wants you to think or live.

Ask God to renew your mind and change your heart so that you can focus on what matters most. Serving people and being a light for Jesus is a great way to stay connected to the Lord's blessings. Spend your time looking for ways to be a blessing to others, and let God handle the blessings He has for you.

---

*Lord, forgive me for spending so much time thinking about myself
and how I can be blessed in this life. Help me to worship You by
forgetting about myself and serving You and others out of a heart
of pure, selfless love. Please give me opportunities to serve others.*

SHOUT FOR JOY!

My lips will shout for joy when I sing praise
to you—I whom you have delivered.
PSALM 71:23 NIV

Think about God and His unfailing love for you. His love is always there to lift you up and remind you that He has delivered you from the power of sin and death. No matter how many mistakes you make, God still loves you and wants to forgive you and cleanse you. His love is there to lift your spirits and keep your heart connected with His.

You can know that your heavenly Father shares in your sadness during your dreary days of sorrow. You can feel secure enough in His love to allow Him to carry all of your burdens. And you can live unshakably for Him when you take His hand and let Him lead you to a place of peace and rest.

Let go of the regrets and grab on to God's compassion. Then you will shout for joy as you remember that He has redeemed you and will bless you through every day and every challenge.

Dear God, thank You for loving me. Remind me daily that You have redeemed me and that I will live with You for all eternity. When I think on those things, I will shout with joy as I praise Your wonderful name.

A RELATIONSHIP WITH GOD

"There will be more rejoicing in heaven over one sinner who repents than over ninety-nine righteous persons who do not need to repent."
LUKE 15:7 NIV

It's clear from reading the four Gospels that relationships with people were at the heart of Jesus' earthly ministry. From the very beginning in Eden, God made people to be in relationship with Him.

In today's scripture verse, Jesus reminded His followers how very important it is to Him—and to all of heaven—when one sinner repents and is brought into a relationship with the heavenly Father.

Jesus gave His followers the Great Commission so they could know their purpose in life. Leading people to Jesus usually takes time, because it takes time to build relationships. When people know you really care, they will trust that you have their best interests in mind. Sharing the Gospel at that point is a natural next step and will be received much more easily than if you didn't have a relationship.

Let people know that Jesus is your King and that He is the most important person in your life. God made you and wants to bless you so you can be a blessing to others. Stay connected to Jesus and boldly share His love with a broken world.

Lord, help me be intentional in seeking out people who are hurting and need You. Give me the courage to share my faith. Show me how to love them like You do.

FULFILLED PROMISES

*Not one of all the LORD's good promises to
Israel failed; every one was fulfilled.*
JOSHUA 21:45 NIV

God is a promise maker and a promise keeper. He made you and promised never to leave you. He saved you and keeps His promise by never letting you go.

Today's verse makes a remarkable claim—namely, that God kept every one of His many promises to the people of Israel. That is an overarching theme throughout the rest of the Bible too—that God keeps *all* of His promises.

God promises to bless you and to reveal good and helpful plans for you. Is there an area in your life where you need Him to do something or provide something for you? Are you comfortable enough and secure enough in His love to tell Him what you need?

Don't forget that God has promised to take care of you. He is looking at you right now and making great plans to satisfy you so completely that you won't have a reason to feel anxious about anything. Trust Him and take Him at His word. Live unshakably, knowing that when God makes a promise, He keeps it—always.

*God, thank You for Your unfailing love. Thank You for
promising to be with me always and to take care of all my
needs. Help me to trust that You keep all Your promises.*

PURE IN HEART

Surely God is good to Israel, to those who are pure in heart.
PSALM 73:1 NIV

———◆———◆———◆———

What do you need to do to place yourself in a position to receive all God has for you? That's a great question to help you realign your priorities so that Jesus is first in every area of your life—so that you are "pure in heart."

When you commit yourself wholly to the Lord, you can be confident that nothing in the world can defeat you. When you stay connected to Him, when you keep your heart pure and humble and tell Him with sincerity that He means everything to you, you'll remain right in the middle of His goodness.

Do a quick inventory of the things that are most important to you. When Jesus is first on that list, you can be sure that your heart will be in step with His priorities. Not only that, but you'll put yourself in the right place to receive all He has for you.

Stay anchored to God's heart because His heart is for you. When you do that, His goodness will rain over you every day.

Lord Jesus, I want You to be my everything. Purify my heart so I can give You the worship You deserve. Help me make my life all about You. Please show me how to put myself—and keep myself— in a place where I can experience Your goodness in my life.

REAL FAITH

"If you have faith as small as a mustard seed, you can say to this mulberry tree, 'Be uprooted and planted in the sea,' and it will obey you."

LUKE 17:6 NIV

The Bible has much to say about what faith can do for you. Faith is at the heart of God's work of saving you for eternity. Faith is what moves God to empower you to serve Him and do the work He has called you to do. And faith is necessary to receive the things God has promised to provide for you.

Faith is simply believing God and taking Him at His word. Faith keeps you praying about the things that can keep you up at night. Faith gives you the perseverance you need to keep praying, even when things aren't happening as quickly as you'd like. And faith helps keep you doing what God wants you to do.

Take some quiet time to reflect on everything God has already done for you—and then let that build up your faith. Let your faith assure you that He is working in your heart right now to make you into the man He created you to be.

God, help me to have stronger faith. Remind me that there is never a time You leave me alone to try to figure things out for myself. Thank You, Lord, for loving me and caring for me.

A BEAUTIFUL THING

*My flesh and my heart may fail, but God is the
strength of my heart and my portion forever.*
PSALM 73:26 NIV

Sometimes life feels like a roller coaster, with a million ups and downs—and more downs than ups. But you can take encouragement in the truth that God wants to be your "enough" in every situation—or, as today's verse puts it, "the strength of [your] heart and [your] portion forever."

Believe that your heavenly Father is working right now to create a beautiful thing in you and through you—even though you feel like your flesh and heart are failing. The enemy wants you to feel the weight of all your past failures, but you can trust that God has forgiven you. When He sees you, He sees the work Jesus did on the cross.

Think about God's grace and mercy, and let those be the things that make your heart glad and cause you to sing a new song to your beautiful, faithful Lord. From that heart position, go into today grateful. Keep your eyes open to all the ways God shows you His love.

*Lord, I know You love me and that I need to remember
what You consider important in this life. Your Word reminds
me to love You with everything I have. Lift me up when I
can't feel Your presence, and forgive me for my lack of faith.*

GOD'S WONDERFUL MERCY

"God, have mercy on me, a sinner."
LUKE 18:13 NIV

◆ ◆ ◆

Staying unshakably connected to God means understanding that your loving heavenly Father desires to shower His grace and mercy on those who humbly confess that they are sinners who are lost without Him.

Jesus told a story about two very different men who went to the temple to pray. One was a local religious leader, and the other was a much-hated tax collector. The religious leader used his prayer to thank God that he wasn't like sinners, while the tax collector confessed that he was a sinner and begged God for mercy. Jesus told His followers that it was the tax collector, not the self-righteous religious leader, who was justified before God.

Christians should always have the same humility the tax collector showed before God. That means approaching Him with a contrite heart and teachable spirit. Coming to God this way will put you in a position to receive His wonderful mercy.

God, thank You for Your gift of mercy when I come to You with a humble, contrite heart. Help me never to think of myself as better than anyone else but instead as a man who needs Your mercy every day. Teach me to understand that Your ways are always better. Teach me to have a humble heart and know that You are my loving and merciful King.

TRUE TREASURE

*"Sell everything you have and give to the poor, and you
will have treasure in heaven. Then come, follow me."*
LUKE 18:22 NIV

◆———————◆———————◆

Where is your treasure? It's a question that never loses power because it's one that helps you pursue God's grace and mercy. When your most important treasure is Jesus, your life will be powerfully transformed.

God created you to be in fellowship with Him always. Many things in this world, however, don't bring eternal benefit but instead can take you off track in your relationship with God. That's where the enemy slips in and tempts you to believe that you can do anything you want and still serve Jesus. But God calls you to a life focused on obedience to Him, a life in which you pursue true treasure.

Pray and ask God to help you inventory the things you give your time and heart to. Spend your time praising instead of planning. Ask Him to show you how you can best store up true treasure, the kind that lasts forever.

*Lord, show me what I need to get out of my life so that I can
follow and serve You wholeheartedly. I don't want to waste my
life chasing after things You're not a part of. Show me what to
concentrate on, and help me to store up treasures in heaven.*

YOUR KING

God is my King from long ago; he brings salvation on the earth.
PSALM 74:12 NIV

◆———◆———◆

Long before you were born, God thought about you and about the ways He would use you to bring Him glory. He carefully considered all the ways He would make you different from everyone else He created. There's only one you, and there will never be another.

Make today a day of celebration as you remember everything God has done in your life. He saved you from the chains of sin, from the darkness that threatened to swallow you. Because of Jesus, your sins are forgiven and you are eternally free to worship and serve your King.

Today is a new chance to reconnect with your King. Rejoice as you see and feel His presence and His never-ending love for you. Reflect on His unfailing love and step out in faith today, knowing that the King of kings has you in His hands and will never let you go.

My King, multiply my time so I can worship You longer and praise Your name with all that I have. Bring me to a place of rest so I may consider all the ways You love me and shower me with grace. Hold me so I can be reminded of Your steadfast love. Open my eyes to Your grace so that I never feel like giving in to fear.

FROM THE HEART

"If they keep quiet, the stones will cry out."
LUKE 19:40 NIV

◆ ◆ ◆

Today is a new day God has given you. Use it to praise Him with your words, your thoughts, and your actions. That would make for a day well spent!

God loves when you praise Him because your praise brings you closer to Him. When you praise the Lord, you acknowledge His goodness and His love for you. When you praise Him from your heart, you express what His greatness means to you.

One day, Jesus' followers praised Him loudly and boldly. The religious leaders wanted Him to tell the people to stop, but Jesus told them that if no one praised Him, the rocks would. Do your thoughts and actions lift Jesus high, or are the stones praising Him because you aren't?

God has so much for you. Lean in and let Him guide you to peaceful places where your heart and soul will be filled with more of His love—places where you can praise Him with everything that is in you. Find courage in Him, praise His name, and be bold for His glory.

Jesus, please help me praise You more and more. I want to fall in love with You and stop running after things that don't matter. You've been so good to me. I can't praise You enough.

PAYDAY WINCES AND SMILES

*He [Jesus] said to them, Then render to Caesar the things
that are Caesar's, and to God the things that are God's.*

LUKE 20:25 AMPC

Each payday, do you smile or wince? Smile at what you took home? Or wince at how much was deducted for taxes? The latter was the default in ancient Roman times, so much so that Jesus was asked if He was *for* or *against* paying taxes to the emperor.

It's important to remember that this question was extremely controversial, highly volatile, and even life-threatening.

If you're *for* paying taxes, the Jews will riot instantly.

If you're *against* paying taxes, the Romans will arrest you just as fast.

So, Jesus, which way is it?

His disciples were deeply divided on this question, at least until they heard His answer. And what an answer it was! After all, Jesus wasn't relying on mere human knowledge and ingenuity. Instead, as God's Son, He proclaimed the inspired, divine, steadfast wisdom and ways of God.

Are you willing to see your paycheck in the light of what the Lord Jesus Christ said and did? If so, how does that change the way you see it?

*Unshakable God, may I take what Jesus said to heart now
and always. The government that makes money demands
some of it back. But You, Lord, own everything.*

LOVING THE LORD AND WIDOWS

[Jesus said,] "Beware of these teachers of religious law!
For they like to parade around in flowing robes and love to receive
respectful greetings as they walk in the marketplaces. And how
they love the seats of honor in the synagogues and the head table
at banquets. Yet they shamelessly cheat widows out of their
property and then pretend to be pious by making long prayers
in public. Because of this, they will be severely punished."
Luke 20:46–47 nlt

I n the days of Jesus on earth, the Sadducees and other Jewish religious leaders controlled the judicial system, which barred women from bringing a case to court. When a woman's husband died, therefore, she couldn't do anything to protect her family's property from being seized "legally." How wicked. Jesus condemned these religious scam artists in no uncertain terms (today's passage and Mark 12:38–40).

Today's New Testament reading, Luke 20:27–47, takes place in the crucible of Jerusalem only three days before Jesus lays down His life. To say the least, the Sadducees had no love for the Lord. They also felt repulsed by the common people. Proof? Their favorite joke made a mockery of childless widows. Again, how wicked.

Do you love widows? If so, which particular widow(s)?

Omniscient Lord, You want unshakable men to love
widows. Which widow can I show love to today?

VALUING WIDOWS

While Jesus was in the Temple, he watched the rich people dropping
their gifts in the collection box. Then a poor widow came by and
dropped in two small coins. "I tell you the truth," Jesus said,
"this poor widow has given more than all the rest of them."

LUKE 21:1–3 NLT

H ow often do widows come up in the Bible? Surprisingly, a lot! The most famous widow's story is found at the beginning of Luke 21. At first, what Jesus appears to do (and not do) causes many readers to wince. Even worse? Religious leaders may have cheated this particular widow out of her rightful property.

In biblical times, loving your neighbor meant giving to the poor on a regular basis—especially widows. What readers sometimes miss in the Gospels: Jesus and His disciples gave alms to the poor regularly and routinely. It's what all godly, good-hearted Jewish people did.

Sadly, however, the poor widow in Luke 21 had been neglected by relatives and overlooked by neighbors. All she has left are two tiny copper coins.

Jesus knew this widow well. Yes, it's true, He knows all widows. Therefore, since it was something He did often, Jesus probably motioned for one of His disciples to follow after her and quietly give her several large silver coins.

Omnipresent Lord, You want men to give generously to poor
widows. Which widow could I help financially today?

YOU CAN CHANGE

Human defiance only enhances your glory, for you use it as a weapon.
PSALM 76:10 NLT

———◆———◆———◆———

Augustine's *Confessions* was the very first Western autobiography. Countless others have followed. One of the newest is by Brent C. Hofer. His book is titled *Confessions of an Angry Man*. Relevant to every man? Indeed. Take a look at Brent's hard-earned wisdom:

> I came to believe that God was working for my good and His glory. He didn't want me angry and dominating my wife, Sherry, and our children. He wanted me changed and He had not given up on me. My life was not over and I was not alone in the dark. I had no idea how long it would take. Often I asked God if anything good was happening, but deep inside I sensed hope.
>
> In time, I recognized that Sherry is the greatest venue for positive transformation of my life. Always. If I will listen. The result of learning to love Sherry brought healing to her heart and reconciliation in our relationship. The result of realizing God loved me transformed my life. This is the miracle I live with every day.
>
> If you are an angry man, I plead with you to do the one act that no one else can do for you. Be willing to change.*

Omnipotent God, I'll do whatever You want so
You can change and transform me.

---

* Extended text used by written permission of Brent C. Hofer.

TAKE DOUBTS AND
QUESTIONS TO GOD

I cry out to God; yes, I shout. Oh, that God would listen to me!
PSALM 77:1 NLT

◆———◆———◆

Asaph, the author of Psalm 77, was an honest, courageous pray-er. Yet even the strongest believers can struggle with big questions and serious doubts.

Asaph spent his life serving God. But that didn't shelter him from the harsh realities of life. Slowly, the injustice he saw around him—the prosperity of wicked people who lived their lives for themselves and reaped all the benefits—began to wear on Asaph. His faith was shaken. *Why waste my time obeying and serving God*, Asaph wondered, *when others disobey and prosper and live to boast about it?*

Asaph's doubts were not unique, but his response was right on target. He was a man of faith about to go over the edge—but he was still a man of faith. Stopping to look at the world through God's eyes, he finally understood that the prosperity of the wicked was only temporary. And he saw himself—foolish for a moment, but loved and guided by God.

So what if I don't get all the perks in this life? Asaph realized. *If I have God, I can know true satisfaction and will enjoy great rewards in the life to come.*

Steadfast Lord, I too struggle with big questions and serious doubts.
Use Your Word and these pages to solidify my faith in You.

TEMPTED? ASK GOD FOR DAILY HELP

[Jesus said,] "Pray that you may not enter into temptation."
LUKE 22:40 ESV

◆━━━━◆━━━━◆

When a hurricane or tropical storm slams into a harbor, which ships take the worst battering? Often the ships that can't sink. Like such ships, Jesus couldn't sin (Hebrews 4:15), but that only intensified His temptations (Hebrews 5:7–9). Christian men have always faced temptation. Repeatedly in Matthew, Mark, and here in Luke, Jesus admonishes His disciples with the words above.

Practically, how does praying help you "not enter into temptation"?

First, start with the Lord's Prayer in Luke 11:1–4 and especially Matthew 6:9–13 (ESV). Both are addressed to the heavenly Father. Both end with the petition, "And lead us not into temptation [or testing]," with Matthew adding, "but deliver us from evil." The top priority is *who* hears your prayers. He is able!

Second, continue with the Lord's most famous parable in Luke 15, especially verses 11–24. Jesus describes a rebellious son and a compassionate father, who in many ways represents the heavenly Father. The father can't wait to forgive his son, who doesn't even get to finish apologizing. Amazing life transformation takes place. And the father can't wait to start a great celebration that very evening. No fear should ever keep you from asking God to forgive you. He is ready!

Unwavering Lord, steer me clear of temptation, deliver me from evil, and forgive me when I fail You.

ATHEISM'S FAVORITE "PROOF" OF BIBLE ERRORS

But Peter denied it. "Woman," he said, "I don't even know him!"
LUKE 22:57 NLT

❖

One of the few episodes that all four Gospels record is Peter's three denials the night before Jesus' crucifixion—in Matthew 26:69–75; Mark 14:66–72; Luke 22:55–62; and John 18:16–27. But to whom did Peter deny the Lord? The four Gospel writers give differing accounts. Do their differences contradict each other?

Like any sports journalist, each Gospel writer had a specific purpose for writing his account. He had a specific audience in mind. By definition, he had to leave out most of what he knew (otherwise, he never would have finished writing!). Leaving out secondary and tertiary details isn't wrong—it's what every good writer does.

Actually, their differences don't contradict; they *complement* each other.

So to whom did Peter deny Jesus Christ? Any good sports journalist can harmonize the four Gospel accounts fairly easily.

- First denial: one maid who talked to a second maid about Peter
- Second denial: the two maids plus others who confronted Peter
- Third denial: a larger group of bystanders, including a servant who was upset with Peter

Bottom line: Over the years, critics have cited Peter's three denials as the "ultimate proof" that the Bible contains errors. Their adamant remarks, however, haven't proven anything.

Yes, immutable Lord, I want to say "Thank You!" that professional sports reporting helps me quickly and easily resolve differing accounts within the Gospels.

GOD DOESN'T WANT ANY TO PERISH

Then he [the second criminal] said, "Jesus, remember
me when you come into your Kingdom."
LUKE 23:42 NLT

The young man leaned over the bed, his strong hands surrounding the old man's frail ones. "Do you believe Jesus died for you, Grandpa? Do you want to trust Him to save you?" The old man nodded his head and gave up his lifelong antagonism toward his Creator. He whispered, "Yes, I do want Jesus to be my Savior." Once again, God's mercy pursued a sinner right to death's door.

A criminal hung contorted and writhing for breath on a Roman cross. Anger and hatred raged in his bursting heart. Until he realized the identity of the man hanging beside him. Was it something Jesus said or the sheer presence of God that convinced him? The thief quieted down, had a complete change of heart, and offered an amazing prayer to the One dying beside him.

Jesus gave the thief his simple request—and more! "Today you will be with me in paradise" (Luke 23:43 NLT). There was no time for probation or restitution for this man, but salvation came immediately. Right then Jesus was paying for his sins. That day Jesus would walk with him in paradise!

Augustine once observed, "There is one case of death-bed repentance recorded, that of the penitent thief, that none should despair; and only one that none should presume."

Immovable God, before it's too late, please save.

WHY DOES JESUS LOVE MEALTIMES?

Then he [Jesus] asked them, "Do you have anything here to eat?"
They gave him a piece of broiled fish, and he ate it as they watched.
LUKE 24:41–43 NLT

◆────────◆────────◆

Doesn't it seem a bit unusual that Jesus spent so much time eating and drinking with His disciples? What does stopping to have a meal have to do with anything? It's something people do all the time—which is exactly why Jesus seized upon it.

Repeatedly throughout His earthly ministry, Jesus talked about the wonderful feast in the kingdom of heaven, when the Lord would celebrate with believers from all ages in glory. It's a banquet no one wants to miss! Then, right before His death, Jesus transformed the bread and wine of the Passover feast into powerful symbols of what the Christian faith is all about.

After His resurrection, Jesus kept right on eating with His disciples. His first meal was with an otherwise unknown disciple named Cleopas, who never looked at food and drink the same again. Every piece of broiled fish, every slice of fresh-baked bread, and every cup of wine became an instant reminder to thank the risen Lord!

Unswerving Lord, I can't wait to eat with You at the marriage supper of the Lamb. In the meantime, change how I look at every meal.

BETWEEN TESTAMENTS, DOES THE LORD CHANGE?

For the law was given through Moses, but God's unfailing love and faithfulness came through Jesus Christ.

JOHN 1:17 NLT

Many Christian men have read Genesis, Exodus, part of Leviticus, Psalms and Proverbs, the four Gospels (Matthew, Mark, Luke, and John), and a few other New Testament books. They're not Bible teachers or scholars, to be sure. But they've started to notice some of the differences between the two testaments.

Some wonder, *Does the Lord change? I feel some disconnect.* If only they had kept reading their Bibles!

Most teaching sections in the New Testament allude back to, indirectly quote, or directly quote the Old Testament (Hebrew scriptures). Take today's key verse.

First, "For the law was given through Moses" and similar statements appear dozens of times from Exodus 20 to Malachi 4:4 and more dozens of times from Matthew 5 to Hebrews 10:28.

Second, "God's unfailing love and faithfulness" and similar descriptions appear two dozen times from Genesis 24 to Micah 7:20 and then in John 1:17 (quoted above) and John 1:14 ("He [Jesus] was full of unfailing love and faithfulness" [NLT]).

Bottom line: Does the Lord *change* between testaments? No, instead the Lord *came!*

Unchanging God, how good to know that You are the same yesterday, today, and forever. Therefore, I never need be shaken as I read Your Word, the Bible. You wrote it all.

ARE YOU LIKE NATHANAEL?

*Jesus answered him [Nathanael], "Before Philip called
you, when you were under the fig tree, I saw you."*
JOHN 1:48 ESV

A number of biblical scholars believe Nathanael also went by the name of Bartholomew, much as Matthew also went by Levi, and Peter also went by Simon. Like the apostles Matthew, James, John, Andrew, Peter, and Philip, Nathanael had an intriguing first encounter with the Lord Jesus.

John tells us that Nathanael was under a fig tree when Philip interrupted him and said, "We have found the very person Moses and the prophets wrote about!" What was Nathanael doing under that fig tree? Presumably, he was resting. It's very possible he was praying. Perhaps he was asking the Lord to make him an honest man—a true son of Israel. Perhaps he was meditating on a prophetic passage from Isaiah's scroll read at the synagogue the previous Sabbath. Or perhaps he was dreaming about the day when the Messiah would come and fruit trees would bear "fresh fruit every month" (Ezekiel 47:12 ESV). In any case, God was preparing Nathanael's heart.

When Philip and Nathanael walked toward Jesus, the Lord said straight-out what kind of man Nathanael was and where he just came from. Nathanael was amazed!

No wonder Nathanael immediately declared his faith in the Lord Jesus.

*Unwavering Lord, thank You that You always know where
I am and what's on my heart. Amazing indeed!*

"DO WHATEVER HE TELLS YOU"

His [Jesus'] mother said to the servants, "Do whatever he tells you." Now there were six stone water jars there for the Jewish rites of purification, each holding twenty or thirty gallons. Jesus said to the servants, "Fill the jars with water." And they filled them up to the brim. And he said to them, "Now draw some out and take it to the master of the feast." So they took it.

JOHN 2:5–8 ESV

W ho wants to be told what to do at every turn? Well, in New Testament times, half of the Roman Empire's population experienced just that. They did what they were told—or else!

Into this world Jesus came as a servant to all. The Son of God humbled Himself to the fullest extent possible. What a strange way for the Lord to come. Not only that, but—in scores of verses from Matthew 8 to John 18:36—Jesus explained that His disciples were to be servants too. They were to do whatever He told them to do.

In today's New Testament Bible reading, right before Jesus starts His public ministry, He graciously acquiesces to His earthly mother's wishes. Notice how the servants responded. They filled each large clay jar "to the brim." Their wholehearted obedience was almost instantly rewarded.

Do you want to feel like a servant? If so, to whom and why?

Unvarying Lord, yes, I want to be Your servant.
I want to do what You say. Help me!

ARE YOU LIKE NICODEMUS?

*Now there was a Pharisee, a man named Nicodemus who
was a member of the Jewish ruling council. He came to
Jesus at night and said, "Rabbi, we know that you are a
teacher who has come from God. For no one could perform
the signs you are doing if God were not with him."*

JOHN 3:1–2 NIV

Nicodemus had been trying to get into God's kingdom by dependence on his Jewish lineage and slavery to human traditions—and was frustrated. "You'll never get there that way," Jesus told him. "Time to change direction. You can only get where you want to go by being born again." Nicodemus had no idea what Jesus was talking about, but God already had said repeatedly that people would need new hearts.

To make sure Nicodemus wouldn't miss a single turn, Jesus patiently explained the way in even more detail. Jesus said, in effect: "In a mysterious way, the Holy Spirit brings about new birth. It happens when you believe in Me, for I will be lifted up so you can be healed from all sin. When you trust in Me, I'll give you eternal life. The only way you can get to heaven from here is if I take you. Believe Me, I've been there before and I'm definitely going back."

Spoiler alert: Nicodemus believed!

*Resolute God, I don't want to take any wrong turns. I believe You.
Please keep me following You—the Way, the Truth, and the Life.*

ARE YOU LIKE JOHN THE BAPTIST?

[John the Baptist said,] "He [Jesus] must increase, but I must decrease."
JOHN 3:30 ESV

◆━━━━━◆━━━━━◆

J ohn the Baptist didn't care what others thought of him—his wild appearance, eccentric diet, prophetic speech, and all. John knew he was just a messenger—it was the Messiah's image and esteem John was interested in boosting and exalting.

John the Baptist had no lack of confidence as he bucked society's fashions and conventions to proclaim a radical message from his wilderness platform. He wasn't afraid to insult the establishment and challenge religious leaders who shackled the people with tradition yet lived in covert rebellion against God. Yet this prophet wasn't interested in gaining a following for himself.

Instead, this fiery man thundered out the call for people to repent and turn to the Lord. Then, in the waters of the Jordan River, he baptized those who meant business.

John's intensity and bold actions weren't a by-product of climbing his own ladder to fame and success. And his obvious humility didn't spring from self-hate or low self-esteem either. He simply recognized that this life wasn't all about John—it was all about Jesus.

Granted, the short-term benefits of exalting Jesus Christ above self seemed bleak at best. Yet John the Baptist reaped rich, eternal rewards. Jesus Himself honored John, declaring that no prophet—not even Moses—was greater. Amazing!

Unflinching Lord, my life is all about Jesus. At least it's supposed to be. May I honor You today and always.

ARE YOU LIKE THE SAMARITAN WOMAN?

Then, leaving her water jar, the woman went back to the town and said to the people, "Come, see a man who told me everything I ever did. Could this be the Messiah?"

JOHN 4:28–29 NIV

When the Samaritan woman came to the well, she met a man who promised to fill her with living water that would never run dry. A minute or two later, Jesus told her something He hadn't told anyone else straight-out: He was the Messiah.

But why should this foreigner believe Him? After all, Jesus had asked her for water, then claimed He had something better. He then declared her national religion inadequate and revealed the pain and shame of her life. Yet in exposing all her insufficiencies, Jesus also shared a beautiful secret—the Father was looking for individuals who would worship Him in spirit and in truth.

Instead of running back to the safety of her sin and dysfunctional way of life, this hurting woman grabbed hold of Jesus' invitation to come into a love relationship with the Father. A minute later, she forgot all about her empty water jug in her excitement to run back to town and tell others about her newfound Savior. What clear evidence that the water of eternal life already was welling up within her!

Unbending God, only You can satisfy the human heart and all its longings. May I always seek true satisfaction in You alone.

WHO EXACTLY IS JESUS CHRIST?

The Samaritans. . .urged him [Jesus] to stay with them, and he
stayed two days. And because of his words many more became
believers. They said to the woman, "We no longer believe just
because of what you said; now we have heard for ourselves, and
we know that this man really is the Savior of the world."

JOHN 4:40–42 NIV

◆———◆———◆

T he Bible doesn't leave today's important title question up in the air. Instead, it clearly says Jesus is the Son of God, equal with God, and fully God. Jesus is a member of the Trinity: Father, Son, and Holy Spirit. Jesus is infinite and eternal. Jesus made all things, by Him all things exist, and God the Father has put all things under Him.

Scripture also says Jesus is the Teacher, Rabbi, and Master. He is the King of kings and Lord of lords. He is Lord of all—Jew and Gentile, male and female, and free and slave. He is Ruler of all—rich and not, civilized and not, and educated and not.

What's more, God's Word says Jesus is the Savior, Deliverer, Redeemer. He died on a Roman cross—a horrible way to die. He died "for our sins, and not only for ours but also for the sins of the whole world" (1 John 2:2 NIV). In every way, Jesus truly "is the Savior of the world."

Unflinching Lord, You are my God, my King, and my Savior indeed!

THE FATHER AND SON: TRULY ONE

*Jesus said to them, "My Father is always at his work to this
very day, and I too am working.". . . "The Son can do nothing
by himself; he can do only what he sees his Father doing, because
whatever the Father does the Son also does. For the Father loves
the Son and shows him all he does. Yes, and he will show him
even greater works than these, so that you will be amazed."*

JOHN 5:17, 19–20 NIV

After God the Father speaks and the Holy Spirit descends on Jesus at
His baptism, readers might be tempted to think Jesus was pretty much
on His own here on earth. After all, that's how most men live their lives.

But make no mistake: Jesus was anything but a rugged individualist.
Just the opposite!

In the key verses above, Jesus said He was unable to do anything, anywhere,
on His own. Jesus only did things where He observed the Father already
at work. That was true of His miracles, parables, sin-forgiveness, teachings,
and travels. He journeyed throughout the twelve tribes of Israel, repeatedly
crossing national borders. Back and forth. Here and there. Always, always
following the Father's directions.

Unlike Jesus, do you tend to live as a rugged individualist? Either way,
now are you willing to pray like Jesus?

*Our Father in heaven, hallowed be Your name. Your kingdom
come, Your will be done, on earth as it is in heaven.*

THE LORD'S JUDGMENTS ARE JUST

*[Jesus said,] "I can do nothing on my own. As I hear,
I judge, and my judgment is just, because I seek not
my own will but the will of him who sent me."*

John 5:30 esv

S ince the Garden of Eden, Satan has tried to fool people into believing his first lie—that the Lord is unjust. Don't believe it!

Then again, many Christian men cringe when they think of the Lord's judgments in Genesis (think fire and brimstone), Exodus (ten plagues), Leviticus (fire from the Lord), Numbers (plagues), Deuteronomy (death before entering the Promised Land), Joshua (conquered nations). . .the death and destruction of those who defiantly opposed the Lord and His word, will, and ways.

The Lord Himself, however, has the first word on these judgments, declaring that He does "righteousness and justice" (Genesis 18:19 esv). In regard to the righteous, Abraham asks one of the world's most important rhetorical questions: "Shall not the Judge of all the earth do what is just?" (Genesis 18:25 esv). This question is worth memorizing and repeating—often!

At the end of history, great multitudes in heaven will have the last word, so to speak. They will proclaim, "Salvation and glory and power belong to our God, for his judgments are true and just" (Revelation 19:1–2 esv). Indeed!

*Unshakable Lord, keep me from doubting Your justice. Make me a righteous
man who trusts You with all my heart, soul, strength, and mind.*

ONE SMALL BOY'S FISH AND CHIPS

Another of His disciples, Andrew, Simon Peter's brother, said to Him,
There is a little boy here, who has [with him] five barley loaves,
and two small fish; but what are they among so many people?
JOHN 6:8–9 AMPC

❖ ❖ ❖

I n John's Gospel we find fewer stories and many more lengthy teachings by Jesus. Yet the average guy remembers more of John's stories over against Luke's, Mark's, and Matthew's. What's more, they typically have memorized some of his teaching verses as well (John 3:16 is the first!). So don't neglect the value of the teaching chapters!

In the context of such rich, powerful teachings are miracle stories. They prove to be the most vivid, moving, and memorable portions of John's Gospel. He calls seven of them "signs."

Why "signs"? Because John clearly wants to demonstrate who Jesus is—the Word of God, the Lamb of God, the very Son of God, the "I Am," the Savior of the world, and more.

In the middle of the seven "signs," Jesus feeds five thousand men plus women and children. Perhaps because he is writing to "whosoever" of all ages, John talks about one particular child. The lesson: If you sacrifice what you have, the Lord will multiply it greatly!

Omniscient Lord, I sometimes ask myself, How can what I give possibly
make a difference? At such times, remind me of one small boy's fish and chips.

NO OTHER SO-CALLED GODS

*"There shall be no strange god among you; you shall not bow
down to a foreign god. I am the Lord your God, who brought you up
out of the land of Egypt. Open your mouth wide, and I will fill it."*
Psalm 81:9–10 esv

W hen reading the Old Testament, it's smart to assume that Joshua and other writers frequently allude to, indirectly quote, or directly quote from the five books of Moses, Genesis through Deuteronomy. That's certainly the case in today's psalm reading.

The key verses above reiterate the opening verses of the Ten Commandments. The Lord had just brought the Israelites out of Egypt. Now, at Mount Sinai, He dictates the unshakable foundation of all biblical commands, morality, and ethics.

Then, at the end of verse 10, the Lord says: "Open your mouth wide, and I will fill it." Fill it with judgment if they disobey? No, the context here and in Exodus 20 indicates filling with blessing upon blessing if they obey.

When Mom serves something new for dinner, boys are quick to hold their nose, close their mouth, and grimace. That's what you should do at the very idea of worshipping anything besides the Lord God, Creator and Maker of heaven and earth, who formed you and breathed His life into you.

Instead, whenever you worship the Lord, be quick to open your mouth in eager anticipation.

*Omnipotent God, I eagerly anticipate Your washing,
filling, renewing, and manifold blessings.*

THE TURNING POINT

Jesus was aware that his disciples [followers, not apostles] were complaining, so he said to them, "Does this offend you? Then what will you think if you see the Son of Man ascend to heaven again? The Spirit alone gives eternal life. Human effort accomplishes nothing. And the very words I have spoken to you are spirit and life. But some of you do not believe me."
JOHN 6:61–64 NLT

Many people who haven't carefully read John's Gospel imagine that Jesus was a populist, attracting larger and larger crowds throughout His public ministry. What a false impression!

If you want to see this for yourself, invite a friend, colleague, or neighbor to read John's Gospel with you. Don't tell them what it says or means. Instead, ask them questions about what *they* think it says and means. If they make it past John 6, there's a good chance they will embrace saving faith as a gift from their new, true God and Lord.

Then again, don't be surprised if your friend quits before the end of John 6. The Lord doesn't want anyone to perish, but sadly, not all come to repentance. They don't trust what He says, doubt what He does, won't embrace true spirituality, and soon walk away.

What about you?

Steadfast Lord, You know how shakable, tentative, wavering, and wayward I can be. May the words of Jesus come alive to me, I pray.

GOD JUDGES UNJUST "GODS"

God presides in the great assembly; he renders judgment among the "gods."
PSALM 82:1 NIV

◆————————◆————————◆

Jesus loved quoting from Psalm 82. What He quoted infuriated the religious leaders badgering Him. Most people, however, are simply puzzled. Why is God talking about "gods"? Isn't the Lord the one and only true God?

First, notice the quotation marks around "gods." The Lord is speaking to those who judge wickedly and unjustly. God is warning earthly rulers, especially religious leaders. Wickedness and injustice can start man to man, but they more widely and systemically start from the top down. Unjust "gods" abound today. They purposefully "defend the unjust and show partiality to the wicked" (82:2 NIV).

Second, these "gods" have forgotten their God-given mandate: "Defend the weak and the fatherless; uphold the cause of the poor and the oppressed. Rescue the weak and the needy; deliver them from the hand of the wicked" (82:3–4 NIV).

Third, these "gods" are deluded: "The 'gods' know nothing, they understand nothing. They walk about in darkness; all the foundations of the earth are shaken" (82:5 NIV).

Fourth, these "gods" will perish: "[A minute ago] I said, 'You are "gods"; you are all sons of the Most High.' But you will die like mere mortals; you will fall like every other ruler" (82:6–7 NIV).

Omnipresent God, the foundations of justice truly have been shaken by "gods." May many repent and do Your will. May I do so too.

THE ADULTEROUS WOMAN AND JESUS

They [the religious leaders] said to him [Jesus], "Teacher, this woman has been caught in the act of adultery. Now in the Law, Moses commanded us to stone such women. So what do you say?"
JOHN 8:4–5 ESV

◆―――◆―――◆

G uilty as charged"—no doubt about it. Dragged weeping from her bedroom to the temple grounds, she needed no lawyer—because she had no excuse. God's law clearly commanded, "You shall not commit adultery" (Exodus 20:14 ESV). She couldn't deny the sordid facts.

Of course, the religious leaders cared little for the woman's fate. They cared even less for Moses' law that required punishing both the woman *and* the man caught in adultery (Leviticus 20:10). Their evil purpose: trap Jesus after demanding that He pass judgment on her behavior.

They thought they had Him either way. But Jesus ignored their twisted game, stooped down, and wrote out His verdict. After realizing *their* sins had been exposed, they quickly slipped from the crowd. Jesus kept writing on the ground. The adulterous woman sat there quietly as the Lord spoke to her heart. Her epiphany: Jesus cared as much about not breaking God's law as about not breaking God's heart. Quietly, she repented.

When He stood up, Jesus declared her forgiven and cleansed—a new woman. But what about the *other* adulterer—the man?

Unwavering God, please forgive me for my adulterous heart, which is anything but wholeheartedly in love with You. I'm so sorry, Lord.

ARE YOU LIKE KORAH'S SONS?

A Psalm of the Sons of Korah. How lovely is your dwelling place,
O LORD of hosts! My soul longs, yes, faints for the courts of
the LORD; my heart and flesh sing for joy to the living God.
PSALM 84:1–2 ESV

Who are these "Sons of Korah"? You may recall seeing their collective name a few weeks ago. These noble men wrote most of Psalms 42–49. They also wrote most of Psalms 84–88, with the last specifically attributed to one of their multitalented leaders, Heman the Ezrahite.

Still, who are these "Sons of Korah"? Near the very end of the Bible, Jude 1:11 (ESV) talks about the wicked who "perished in Korah's rebellion." Jude assumed that his readers knew the story, which you'll find in Numbers 16 and reiterated in Numbers 26:9–10.

A plain reading up to that point begs the question "Didn't all of Korah's kin perish?" The very next verse says: "But the sons of Korah did not die" (Numbers 26:11 ESV).

Instead of perishing, many of the sons of Korah were upright and godly men. They went on to become composers, musicians, singers, worship leaders, and prophets.

These men serve as exhibit A that an ungodly, rebellious, and wicked father doesn't dictate his son's character or destiny.

Unswerving God, You know my father. You know what he was
(is) like. May You shape my character, faith, and love for You.

ABRAHAM AND JESUS, TOGETHER?

[Jesus said to the religious leaders,] "Your father Abraham rejoiced at the thought of seeing my day; he saw it and was glad." "You are not yet fifty years old," they said to him, "and you have seen Abraham!" "Very truly I tell you," Jesus answered, "before Abraham was born, I am!" At this, they picked up stones to stone him, but Jesus hid himself.

JOHN 8:56–59 NIV

When the Lord walks in the Garden of Eden with Adam and Eve, when He instructs Noah how to build an ark, and when He invites Abraham to look at the sky, most readers have a hard time "seeing" the Lord. It's because they don't see Jesus.

Yes, Jesus visited planet Earth many times before His incarnation. Granted, Abraham didn't think of Him as "Jesus." But he still saw Him! What's more, Jesus talked at length with Abraham about his "seed." He spoke of many descendants. He also spoke of "seed" singular—referring to Himself (Galatians 3:16).

In today's key verses, Jesus says Abraham responded to all this by rejoicing. That's the exact opposite response of the religious leaders. They understand Jesus, in saying "I am," to be claiming He's God's Son, the Lord incarnate. They are correct. But unlike Abraham, they doubt, and their evil, wicked, unbelieving hearts see red.

Were Abraham and Jesus ever together? You can believe it.

Unchanging Lord, I believe every word Jesus said. Help me overcome my unbelief.

THE BLIND MAN'S AMAZING TRANSFORMATION

The man answered, "Now that is remarkable! You don't know where he comes from, yet he opened my eyes. We know that God does not listen to sinners. He listens to the godly person who does his will. Nobody has ever heard of opening the eyes of a man born blind. If this man were not from God, he could do nothing."

JOHN 9:30–33 NIV

The man with restored sight was right: The Hebrew scriptures never talk about any man born blind. The Christian scriptures don't mention this particular man's name, but tradition says his name was Celidonius.

Readers of John 9:13–34 (today's New Testament reading) can't help noticing this formerly blind man's amazing transformation before the Pharisees assembled to judge this man and his healer.

In verse 17 (NIV) the formerly blind man says of Jesus, "He is a prophet."

In verse 25 (NIV) the man rebuts their claim that Jesus is a sinner. Then he adds, "One thing I do know. I was blind but now I see!"

In verse 27 (NIV) he taunts them, saying, "Do you want to become his disciples too?"

Finally, in the key verses quoted above, this man describes Jesus as godly, not a sinner. Not only that, but he goes on to say Jesus obviously has come from God and therefore can work unprecedented, God-honoring miracles.

So who do *you* say Jesus is?

Triune God, thank You so much for sending Your only Son, Jesus. May I be His faithful disciple too.

BLESSINGS FROM
HEAVEN TO EARTH

*Surely his salvation is near to those who fear him, so our land will be
filled with his glory. Unfailing love and truth have met together.
Righteousness and peace have kissed! Truth springs up from
the earth, and righteousness smiles down from heaven.*

PSALM 85:9–11 NLT

D o you remember last Friday's opening lines? When you read the Old
Testament, it's smart to assume that the writers frequently allude to,
indirectly quote, or directly quote from the books of Moses. That's the case
again in today's psalm reading.

In this psalm, the composers repeatedly allude to the most famous ancient
Hebrew blessing. This threefold blessing is found in Numbers 6:24–26. Each
blessing is from the happy Lord looking upon His godly people here on earth.
What's more, each blessing produces tangible results for those people.

How happy is the Lord? First, He sends the blessings of salvation,
including protection. Second, He smiles on His godly people and sends
gracious provisions to meet all their needs. Third, He shows His favor and
gives His people *shalom* (peace).

The poetic key verses quoted above reiterate each aspect of the Jewish
people's favorite blessing. Now, imagine hearing the Lord speak it over you!
Better yet, why not share it with someone else today?

*Unvarying God, You are the same yesterday, today, and forever. Your
blessings never cease. May I become a godlier man with each passing day.*

WHO IS YOUR UNSHAKABLE LORD?

*For you, O Lord, are good and forgiving, abounding
in steadfast love to all who call upon you.*
PSALM 86:5 ESV

———◆———◆———◆———

Sometimes it's helpful to consider when and where the Bible first tells readers about specific aspects of who the Lord is.

First, consider "good." You need look no further than the opening pages of God's Word, which repeatedly say the Lord makes what is good. That is, the good Lord delights to make what reflects His goodness.

Second, consider "forgiving." If you turn to Exodus 34:6–7, you'll see that the Lord declares His amazing, marvelous name. In the second verse, the Lord talks about His forgiving nature. He wants to forgive iniquity, transgression, and sin. What a merciful and gracious God He is!

Third, consider "abounding in steadfast love." Again, look at Exodus 34:6–7, where the Lord uses that same exact phrase to describe Himself. He then adds, "keeping steadfast love for thousands."

Fourth, consider "call upon you." If you go back to the opening pages of God's Word, you'll find this important statement: "At that time people began to call upon the name of the LORD" (Genesis 4:26 ESV). This statement appears immediately after the record of the birth of Adam and Eve's first grandson, Enosh ben Seth. In other words, prayer became the primary way to talk to (and with) the Lord God.

*Immutable Lord, I'm calling on You. I want to experience more
of Your goodness, forgiveness, and steadfast love today!*

CAN SOMEONE BREAK ONLY ONE COMMAND?

"Is not this Bathsheba, the daughter of Eliam,
the wife of Uriah the Hittite?"
2 SAMUEL 11:3 ESV

◆———————◆———————◆

A man who walks his own way, outside the will of God, tends to start breaking the Ten Commandments one after the other. Consider the infamous story of King David breaking each of the last five of the Ten Commandments in his affair with Bathsheba.

First, "Thou shalt not kill" (Exodus 20:13 KJV): David had one of his most loyal men, Uriah the Hittite, cut down and killed in an evil plot (2 Samuel 11:15).

Second, "Thou shalt not commit adultery" (Exodus 20:14 KJV): David sent his men to fetch Bathsheba, took her into his bedroom, and lay with her (2 Samuel 11:4).

Third, "Thou shalt not steal" (Exodus 20:15 KJV): again, David took Bathsheba away from her husband.

Fourth, "Thou shalt not bear false witness against thy neighbour" (Exodus 20:16 KJV): David tried to pin Bathsheba's pregnancy on Uriah (2 Samuel 11:8) and then tried to pin Uriah's death on random chance or God's will (2 Samuel 11:21).

Fifth, "Thou shalt not covet thy neighbour's wife" (Exodus 20:17 KJV): David's coveting got this terrible bundle of sins rolling (2 Samuel 11:2).

Unflinching God, what King David did was reprehensible. Yet I'm
made of flesh too. Keep me walking inside Your will, not mine.

LIFE AND DEATH

Then Jesus shouted, "Lazarus, come out!"
JOHN 11:43 NLT

———◆———◆———◆———

What would you want more than anything after your death?
Throughout the scriptures, the Lord offers the promise of resurrection and eternal life to those who believe in Him. That hope takes the sting out of death, but not the grief.

Before his martyrdom, the apostle Paul admitted: "I'm torn between two desires: I long to go and be with Christ, which would be far better for me. But for your sakes, it is better that I continue to live" (Philippians 1:23–24 NLT).

When they think of going to be with the Lord, many wonder, *What about all the loved ones I'll leave behind?*

Lazarus had the unique privilege of being reunited with his loved ones *and* still being with the Lord.

Like his sisters, Lazarus had a deep love for and faith in the Lord Jesus. They looked forward to the resurrection. Still, Lazarus must have hoped and prayed that Jesus would arrive before he died.

Like people in Jesus' day, you may not understand why the Lord heals some and allows others to die. You or a loved one may face the prospect of an early death.

Like Lazarus, never lose the hope and joy of knowing that after this life "we will be at home with the Lord" (2 Corinthians 5:8 NLT).

*Resolute Lord, thank You so much that I
can trust Your promise of life eternal!*

GOD'S TOOLS TO SHAPE YOUR HEART

You have thrown me into the lowest pit, into the darkest depths.
PSALM 88:6 NLT

◆———◆———◆

Today's psalm is the only one written by Heman the Ezrahite, whom 1 Chronicles describes as a multitalented Levite: a composer, musician, singer, worship leader, and prophet.

Sadly, many such gifted men suffer from discouragement, depression, and despair. On one such occasion, Heman started composing Psalm 88. Unlike every other psalm, however, it offers not even a hint of an uplifting note of hope, hallelujah, or inspiration. The composer is super down, and pretty soon you are too!

A. W. Tozer admitted, "It is doubtful whether God can bless a man greatly until He has hurt him deeply." In other words, you need to expect and embrace discouragement, depression, and despair. They are three of God's tools to chip away at the rough parts of your heart, the wrong thinking in your head, and the wayward tendencies of your hands and feet.

Like a world-class lapidary, the Lord wants to make you a million-dollar trophy of His loving-kindness, mercy, and grace—now and for eternity. Let Him!

---

*Thank You, unshakable God, that out of deep pain can
come hope. Out of deep pain can come a much richer sense
of Your providential love. Out of deep pain can come a
bridge to one's destiny. So please do Your good work in me.*

HATING LIFE?

"Anyone who loves their life will lose it, while anyone who hates their life in this world will keep it for eternal life."

JOHN 12:25 NIV

H ave you ever known someone who, during an especially difficult season, said something like, "I hate this life"? That sounds like a man who is seriously discouraged—even depressed—doesn't it?

On the other hand, didn't Jesus tell His followers to "hate their life in this world"? But Jesus wasn't saying you should go through life with a long face, hating the fact that you're stuck here on earth. That's *not* the "abundant life" He promised those who love and faithfully follow Him (John 10:10).

You'll live an unshakable, abundant life of faith here on earth when you remember that this life is nothing compared with what God has for you beyond the here and now: your forever home in a place Jesus called "paradise."

God has given you a precious life here on earth. You can express your gratitude by giving your every day to Him as a sacrifice of praise and thanksgiving.

Lord, thank You for giving me physical life. But help me to remember that there's much more than the short time I get to spend here on earth. Remind me daily that You call me to serve You and honor You while I'm here.

UNFAILING LOVE AND FAITHFULNESS

I will sing of the LORD's unfailing love forever! Young and old
will hear of your faithfulness. Your unfailing love will last forever.
Your faithfulness is as enduring as the heavens.

PSALM 89:1–2 NLT

P salm 89, written by a man named Ethan, includes accounts of many troubles, but the writer starts with this wonderful premise: "I will sing of the LORD's unfailing love forever!"

When you are going through difficulties—as every man living on this earth most certainly does!—do you allow yourself to feel down and defeated? Do you find yourself grumbling and complaining? Well, Ethan had a better—*much* better—approach to staying grounded during tough times: focusing on and speaking about God's goodness.

Part of living a steadfast life of faith is focusing on God's amazing love and faithfulness. . .and then giving voice to what you see. Ethan didn't see his joy and gratitude as something to keep under his hat. He wanted others—young and old alike—to hear about God's goodness, love, and faithfulness. What can you do today to follow the psalmist's example?

Lord, You are so good to me in every way, and I thank You
for the privilege of speaking words of praise and thanksgiving
for Your unfailing love. May I speak those words so others
will hear them and learn of Your goodness.

AS I HAVE LOVED YOU

I give you a new commandment: that you should love one another.
Just as I have loved you, so you too should love one another. By this
shall all [men] know that you are My disciples, if you love one
another [if you keep on showing love among yourselves].
JOHN 13:34–35 AMPC

◆———◆———◆

Love was so important to Jesus that He quoted directly from the book of Leviticus when He named loving your neighbors as yourself as one of the two greatest commandments (Mark 12:31). But not long before He died on a wooden cross, He instructed His followers to take their love for others to a whole new level.

God's commandment to love was hardly new, but Jesus' five words—"as I have loved you"—placed emphasis on loving fellow Christians by following His *example* of selfless, sacrificial love. It would have been one thing had Jesus simply said, "Love one another," but He set the perfect example of love for all to see.

The great nineteenth-century English preacher Charles Spurgeon once said, "We are to love our neighbor as ourselves, but we are to love our fellow-Christians as Christ loved us, and that is far more than we love ourselves." So love your brothers and sisters in Christ—selflessly, sacrificially. . .unshakably.

Lord Jesus, show me ways—today and every day—I can express
my love for my Christian brothers and sisters. Thank You for
loving me first so that I can love others.

WITH JESUS–FOREVER

"My Father's house has many rooms; if that were not so, would I
have told you that I am going there to prepare a place for you?
And if I go and prepare a place for you, I will come back and
take you to be with me that you also may be where I am."

John 14:2–3 niv

J esus knew that His time on earth was short. He had spent the past three years healing the sick, feeding the hungry, and delivering life-changing teaching about the kingdom of God. But it wouldn't be long before He completed the most important task of His time on earth: dying on a cross and then being raised from the dead.

But Jesus didn't stop His work after He returned to heaven. Before He left His disciples behind to complete His work here on earth, Jesus promised them—and you—that He would prepare a place where they could be with Him. . .forever.

Loving someone means wanting to be with that person, doesn't it? And Jesus wants to spend eternity with those He loves, including you.

You can live unshakably in your confidence in Jesus and His promises. Always remember: He's preparing a place—a place just for you!

Lord Jesus, in a very real way, knowing that I will be with
You forever helps me to live every day unshakably for You. Thank
You for the wonderful promise of eternal life with You.

UNSHAKABLE GRATITUDE

*David sang to the LORD the words of this song when the LORD
delivered him from the hand of all his enemies and from the
hand of Saul. He said: "The LORD is my rock, my fortress and my
deliverer; my God is my rock, in whom I take refuge, my shield
and the horn of my salvation. He is my stronghold, my refuge
and my savior—from violent people you save me."*

2 SAMUEL 22:1–3 NIV

Luke 17:11–19 tells the wonderful—and sad—story of Jesus healing ten
men afflicted with leprosy, a terrible skin disease. These men had called
out to Jesus and asked Him to have mercy on them. Jesus answered their
prayer by healing every one of them. That's the wonderful part of this account.

Now comes the sad part. Jesus healed ten men that day, but only one of
them came back to Jesus to express his gratitude. The other nine just went
on their way, seemingly unaware that God in the flesh Himself had done an
amazing miracle for them.

You should make sure you aren't like those nine ungrateful men. Instead,
be like the one who came back to Jesus—and like King David, who spoke the
words of gratitude you just read in today's scripture passage.

*Gracious heavenly Father, remind me daily of the many
wonderful things You have done for me—and help me
remember to speak to You words of deep gratitude.*

A CLEAN CONSCIENCE

But after he had taken the census, David's conscience began to bother him. And he said to the LORD, "I have sinned greatly by taking this census. Please forgive my guilt, LORD, for doing this foolish thing."
2 SAMUEL 24:10 NLT

Remember the old saying "Let your conscience be your guide"? That's actually good advice for a Christian man. Your conscience, when it's in tune with the Lord, can keep you out of trouble and can alert you to sin you need to confess.

King David made a huge mistake when he ordered one of his servants to take a count of all the people of Israel—an act the Law of Moses prohibited. David later realized he had sinned against God, and he confessed his wrongdoing. Still, the people of Israel suffered greatly because of their leader's sin.

Living unshakably requires that you keep your conscience clean and sensitive to what God is saying to you through the written Word and through the Holy Spirit. So listen to God and always go to Him immediately when your conscience tells you that it's time to make things right with your heavenly Father.

Lord, thank You for giving me a conscience so that I can know when I'm veering off the life course You have for me. When my conscience bothers me, help me to come to You immediately so You can forgive me and get me back on track.

IN JESUS' NAME

"At that time you won't need to ask me for anything. I tell you the truth, you will ask the Father directly, and he will grant your request because you use my name. You haven't done this before. Ask, using my name, and you will receive, and you will have abundant joy."

JOHN 16:23–24 NLT

When Jesus came to earth, He brought with Him a message of change. From that time forward, the way people receive God's forgiveness, the way they have fellowship with their Creator, the way they worship Him. . .all of that would change. Even the way people pray would change.

You've no doubt heard people (ministers and laypeople alike) end prayers with the words "In Jesus' name, amen!" Today's scripture passage shows us that this isn't just a nice-sounding platitude. These words mean something very important and very powerful.

Jesus told His followers that when they prayed using His name, they would receive what they asked for. That is because of the world-changing work He did when He died on the cross and then was raised from the dead three days later. From that time forward, they had full access to God the Father through Jesus.

So do you!

When you pray, remember whose you are—and then make your requests in His powerful, wonderful name.

Thank You, Lord, for the amazing privilege of receiving what I need when I simply ask You in Jesus' name. May my requests always honor You.

A LEGACY OF OBEDIENCE

*When the time drew near for David to die, he gave a charge to
Solomon his son. "I am about to go the way of all the earth," he said.
"So be strong, act like a man, and observe what the LORD your God
requires: Walk in obedience to him, and keep his decrees and commands,
his laws and regulations, as written in the Law of Moses."*

1 KINGS 2:1–3 NIV

When the time drew near for Solomon to take the throne as king of
Israel (after David's death), David encouraged his son to walk in
obedience to God and obey all His laws and regulations from the Law of Moses.

King David was very far from a perfect man, but he was able to learn the
lessons God had taught him through his many mistakes. David knew Solomon
would face the same kinds of temptations he faced during his forty years as
king. Despite his weaknesses and mistakes, he wanted to leave Solomon a
legacy of obedience to God.

God wants you to establish that same kind of legacy—for your children or
for others. You can do that when you commit yourself to obeying and loving
God with your whole heart, mind, and body.

---

*Heavenly Father, David offered his son Solomon some great advice
for life: obey his God in every way. That's wise counsel for me too.
May I live a life of obedience every day and in every way.*

SOMETHING EVERY GUY NEEDS

The Lord was pleased that Solomon had asked for wisdom.
So God replied, "Because you have asked for wisdom in
governing my people with justice and have not asked for a long
life or wealth or the death of your enemies—I will give you
what you asked for! I will give you a wise and understanding
heart such as no one else has had or ever will have!"

1 Kings 3:10–12 nlt

In the New Testament, James 1:5 (nlt) begins with these words: "If you need wisdom." Maybe it's good to personalize this verse by imagining it saying, "*When* you need wisdom." Between work, family, ministry, and other important parts of your life, you have a lot on your plate—and you *need* wisdom every day. Every guy does!

You need wisdom to live an unshakable life. And the good news is that God *wants* to give it to you—just like He wanted to give it to Solomon. He'll never look down on you when you ask for wisdom, and He'll always give it to you so that you can grow and flourish in every area of your life. Count on it!

Lord, I need wisdom to lead my family, to do the work You've
given me to do, and to live a godly life. Do what You need to do
in order to give me the wisdom I need—today and every day.

NO HARM OR DISASTER

*If you say, "The LORD is my refuge," and you make the
Most High your dwelling, no harm will overtake you,
no disaster will come near your tent.*

PSALM 91:9–10 NIV

◆———————◆———————◆

As you read today's scripture passage, you might find yourself thinking, *How can this be? A lot of godly men have faced harm and disaster! Is there some kind of typo in these verses?*

It's an absolute fact that many solid Christian men have suffered harm at the hands of other people, and many others have suffered physical disaster. So what is God saying here?

Jesus once warned His followers, "In this world you will have trouble" (John 16:33 NIV). But He also promised, "I have overcome the world." In light of that, you can take today's scripture reading to mean that while you'll encounter many difficulties in this life, you'll ultimately never be defeated when you make the Lord your refuge from this fallen world.

The devil would love nothing more than to leave you shaken and doubting when troubles come. But when you cling tightly to God during those times, He'll never allow the enemy to snatch you out of His hands. Never!

*Father, I live in a fallen world, and a fallen world is a
dangerous world. Thank You for being my refuge from the
danger and for keeping me secure in You, especially when I face
the difficulties You have said are part of life in this world.*

PRIORITIES

*It took Solomon thirteen years, however,
to complete the construction of his palace.*
1 KINGS 7:1 NIV

◆   ◆   ◆

Today's verse is the first in a Bible chapter, so the word *however* might seem a little out of place. But if you go back to the previous verse—1 Kings 6:38—you'll see that the two verses together make a comparison between the time it took Solomon to build God's temple and the time it took to build Solomon's palace.

Both buildings were magnificent—and important. Some scholars believe this difference was because Solomon made the building of the temple his priority, but others say it was because God had given Solomon perfect instructions for building the temple. Either way, these two verses together say something about *priorities*. God had made the completion of His temple Solomon's top priority because God Himself was to be the nation of Israel's top priority.

God gives every man a list of important responsibilities. You'll be unshakable in meeting those responsibilities when you make God your top priority. Always make sure that spending time with Him in prayer and Bible reading takes precedence over all your other important responsibilities.

*Loving Father, You have given me many responsibilities.
Sometimes it's hard for me to prioritize the things I know You've
given me to do. I know, however, that my relationship with You
is by far my top priority. May I always put You first.*

THRILLED!

You thrill me, LORD, with all you have done for me!
I sing for joy because of what you have done.
PSALM 92:4 NLT

C an you remember the last time you worshipped God with everything you had and then felt overwhelmed with love for Him and gratitude for all the amazing things He does for you every day?

While you shouldn't base your relationship with God on emotion only, you can still enjoy those moments when your heart feels overwhelmed with love and gratitude toward your heavenly Father. He's more than worthy of the smiles, the words of praise, even the tears that pour forth when you feel and enjoy His amazing presence. . .and when you think on the things He has done for you.

When you think long and deep about who God really is, and then about the wonderful things He has done for you (starting with your eternal salvation), you'll find yourself feeling deep gratitude and speaking words of praise to your heavenly Father. That's what being *thrilled* with God really looks and feels like!

Father in heaven, thank You for the many, many things You have
done for me—and continue to do for me daily. May my heart and
mind be filled with gratitude, and may my mouth speak words
of thanks for Your generosity and goodness.

GOD'S PRESENCE

"May the LORD our God be with us as he was with our ancestors; may he never leave us nor forsake us. May he turn our hearts to him, to walk in obedience to him and keep the commands, decrees and laws he gave our ancestors."
1 KINGS 8:57–58 NIV

Today's scripture passage is part of Solomon's blessing over the people of Israel at the dedication of the newly finished temple. In it, Solomon spoke of the people's ancestors and how they enjoyed God's constant presence.

It's no accident that Solomon immediately follows his words about God's presence with a challenge to the people to obey God from the heart and keep His commandments. It's as if he was saying, "Since God has promised to be with us always, we should respond by turning our hearts to Him and obeying His laws and commandments."

Today, you have the privilege of enjoying God's constant, wonderful presence because of what Jesus accomplished when He died on the cross. His promise to the people of Israel still stands for you today: "Never will I leave you; never will I forsake you" (Hebrews 13:5 NIV).

Your gratitude for God's constant presence in your life should motivate you to live an unshakable life of commitment and obedience to Him.

Father, You've promised me Your constant and never-ending presence. I choose to obey Your commands, not because I'm afraid You'll leave me or abandon me, but because I'm so grateful.

SENT

Jesus said, "Peace be with you! As the Father has sent me, I am sending you."
And with that he breathed on them and said, "Receive the Holy Spirit."
JOHN 20:21–22 NIV

Jesus' twelve disciples—also called His "apostles"—spent three years with Him, traveling around the land of Israel, witnessing His astonishing miracles, and hearing His amazing, life-changing teaching.

What the Twelve didn't understand, however, was that Jesus was preparing them to rock the world around them with an eternal life-giving message of God's love and forgiveness. That's why, on the night before He was crucified, He prayed, "As you sent me into the world, I have sent them into the world" (John 17:18 NIV).

After He was raised from the dead, and before He returned to His Father in heaven, Jesus told His disciples (minus Judas) that He was sending them into the world to preach the Gospel message. But before they went, they received the empowerment they would need in the person of the Holy Spirit.

Jesus sent His disciples out on a world-changing mission, and it's the same mission He sends you out on today. With the empowerment of His Holy Spirit, you can do it—unshakably!

Lord Jesus, I know You want me to take Your message of salvation to the world around me. Thank You for giving me Your Holy Spirit to empower me to do what You've called me to do.

LET GOD BE GOD

*O Lord God, You to Whom vengeance belongs, O God, You to
Whom vengeance belongs, shine forth! Rise up, O Judge of the earth;
render to the proud a fit compensation! Lord, how long shall the
wicked, how long shall the wicked triumph and exult?*
PSALM 94:1–3 AMPC

D o you ever look at all the sin and injustice going on in the world around
you and wonder why God doesn't just come down and mete out some
well-deserved punishment and set things right?

The psalmist who wrote today's scripture passage seemed to wonder
the very same thing. He pointedly asked God how He could allow evil
men to continue to prosper and triumph. But he starts out his complaint by
acknowledging one important fact: all vengeance belongs to the Lord.

Vengeance for sin and injustice does not belong to us humans. It is in
the hands of a God who knows all and who possesses the perfect wisdom it
takes to know the right timing in everything He does.

So let God be God—and live unshakably in the knowledge that He has
everything under control.

*Father, I confess that I sometimes wonder why You allow sin and rebellion
to continue on—seemingly unchecked. But I recognize that it's not my job to
worry about those things. . .it's Yours and Yours alone. My job is to remain
unshaken by the sin I see around me and to do all I can to bring sinners to You.*

DOUBTS

When doubts filled my mind, your comfort gave me renewed hope and cheer.
PSALM 94:19 NLT

———◆———◆———◆———

Remember the story of "Doubting Thomas"? He was one of Jesus' twelve disciples—the men who traveled with Him for three years, learning from Him and witnessing His amazing miracles. . .and hearing Him talk about how He would die but would be raised from the dead.

After Jesus was raised from the dead, the other disciples told Thomas they had seen Him. But Thomas didn't believe them. He flatly told them, "Unless I see the nail marks in his hands and put my finger where the nails were, and put my hand into his side, I will not believe" (John 20:25 NIV).

That is some serious doubt, isn't it? But because Thomas was honest about his doubt, Jesus handled it and brought him back to a place of unshakable faith.

When doubt comes knocking at your heart and mind, remember that God is more than capable of handling it when you talk to Him about your struggles. Talk to Him about your doubts—and then let Him comfort you and strengthen your faith.

He did it for Thomas, and He'll do it for you too.

Lord, thank You for comforting me and assuring me when I go through seasons of doubt. Remind me to always bring my doubts to You so that You can strengthen me and give me unshakable faith.

HUMBLE WORSHIP

*Come, let us worship and bow down. Let us kneel before
the LORD our maker, for he is our God. We are the
people he watches over, the flock under his care.*
PSALM 95:6–7 NLT

The first seven verses of Psalm 95 are some of the most beautiful expressions of praise in the whole Bible. As you take the time today to focus on this psalm, you'll see that the writer feels an overwhelming sense of awe at the greatness of God. . .and an even more overwhelming sense of gratitude for his Creator's goodness and love toward His people.

As the psalmist focuses on his God, he is humbled to the point that he encourages his readers to *worship*, *bow down*, and *kneel* before the Lord. This is a word picture of a man who knows that he as the created can do nothing but humbly praise his Creator.

When you focus on the greatness of God and on His goodness toward you, there's nothing for you to do but humbly worship Him as *your* God, as the One who made you and watches over you every second of every day.

He really is worthy, isn't He?

*Loving Creator, I have so many reasons to worship You every day—
starting with the fact that You created me and You redeemed me.
I am Yours, Lord! Thank You for Your love and for the many
ways You express that love to me every day.*

BELIEVING GOD, OBEYING GOD

*She went away and did as Elijah had told her. So there was food
every day for Elijah and for the woman and her family. For the
jar of flour was not used up and the jug of oil did not run dry,
in keeping with the word of the LORD spoken by Elijah.*

1 KINGS 17:15–16 NIV

◆────◆────◆

I magine the faith it took for a poor widow living in a place called Zarephath
to do as the prophet Elijah had commanded her. She was so poor that she
believed she and her son would die of starvation (1 Kings 17:12). Yet she
willingly risked what little she had and did as Elijah had asked, preparing
for him a small loaf of bread.

The Bible doesn't say anything about this woman before she met Elijah.
But it tells us plenty about how her faith directed her actions. Because she
believed Elijah's word from the Lord, God abundantly met her needs.

What would you do if you felt God leading you to give out of what little
you have? God can take just a little and multiply it for you—if you have the
faith it takes to give Him what little you have.

---

*Lord God, I will take a big step of faith. I may not have much to offer
You today, but what I have, I give to You to use as You see fit.*

FEELING ALL ALONE

He replied, "I have been very zealous for the LORD God
Almighty. The Israelites have rejected your covenant, torn down
your altars, and put your prophets to death with the sword.
I am the only one left, and now they are trying to kill me too."
1 KINGS 19:14 NIV

◆━━━━━◆━━━━━◆

The prophet Elijah had just performed an incredible miracle that showed the people of Israel the power of the one true God (see 1 Kings 18:16–40). Yet a short time later, he is alone, having fled because of threats on his life. Elijah is so depressed and discouraged that he complains to God that it is unfair that he, a faithful servant of the Lord, should be alone in his suffering. He believes in his heart that he is the only true prophet of God left in all of Israel.

Elijah wasn't truly alone, and God would later prove that to him. But in his discouragement, Elijah *felt* alone—just as you sometimes may feel alone in serving God faithfully.

When you feel all alone, don't try to keep how you feel from your Father in heaven. Instead, tell Him how you feel and ask Him to encourage you—both with His presence and with the help of some godly friends.

Lord, serving You faithfully sometimes feels like a lonely endeavor.
When I feel alone, bring committed Christian men into my life
so that we can encourage one another.

THE BASICS

*They devoted themselves to the apostles' teaching and
to fellowship, to the breaking of bread and to prayer.*
ACTS 2:42 NIV

O n the day of Pentecost, God did a miracle through the preaching of the apostle Peter. About three thousand people came to faith in Jesus. Afterward, these people started doing things that have stood as examples for Christians for almost two thousand years since.

These people's growth in their faith wasn't complicated. It was built on some basics that have characterized growth in faith for every Christian since then. These basics are the things you should make priorities in your life of faith.

Your faith will become unshakable when you do as the first generation of Christians did: devote yourself to the apostles' teaching (reading and listening to the Word of God), to fellowship (spending time with your Christian brothers and sisters), to the breaking of bread (remembering what Jesus has done for you), and to prayer (talking to and listening to God).

*Lord Jesus, thank You for giving me the example of the early church.
You still use that first generation of Christians to show me the importance
of time spent in Your written Word, fellowship with other believers,
reflection on what You did for me when You died on the cross,
and daily prayer. May I never neglect any of those things.*

SPEAKING THE TRUTH—ALWAYS

Meanwhile, the messenger who went to get Micaiah said to him, "Look, all the prophets are promising victory for the king. Be sure that you agree with them and promise success." But Micaiah replied, "As surely as the LORD lives, I will say only what the LORD tells me to say."

1 KINGS 22:13–14 NLT

◆———◆———◆

Micaiah was a prophet who served God faithfully during a time when four hundred "counselors"—actually false prophets who had no regard for the Lord or His word—were telling King Ahab, the wicked ruler of Israel, only what he wanted to hear. Micaiah, on the other hand, was fully committed to speaking only what God told him to say.

What would you do if God had told you what He wanted you to say in a certain situation, but you felt like others wanted you to speak only words that wouldn't offend? Would you follow the example of Ahab's prophets, or would you follow Micaiah's example?

Too often, men of God fail to speak His truth out of fear that it may cost them more than they are willing to pay. But you will never go wrong when you commit yourself to always speak God's truth.

Father, speaking Your truth can sometimes be uncomfortable—even scary. When I'm in a situation where I know what You want me to say, give me the courage to lovingly and gently speak Your truth.

UNSHAKABLE GENEROSITY

All the believers were one in heart and mind. No one claimed that any of their possessions was their own, but they shared everything they had.
ACTS 4:32 NIV

◆———◆———◆

That first generation of Christians living in Jerusalem set many amazing examples for believers today. Today's scripture verse says that they were united in their love for Jesus and committed to sharing their possessions and financial assets among themselves.

That's love in action, isn't it? But it's also an example of a recognition that God owned everything they had—and therefore they were able to let go of their possessions and money for the good of others.

So what should this example mean to you? Simply that it's a good idea to be alert for opportunities to share with those who need help—to love others with an attitude of *what's mine is yours*.

When you share out of a heart of loving generosity, you not only meet the needs of others but also glorify God. . .and you put yourself in a position to receive His blessings. That's a big win for everyone involved!

Heavenly Father, thank You for giving me the privilege of fellowship with other believers. Help me to always be on the lookout for opportunities to express my love for my brothers and sisters by meeting their needs—whatever they may be. Remind me daily that everything I have belongs to You.

ASKING BIG

*When they had crossed, Elijah said to Elisha, "Tell me, what can
I do for you before I am taken from you?" "Let me inherit
a double portion of your spirit," Elisha replied.*
2 KINGS 2:9 NIV

Elisha knew two things lay ahead for him. First, his friend and mentor would soon be leaving him behind. Second, he would be taking over as Israel's leading prophet.

Elisha knew he would need great power to serve as mightily as Elijah had. So he made one request before Elijah was taken up to heaven. Elisha asked Elijah to allow him to "inherit a double portion of your spirit." Elijah told Elisha that he would have what he had asked for, and then Elijah was taken to heaven.

Because Elisha had summoned up the courage to make such an audacious request, God empowered him to become an amazing, miracle-working servant of the Lord.

Do you believe God has something big for you? Then when you ask Him to prepare you, don't be afraid to ask big! He loves to answer that kind of prayer with a resounding yes!

*God in heaven, thank You for giving me opportunities to serve You. I want
to do big things for You, and that means I'll need big empowerment
from Your Holy Spirit. I ask You to give me that very thing today.*

OBEY GOD FIRST

But Peter and the apostles replied, "We must
obey God rather than any human authority."
ACTS 5:29 NLT

◆━━━━◆━━━━◆

The Bible is clear that Christians are to obey earthly authorities. For example, the apostle Paul wrote, "Let every person be subject to the governing authorities. For there is no authority except from God, and those that exist have been instituted by God. Therefore whoever resists the authorities resists what God has appointed, and those who resist will incur judgment" (Romans 13:1–2 ESV).

But one day, Jewish religious leaders warned the apostle Peter and some of his friends to stop talking to people about Jesus. Peter's response? *We must obey God rather than you.* In saying that, Peter showed incredible courage. He also set an example for all men of God to follow.

You should respect, obey, and pray for earthly authorities because God has placed them in their positions. But when these authorities contradict or oppose the laws of God, it is your duty to respectfully speak up and even disobey if it comes to that. But before you do that, seek God and ask for wisdom in making the best decision.

Father in heaven, I know You want me to obey earthly authorities
because You put them in place. But I also know that I must obey You
over any human institution or authority. When I must choose whom
to obey, give me the wisdom and courage to make the right decision.

CHARACTER VERSUS REPUTATION

*I will be careful to lead a blameless life—when will you come to
me? I will conduct the affairs of my house with a blameless heart.
I will not look with approval on anything that is vile.*

PSALM 101:2–3 NIV

The great UCLA men's basketball coach John Wooden once said, "Be more concerned with your character than with your reputation, because your character is what you really are, while your reputation is merely what others think you are."

Most men, if you asked them if their reputation is important to them, would answer with a resounding "Yes!" But many don't make the connection between reputation and true character, which has been defined as how you behave when no one is watching.

God cares far more about your character than your reputation among humans. He wants you to live, speak, and think in ways that please and glorify Him—even when He is the only One watching.

Unshakable character comes from an unwavering commitment to God's ways, God's commands, and God's written Word. Hold to all those things, and you'll be more likely to enjoy a good reputation.

*Heavenly Father, I know You want me to live a life of unshakable character.
But I also know I can't do that on my own. Strengthen me by Your Holy
Spirit to consistently live, speak, and think in ways that honor You.*

PRAYERS OF THE AFFLICTED

Hear my prayer, LORD; let my cry for help come to you.
Do not hide your face from me when I am in distress.
Turn your ear to me; when I call, answer me quickly.
PSALM 102:1–2 NIV

P salm 102 is the prayer of an unnamed man who is feeling afflicted and sick—physically *and* emotionally. Worse yet, he seems to wonder where God is in his suffering. He knows that God is good and compassionate toward those He loves, but he feels like God is far, far away at this time in his life.

Have you ever felt like this psalmist? Have you ever felt as though God didn't see your suffering or your problems—or if He did see, He wasn't willing to comfort or deliver you? If so, then pray the way the psalmist did. Ask God to assure you that He hears you when you cry out to Him, that He is not hiding from you, and that He wants to answer your prayers.

The Bible says over and over that God sees and hears when His beloved people suffer, that He wants to be there for them during good times and difficult times alike. That's true, no matter how you may *feel* today.

Father, when I'm in a difficult situation and in desperate need of answers, help me to be unshakable in the truth that You want me to call out to You and that You won't hide Yourself from me.

NO TURNING BACK

*"But our ancestors refused to obey him. Instead, they rejected him
and in their hearts turned back to Egypt. They told Aaron, 'Make
us gods who will go before us. As for this fellow Moses who led
us out of Egypt—we don't know what has happened to him!' "*

ACTS 7:39–40 NIV

Today's scripture passage includes some astonishing information about the Israelites who had left their lives of slavery in Egypt under the God-ordained leadership of Moses. It says that in their hearts, they turned back to Egypt and wanted Aaron to make them gods who would go before them.

Many Bible scholars believe that the Israelites didn't literally want to go back to the land of Egypt but instead wanted to resume the idolatrous practices of the Egyptians—practices God wanted them to leave behind as they began their journey to the Promised Land.

God had miraculously freed the Israelites from slavery and from idolatry, yet their hearts were inclined to return to bondage. That's a temptation many Christian men still face to this day.

The Bible teaches that those who don't know Jesus are enslaved to sin, but the apostle Paul wrote, "You have been set free from sin and have become slaves to righteousness" (Romans 6:18 NIV). That means God has set you free. So don't go back to your own personal Egypt—in your heart or with your body.

*Gracious Father, You have freed me from my former life
of bondage to sin. There's no turning back for me!*

RADICAL FORGIVENESS

As they stoned him, Stephen prayed, "Lord Jesus, receive
my spirit." He fell to his knees, shouting, "Lord, don't
charge them with this sin!" And with that, he died.
ACTS 7:59–60 NLT

◆———————◆———————◆

J esus came to earth preaching a message of love and forgiveness, even telling His followers, "I tell you, love your enemies and pray for those who persecute you" (Matthew 5:44 NIV).

It's one thing to love, forgive, and pray for those who love you, but Jesus called His followers to take their love and forgiveness to a radical new level. Moreover, He set an example when He hung from the cross, suffering unimaginable agony, and pleaded with His Father to forgive His tormentors (Luke 23:34).

Stephen, the very first of many people who would die for following and talking about Jesus, followed His example. Stephen's very last words before he died were that God would forgive the men who were putting him to a grisly, agonizing death.

If you're like most men reading this account, you probably find yourself wondering how you could ever do that.

When someone does you wrong, follow Jesus'—and Stephen's—example of loving an enemy deeply enough to earnestly pray for him.

———————————————

Jesus, it's extremely unlikely that I'll face the kind of mistreatment Stephen faced in Jerusalem—or You faced at Golgotha. But when I am mistreated or slandered, help me to respond the way You did: with radical forgiveness.

READY WITH AN ANSWER

Then Philip ran up to the chariot and heard the man reading
Isaiah the prophet. "Do you understand what you are reading?"
Philip asked. "How can I," he said, "unless someone explains it
to me?" So he invited Philip to come up and sit with him.
ACTS 8:30–31 NIV

P hilip the evangelist (not to be confused with Philip, one of Jesus' twelve disciples) was a man who had a heart for telling people about Jesus. And he was also a man who was prepared when God gave him opportunities to tell others about Him.

Acts 8:26–39 tells the story of Philip's encounter with an unnamed Ethiopian man who had been in Jerusalem to worship God. Philip heard the man reading a passage from the book of Isaiah about the Messiah. The Ethiopian didn't understand what he was reading, but Philip did. So Philip sat with him and "began with that very passage of Scripture and told him the good news about Jesus" (verse 35 NIV).

No missed opportunity there!

Ask God today to bring you opportunities to tell others about Jesus. Also ask Him to help prepare you to answer questions they may have about Him—and why they need Him.

Lord, I have two requests today. First, bring people into my life who
need to hear about Your love and forgiveness through Jesus. Second,
help me to be alert and ready when You grant that first request.

FORGIVEN. . .COMPLETELY

*For as high as the heavens are above the earth, so great is his
love for those who fear him; as far as the east is from the
west, so far has he removed our transgressions from us.*
PSALM 103:11–12 NIV

◆━━━━◆━━━━◆

Perhaps nothing keeps a man of God from living an unshakable life of faith more than guilt—guilt over the things he has done and things he has failed to do. He may have confessed his sin and turned completely away from it, yet he suffers under oppressive guilt and an underlying fear that God still holds his misdeeds against him.

Today's scripture passage shows the completeness of God's forgiveness. Focus for a minute on the words "as far as the east is from the west" and then consider this: If you were to start at the northernmost spot on the globe and begin traveling south, eventually you would be traveling north. However, if you were to begin traveling east from any point on earth, you would continue traveling east an infinite distance.

The Bible says that when you confess your sins, God removes your sins from you and casts them far away—*infinitely* far away.

---

*Lord, thank You for Your willingness to forgive me completely when I confess my
sins to You. Help me to learn from my mistakes and bad decisions but never
to dwell in guilt or regret over sins You've already forgiven and forgotten.*

STAND FIRM FOR JESUS

Saul increased all the more in strength, and confounded the Jews who lived in Damascus by proving that Jesus was the Christ.
ACTS 9:22 ESV

◆——◆——◆

You've probably heard cynics say that people cannot change. Once a liar, always a liar. Once an adulterer, always an adulterer. And once a killer, always a killer. But Christ can change even the most hardened killer into a Gospel proclaimer, as we see in today's verse.

Following Saul's dramatic conversion, he spent some time with the believers in Damascus, where his faith was strengthened. Immediately after that, he began proclaiming Jesus in the synagogues. This was the same man who had made a habit out of persecuting and even killing Christians. But the Holy Spirit had done a work in him, giving him a rock-solid resolve to tell others about the soul-saving message of Christ. Naturally, some of the disciples were afraid of him at first. But once they learned about how boldly he was already living out his faith, they embraced him.

If Saul, who was also called Paul (Acts 13:9), could trust God with such resolution in his conviction to share Jesus with others, then any believer can. As you go into your workplace or classroom today, don't hesitate to stand firm for Jesus. Tell others that anybody can be saved from their sins.

Father, give me the resolve of Saul today. Help me not to waver when You present opportunities to share the Gospel.

NO COMPROMISE

For he [King Hezekiah] held fast to the LORD. He did not depart from following him, but kept the commandments that the LORD commanded Moses. And the LORD was with him; wherever he went out, he prospered.

2 KINGS 18:6–7 ESV

King Hezekiah was just twenty-five years old when he began his reign in Judah. His youth didn't stop him from doing what was right in the eyes of the Lord.

The Bible says, "He removed the high places, smashed the sacred stones and cut down the Asherah poles" (2 Kings 18:4 NIV). He even smashed the bronze serpent Moses had made—the one to which Israel had begun making offerings. His trust in God was so strong that scripture says "there was none like him among all the kings of Judah after him, nor among those who were before him" (2 Kings 18:5 ESV).

Doing what is right in the eyes of the Lord can make a man feel like he's standing all alone. And sometimes he will need to, despite the fallout he may face. But God is with the man who does not depart from Him and His commands. He may end up in jail or even worse, but the Lord will be there with him.

You should never compromise your faith in Christ, no matter how much pressure the world puts on you. Stay faithful to Him.

Father, make me a Hezekiah—a man who is willing to follow You at any cost.

START ANEW

*Hezekiah turned his face to the wall and prayed to the LORD, saying,
"Now, O LORD, please remember how I have walked before you in
faithfulness and with a whole heart, and have done what is
good in your sight." And Hezekiah wept bitterly.*
2 KINGS 20:2–3 ESV

King Hezekiah was sick to the point of death when the Lord spoke through Isaiah and told him to set his house in order, for he was about to die. Hezekiah reminded God about his constant faithfulness to Him. He didn't specifically ask for more time, but he certainly implied it. And the Lord granted him fifteen more years.

Imagine living such a faithful life that you could make such a request of God on your own deathbed. Hezekiah's faithfulness was not good enough to "earn" him more time. But his heart was right with the Lord, so much so that he felt comfortable enough to pray such a prayer.

Maybe you are thinking, *I'm no Hezekiah. I could never request such a thing from God.* But because you are a child of God, He will hear your prayers if you are repentant. If you've fallen short, you can start anew today—not because you want to live longer, and not because doing so will better attune God's ear to your requests, but rather because you want to honor Him.

*Father, I earnestly desire to walk faithfully with You,
even though I have fallen short. Help me start anew.*

LOOK TO GOD

All creatures look to you to give them their food at the proper time.
When you give it to them, they gather it up; when you open your hand,
they are satisfied with good things.

PSALM 104:27–28 NIV

❖───────❖───────❖

According to WorldAtlas.com, researchers have documented approximately 1.2 million animal species, which is far short of the 8.7 million they believe exist. Many have gone undiscovered so far and still others have gone extinct. All these animal species instinctively look to their Creator for food. He built that sort of trust into each species.

On this day, when the United States celebrates its independence, Christians would do well to celebrate their *dependence* on God to meet their every need. If He'll care for animals, He'll care for His children.

In Philippians 4:18–19 (NIV), the apostle Paul thanked the church in Philippi for the gifts they had sent him, saying: "I have received full payment and have more than enough. I am amply supplied, now that I have received from Epaphroditus the gifts you sent. They are a fragrant offering, an acceptable sacrifice, pleasing to God. And my God will meet all your needs according to the riches of his glory in Christ Jesus."

Never fear or doubt that God will come through for you. Trust Him to meet your needs.

Father, forgive my doubt during my times of need.
You are a loving God who takes care of His creation.

CONTINUE WITH THE LORD

*When he [Barnabas] arrived and saw what the grace of God had done,
he was glad and encouraged them all to remain true to the Lord with all
their hearts. He was a good man, full of the Holy Spirit and faith, and a
great number of people were brought to the Lord.*

ACTS 11:23–24 NIV

◆———◆———◆

After Stephen was martyred, persecution arose in Jerusalem, causing believers to scatter. As they went, they preached the Word, and a great number of both Jews and Gentiles believed and turned to the Lord. When the news spread to the church in Jerusalem, they sent Barnabas as far as Antioch. When he arrived, he was overjoyed at the sight of new converts, and he encouraged them to continue with the same purpose in their hearts.

You have been scattered in a different fashion—scattered into your workplace, school, or community—and you have opportunities to tell others about Christ. No doubt, you will face opposition at times, and the work can be messy and difficult. But Barnabas would encourage you to purpose your heart to "remain true to the Lord." People will find eternal life in Christ as a result of what you do and say to them today.

*Lord God, give me the heart of the believers who were scattered to Antioch.
They saw their scattering as an opportunity to reach new people. Open the
hearts of those You've placed around me to receive and believe the Gospel.*

A STEADFAST LIFE

He's GOD, our God, in charge of the whole earth. And he
remembers, remembers his Covenant—for a thousand
generations he's been as good as his word.
PSALM 105:7–8 MSG

This history of Israel in the Old Testament can be maddening to read. God's people often turned to idols and engaged in all sorts of wickedness, including practicing sorcery, consulting mediums, and worshipping foreign gods. Generations of His people would forget Him and do what was right in their own eyes before a generation would finally turn back to Him.

There was a time when God overlooked ignorance. In Acts 17:30 (MSG), Paul points out that "God overlooks it [ignorance] as long as you don't know any better—but that time is past. The unknown is now known, and he's calling for a radical life-change."

Amazingly, through Israel's time of ignorance, God remembered His covenant and remained faithful to humanity, even though they didn't deserve it. Now that Jesus has come in the flesh and revealed the heart of the Father, He is indeed calling believers to a steadfast life of courage and obedience—to live differently than the rest of the world.

Father God, I can identify with Israel. Sometimes I am hot in
my faith journey and other times I am cold. But You call for a
radical life-change. May I submit to the Spirit's leading to show
the world what it means to live a consistent Christian life.

SAFE IN THE ARMS OF CHRIST

When they [Israel] were few in number, of little account, and sojourners in it, wandering from nation to nation, from one kingdom to another people, he allowed no one to oppress them; he rebuked kings on their account, saying, "Touch not my anointed ones, do my prophets no harm!"

PSALM 105:12–15 ESV

◆━━━◆━━━◆

Even though Israel often forgot God, He never forgot His people. He protected them, even when they didn't know it, not allowing His anointed ones to suffer harm without His permission—much the same way parents protect their children when they are too young or unaware to protect themselves.

In a different way, you too are unaware. In the spiritual realm, Satan and his legions of demons seek permission from the Father to wreak havoc in your life—to steal, kill, and destroy you (John 10:10). But Jesus is praying for you (Hebrews 7:25), and the Holy Spirit has sealed you with a promise of eternity (2 Corinthians 1:22, Ephesians 1:13–14).

You are safe in the arms of Jesus, no matter what this world does to your body. With this in mind, how can you do anything but remain faithful to Him, just as He is faithful to you? Give little credence to temporal trials or threats. Instead, live with eternity in mind, knowing God is in total control.

Father, my life is Yours. I trust You implicitly to do with it as You will.

STAY THE COURSE

Some of the Jews, however, spurned God's message and poisoned the minds of the Gentiles against Paul and Barnabas. But the apostles stayed there a long time, preaching boldly about the grace of the Lord. And the Lord proved their message was true by giving them power to do miraculous signs and wonders.

ACTS 14:2–3 NLT

Paul and Barnabas were accustomed to resistance during their travels to proclaim the Gospel. The incident in today's scripture passage happened in a place called Iconium, where the Jews worked against them. Some might have become discouraged and left, but the apostles stayed there a long time, preaching boldly—and a great number of both Jews and Greeks were converted.

Are you facing spiritual resistance in a situation right now? Do you sense the Lord's leading and power flowing through you, even though people you are trying to reach aren't necessarily receptive right now? Stay the course. Preach and share boldly for as long as it takes. You are only responsible for telling others about Christ. It's the Spirit's job to draw them and open their spiritual eyes. Rest in that fact and get to work.

Father, I admit to shaking the dust from my sandals too quickly sometimes. Give me a spirit of boldness as I engage with the people You have surrounded me with, and give me patience to stay with them for a long time if necessary.

DESPERATE PRAYERS

They waged war against the Hagrites, Jetur, Naphish and Nodab.
They were helped in fighting them, and God delivered the Hagrites and all
their allies into their hands, because they cried out to him during the battle.
He answered their prayers, because they trusted in him.
1 Chronicles 5:19–20 niv

As the Reubenites, Gadites, and half tribe of Manasseh waged war against the Hagrites, Jetur, Naphish, and Nodab, they cried out to God and He answered them because they trusted in Him. They ended up defeating their enemies and seizing all their livestock "because the battle was God's" (1 Chronicles 5:22 niv), and they occupied the land until the exile. They were unwavering in their faith, and the Lord delivered them.

Prayers of desperation are often likened to a "Hail Mary" pass in football. But the comparison falls far short. When a team lofts a pass toward the end zone, usually as time expires, the coaches and players are really just hoping beyond hope that one of their receivers will come down with the ball and score the winning touchdown. Conversely, when prayers of desperation are offered in faith, believers aren't leaving the situation to chance. God hears His people and He answers them.

What are you praying for right now? Don't give up!

Lord God, just as You heard the prayers of the Reubenites, Gadites,
and Manasseh, hear mine today. Give me the unwavering faith
they had to stand strong as I await an answer.

RESOLUTE OBEDIENCE

He gave them the lands of the nations, and they took possession
of the fruit of the peoples' toil, that they might keep his
statutes and observe his laws. Praise the LORD!
PSALM 105:44–45 ESV

G od didn't stop caring for His people after He delivered them from bondage in Egypt. He covered them by cloud during the day and gave them fire at night. He fed them in abundance. And He remembered His holy promise to Abraham to make his descendants too numerous to count. His end goal was to have an obedient people who were thankful for His deliverance.

"That they might be properly instructed, and properly disciplined," wrote Adam Clarke in his commentary about today's verses. "This is the end proposed by Divine revelation: men are to be made wise unto salvation, and then to be brought under the yoke of obedience. He who is not conformed to God's word shall not enter into Christ's kingdom."

What sort of bondage has Christ delivered you from? How has He cared for you since? His end goal is your obedience. Yes, the covenant of grace is in full effect and your sins are covered by the blood of Christ. That should motivate you to live in resolute obedience.

Father, I thank and praise You for rescuing me from my pit of sin. In response,
I want to live a life of obedience to You. Infuse me with resolve to do so.

WALK HUMBLY

So Saul died for his breach of faith. He broke faith with the LORD in that he did not keep the command of the LORD, and also consulted a medium, seeking guidance. He did not seek guidance from the LORD.

1 Chronicles 10:13–14 esv

K ing Saul serves as a long-standing example of how not to live the life of faith. He failed to wait for Samuel, as he had been instructed, before offering an unauthorized sacrifice, and he spared the Amalekites when he had been instructed not to. Today's verses add another grave sin to the list; he consulted a medium, seeking guidance, rather than seeking the guidance of the Lord.

A Christian would do well to ask himself if there are any commands in scripture that he is willfully disobeying—in addition to asking himself where he is seeking guidance. If the answer to either of those self-tests is incorrect, he is in jeopardy of stumbling. Saul died for his breach of faith. Your consequences might not be so severe, but they might cost you more than you would ever dream of paying in your relationships, work situation, or even freedom.

Micah 6:8 (esv) explains how to stay on track spiritually: "He has told you, O man, what is good; and what does the LORD require of you but to do justice, and to love kindness, and to walk humbly with your God?"

Lord, may I walk humbly with You today.

IN TUNE WITH THE SPIRIT

Paul and Silas passed through the territory of Phrygia and Galatia, having been forbidden by the Holy Spirit to proclaim the Word in [the province of] Asia.
ACTS 16:6 AMPC

P aul and Silas wanted to strengthen the churches in Asia, just as they had been doing in other towns, but were forbidden by the Holy Spirit from entering. Maybe they would have been entering an even more dangerous situation, or maybe God intended for them to take the Gospel beyond Asia Minor and on into Greece. Whatever the reason, the Spirit expected and received their complete cooperation.

Think about the last time you were prompted by the Spirit to do something contrary to what you were planning. How quick were you to obey? What did your obedience or disobedience reveal about your trust in God?

Living a life of faithful obedience means being in tune with the Spirit's promptings. How well do you hear the Spirit's voice? Do you ever have doubts when you believe He is speaking to you? How might your faith increase if you were to obey Him without any questions?

The Lord often gives His children everything they need to know, exactly when they need to know it. When believers act in faith, He provides further instruction.

Lord, I want to walk in obedience to Your voice. Tune my ear to hear only You, Father, so that Your kingdom can be advanced through me.

A STRONG WITNESS

About midnight Paul and Silas were praying and singing hymns to God, and the prisoners were listening to them.
ACTS 16:25 ESV

W hen Paul cast out a demon from the slave girl in Philippi, his action upset her owners, who benefited financially from her fortune-telling. That led to Paul and Silas being tossed in jail for advocating religious customs that were not legal in Rome. The jailer fastened them into the inner prison and secured their feet in stocks. In response, they didn't demand their rights. Instead, they prayed and sang hymns—presumably while still in stocks—while the other prisoners listened. And God moved in the form of an earthquake.

What is your initial response when someone tries to silence you from talking about Christ? Are you quick to point out your religious liberties? Where do prayer and hymn singing rank in your order of responses? Do you know enough hymns to sing a few by heart if you were in a similar situation to that of Paul and Silas?

Sometimes as Christians, it's better to lay down your own rights and privileges for the Gospel's sake, knowing that God can and will act on your behalf. And doing so is often a better witness to surrounding unbelievers.

Father, the next time a situation arises in which my religious liberties are being taken away from me, remind me of Paul and Silas's response. And show up in a mighty way.

A FAITHFUL GOD

*Remember his covenant forever—the commitment he made to a
thousand generations. This is the covenant he made with Abraham
and the oath he swore to Isaac. He confirmed it to Jacob as a decree,
and to the people of Israel as a never-ending covenant.*
1 CHRONICLES 16:15–17 NLT

I srael brought the ark of God to the special tent that David had prepared for it. After the priests presented burnt and peace offerings, then offered sacrifices, it was time for worship. Today's verses contain lyrics David gave to Asaph and his fellow Levites to sing during that time of worship.

One of the best ways to remain unshakable in your faith is to do what David did—worship the Lord while remembering His faithfulness to a thousand generations. How far back can you trace your family's spiritual legacy? One generation? Two? Maybe more? Even if you are a first-generation Christian, someone with a spiritual heritage shared the Gospel with you. The point is God was at work in people long before you were born and will continue to be after you have entered glory.

If that sort of perspective doesn't encourage you to remain faithful, it's possible that you have lost sight of it. If you have, reread 1 Chronicles 16:8–36 and make it the song of your heart.

*Father, You're faithful to a thousand generations.
How can I be anything other than faithful in return?*

HOLD FAST

*When they [the men of Athens] heard about the resurrection of the dead,
some of them sneered, but others said, "We want to hear you again on
this subject." At that, Paul left the Council. Some of the people
became followers of Paul and believed.*

Acts 17:32–34 NIV

D o you have friends, coworkers, classmates, or acquaintances who simply refuse to believe any of the supernatural elements of Christianity? Maybe they don't believe in angels or the virgin birth or the resurrection of the dead. If so, you aren't alone.

Paul spoke to the men of Athens and stood strong as he heralded the resurrection of the dead. Yes, he faced mockers. But don't miss out on the fact that he also gained a hearing among some—so much so that some of the men joined him and believed. That's amazing if you think about it. And it was proof that God was at work even in a place where people worshipped an unknown god.

It's easy to say you believe the Word of God when you're among fellow believers. It's not so easy to hold fast to the truth when you're surrounded by mockers. Don't focus on them. Instead, hold fast to the faith and rejoice over those who want to hear more about a Messiah who has conquered sin and death.

*Father, in the past I've allowed mockers to distract me from sharing the truth.
Shape me into someone like Paul, who continued sharing despite opposition.*

SHARE YOUR TESTIMONY

*Let the redeemed of the LORD say so, whom he hath
redeemed from the hand of the enemy.*
PSALM 107:2 KJV

◆━━━◆━━━◆

The enemy often tempts believers to stay quiet about their faith. He knows that if he is successful, then not only will those around us not turn to us for spiritual answers, but our hesitation to declare Christ's redeeming power will result in a weakening of our own faith. Today's verse is a call for the redeemed of the Lord to say so.

In Matthew 5:14–15 (KJV), Jesus said, "Ye are the light of the world. A city that is set on an hill cannot be hid. Neither do men light a candle, and put it under a bushel, but on a candlestick; and it giveth light unto all that are in the house."

In what ways are you lighting a candle and putting it on a candlestick to light the sphere of influence God has placed you in? Are you praying for such opportunities before you start your normal daily routines that take you around those who are not redeemed? You have been redeemed from the hand of Satan. It's time to tell other captives about the freedom they can experience in Christ. As you do, you'll find that your faith becomes stronger—more unshakable.

*Father, provide an opportunity for me to share my testimony with someone
today. Strengthen my faith as I do.*

FIERY ENTHUSIASM

He [Apollos] was particularly effective in public debate with the Jews [in Achaia province] as he brought out proof after convincing proof from the Scriptures that Jesus was in fact God's Messiah.

ACTS 18:28 MSG

Apollos—a Jew from Alexandria, Egypt—was a great speaker who was eloquent and powerful in his preaching of the scriptures. He was also well educated in the way of Christ and was known for being fiery in his enthusiasm. He traveled to the Achaia region (present-day western Greece), where he debated with Jews about the Messiah, using the scriptures.

Apollos was gifted in his presentation, but don't miss his enthusiasm, which surely led to his dedication to the scriptures. The two go hand in hand. Every day, you have opportunities to defend the faith and to point people toward the Messiah. You don't have to be an expert theologian to do so. But knowing the scriptures well is important.

If fellow Christians in your small circle were to describe your faith, what would they say? It would take a lot of courage, but it might be worth asking them to give you an honest assessment. Then take the results to the Lord in prayer, devoting yourself to a stronger commitment to Christ and the scriptures.

Father, make me into a modern-day Apollos. I want to shine brightly for You and be able to give the world an answer for the hope I have in Christ.

FAITH-BUILDING STORMS

He stilled the storm to a whisper; the waves of the sea were hushed. They were glad when it grew calm, and he guided them to their desired haven.
PSALM 107:29–30 NIV

◆———◆———◆

Strong faith requires tests. In today's portion of scripture, those who did business on the water experienced turbulent seas. Those who were on board reeled to and fro, staggering like drunk men. They cried out to the Lord and He calmed the storm, strengthening their faith before the next storm they would surely encounter.

In Romans 5:3–4 (NIV), Paul wrote, "But we also glory in our sufferings, because we know that suffering produces perseverance; perseverance, character; and character, hope." Such hope builds trust in the Lord because a believer has experienced His guiding hand.

Are you in the middle of a storm right now? Know that it is designed to lead you to hope in the Lord. Don't get so caught up in how high the waves are that you can't see Jesus as He extends His hand toward you. He is there, just waiting for you to call out to Him. Once you do, you can trust Him—both in your current storm and in all your future ones.

Father, I'm just like the people on this ship in today's verses. I see the high waves and strong wind and I fear they will overwhelm me. Help me to see that You are always with me in the storms I'm facing.

WHOLEHEARTED DEVOTION

"And you, my son Solomon, acknowledge the God of your father, and serve him with wholehearted devotion and with a willing mind, for the LORD searches every heart and understands every desire and every thought."
1 CHRONICLES 28:9 NIV

C hristians can never sin cheaply; they pay a heavy price for iniquity," wrote Charles Spurgeon in his *Morning and Evening* devotional. "Transgression destroys peace of mind, obscures fellowship with Jesus, hinders prayer, brings darkness over the soul; therefore be not the serf and bondman of sin."

David seemed to understand that truth when he spoke to his son Solomon, encouraging him to serve the Lord wholeheartedly with a willing mind, for the Lord searches every heart and understands every desire and thought. A mind and heart that are harboring sin are unable to serve Him wholeheartedly.

You will never be fully free from sin on this side of heaven, but if you are quick to confess your sin, you exhibit a heart that is fully devoted to God. Holding on to pet sins is an indicator that your heart has been pulled away from Him. What does the Lord see right now when He searches your heart, your desires, and your every thought? If He sees any darkness, confess it to Him right now.

Father God, at times I get so discouraged over my sin. When You examine my heart, I want You to see someone who is completely sold out for You.

WHAT DO YOU WANT?

"Give me [Solomon] the wisdom and knowledge to lead them properly,
for who could possibly govern this great people of yours?"

2 CHRONICLES 1:10 NLT

◆───────◆───────◆

After Solomon took control of his kingdom, he called together the leaders of Israel, and they gathered in front of the tabernacle of the Lord to consult Him. That night, God appeared to Solomon and said, "What do you want? Ask, and I will give it to you!" (2 Chronicles 1:7 NLT). Solomon could've asked for riches or fame, but he asked for wisdom and knowledge to lead God's people properly.

God responded by giving him not only what he asked for but also riches and fame such as no other king before or after him ever received.

If God asked you what you wanted, what would your answer reveal about your faith in Him? Would it show commitment and humility, like Solomon exhibited? Or would it show that your heart is far from God? Even if it's the latter, you desire to love and serve Him. That's why you're meeting with Him this morning. Pray a prayer similar to the one Solomon prayed and eagerly expect an answer.

Father, my devotion to You is sometimes lacking. But I pray that You would give me the wisdom and knowledge to lead my family properly, for You have graciously given them to me to lead and guide them for Your glory.

FINISHING WELL

"I do not account my life of any value nor as precious to myself, if only I may finish my course and the ministry that I received from the Lord Jesus, to testify to the gospel of the grace of God."

ACTS 20:24 ESV

◆———————◆———————◆

The apostle Paul knew what awaited him when he arrived in Jerusalem. He'd called for the elders of the church in Ephesus and explained that the Spirit had told him he would face imprisonment and afflictions. Yet he didn't account his life as precious to himself. Instead, he would stare down death because his earnest desire was to stay faithful to the end.

Throughout the centuries, Christians have been willing to die as martyrs for Christ. It's not that they didn't value their lives; they valued the ministry that God had given them more. Christ died for them. The least they could do was offer up their lives for Him if the situation arose. Such a spirit is still alive and well in believers all around the world who want to finish well in countries that are hostile to the Gospel.

What would finishing well look like for you? What ministry has Christ given you, and how determined are you to complete it? What steps do you need to take today?

Lord, give me the determination and unswerving dedication that Paul mentioned in today's verse to finish the ministry You have given me. I want to finish well, for Your glory.

DEVOUT PRAYERS

Listen to my prayers, energetic and devout. . . . Keep your eyes open to this Temple day and night, this place you promised to dignify with your Name. And listen to the prayers that I pray in this place. And listen to your people Israel when they pray at this place.

2 CHRONICLES 6:19–21 MSG

Solomon was a lot of things. He was a king, a husband, and a father. He was also a writer, a lyricist, and the wisest man who ever lived. With all of that said, he had his faults. He allowed his many wives and concubines to turn his heart away from the Lord. Maybe that's why he also had such a heart for intercessory prayer. He knew how easily humans could be drawn away from the Lord. In today's verses, he prayed for the Lord to hear the prayers His people offered in the temple.

What sort of devout prayers are you praying right now? Who or what are they for? Are you asking the Father to answer other people's prayers, then maybe checking in with them occasionally to see how God is responding? If not, take a page out of Solomon's book and begin doing so today, putting your whole heart into such prayers.

Father, hear the prayers of my family today. Attune Your ears to their requests. Please do the same for my friends and even my enemies.

FOR HIS NAME'S SAKE

But you, O GOD my Lord, deal on my behalf for your name's sake;
because your steadfast love is good, deliver me!
PSALM 109:21 ESV

In today's verse, David wasn't simply calling out to the Lord to save him from his enemies for David's sake. David wanted God to fight for him for His name's sake, which makes his motive pure and shows how strongly he believed in God's love for him.

"That is, Interpose for me; exert thy power in my behalf," wrote Albert Barnes in his *Notes on the Bible*. "The phrase 'for thy name's sake' implies that the motive which prompted him was a desire that God might be honored. It was not primarily or mainly for his own happiness; it was that God might be glorified, that his character might be illustrated, that his plans might be accomplished."

Don't view your circumstances with only physical eyes, but instead look at them with spiritual eyes. God is seeking to glorify Himself through you in the midst of your trials.

Are you receiving pushback at work or in your circle of friends for doing something that honors God? Have you considered asking God to deal on your behalf for His name's sake? After all, the battle belongs to the Lord.

Father, I know I'll receive criticism or even persecution for living for You.
Your steadfast love is good, Lord. Deliver me, for Your name's sake.

YOU ARE CHRIST'S AMBASSADOR

"The God of our ancestors has chosen you to know his will and to see the Righteous One and to hear words from his mouth. You will be his witness to all people of what you have seen and heard."

ACTS 22:14–15 NIV

◆━━━━◆━━━━◆

Ananias had a message for Paul after Paul's dramatic conversion to Christ, and Paul recounted that message for a crowd after being arrested in the temple, as we read in today's scripture passage. Ananias wanted Paul to know that God had chosen him as an ambassador. He was to be a witness to everyone of what he had seen and heard.

Now that the church has the completed canon (both the Old and New Testaments), all believers are to be ambassadors for Christ. Second Corinthians 5:20 (NIV) says, "We are therefore Christ's ambassadors, as though God were making his appeal through us. We implore you on Christ's behalf: Be reconciled to God."

In recent weeks, you've been reading about how both David and Paul stood strong when facing opposition as they sought to glorify God by proclaiming His Word. Remember, though, that Jesus said, "If the world hates you, keep in mind that it hated me first" (John 15:18 NIV). The fact that the world opposes you means it can see Christ in you. Rejoice!

Father, thank You for making me one of Christ's ambassadors. How can I do anything other than rejoice when people see You in me?

SOUND YOUR BATTLE CRY

*When Judah realized that they were being attacked from the front
and the rear, they cried out to the LORD for help. Then the priests blew
the trumpets, and the men of Judah began to shout. At the sound
of their battle cry, God defeated Jeroboam and all Israel.*

2 CHRONICLES 13:14–15 NLT

King Abijah probably doesn't get his just due. He only reigned over Judah for three years, during the time Jeroboam reigned over Israel. When war broke out between the two nations, Israel had double the number of troops (800,000 versus 400,000). Abijah tried to warn Israel that the Lord had made an everlasting covenant with David, giving him and his descendants the true throne, but Jeroboam wouldn't listen, and he paid dearly; 500,000 of his troops died during battle.

God's people are usually outnumbered in any situation. The culture scoffs and laughs at the church whenever believers try to point it in the right direction, according to God's Word. Today we live in what could be considered another dark age. Yet God is still faithful to His church. He still defends her. Don't lose heart, no matter what your eyes tell you. Cry out to the Lord for help in pushing back the darkness. Blow your proverbial trumpet and then leave the results to God.

*Father, may I continue to shine my light for Jesus even when the
circumstances around me seem bleak. I will trust in You.*

A FRESH COMMITMENT

The works of the LORD are great, sought out of all them that
have pleasure therein. His work is honourable and glorious:
and his righteousness endureth for ever.
PSALM 111:2–3 KJV

Have you ever sat around a breakfast or dinner table with a group of Christian men and discussed the works of the Lord—things like creation, redemption, the virgin birth, resurrection, or heaven—in light of what the scriptures say about them? Each topic would take a lifetime to unpack, which is one of the things that fascinates the believer to the point of endless study.

Notice the connection in today's verse between studying God's works (as recorded in the Bible) and pleasure. If you had to describe your Bible study habits in one word, what would it be? Does it fall short of pleasure? Sometimes believers encounter periods of spiritual dryness, but God breaks through it at some point if the person keeps seeking Him.

If your time in the Word has been lacking, will you make a fresh commitment to reading and studying it regularly? You are already reading through the Bible as part of this book's reading plan, and that's an excellent start. But don't forget to go deeper by *studying* the Word. If you aren't sure how, ask a leader at your church or a trusted Christian friend.

Father, I want what the psalmist described—pleasure in studying Your
great works. Help me to make this a priority in my life.

REMAIN FAITHFUL

"Didn't I tell you?" the king of Israel [Ahab] exclaimed to Jehoshaphat.
"He never prophesies anything but trouble for me."
2 CHRONICLES 18:17 NLT

King Ahab had a long history of committing evil before the Lord. In fact, 1 Kings 16:30 (NLT) says he "did what was evil in the LORD's sight, even more than any of the kings before him." So it was no surprise he wasn't pleased when the prophet Micaiah, who apparently often spoke against the king and his actions, said that King Ahab would die in battle.

The role of prophet was often a lonely one. Imagine being summoned by a king and asked to inquire of the Lord, only to hear Him tell you something that the king wouldn't like. Then imagine that you are serving a wicked king whom God opposes at every turn. Micaiah, a lesser-known prophet, had the courage to do so. And his prophecy about King Ahab dying in battle came true.

While you may not be a prophet, you are a follower of Christ who is spending time in the Word of God. Your responses to people won't always make you popular. But like Micaiah, you can honor the Lord by remaining true to what you know to be right.

Lord God, give me Micaiah's courage in the face of opposition. May I always remain true to You, no matter how unpopular my message is.

PRAISE THE LORD!

Let the name of the LORD be praised, both now and forevermore.
From the rising of the sun to the place where it sets,
the name of the LORD is to be praised.
PSALM 113:2–3 NIV

❖

Some faith traditions seem to place a high value on church attendance, as if living for God one hour each week is enough. In reality, the Christian life is one that lives *coram Deo*, a Latin phrase that means to live before the face of God. As such, the Christian lives to honor and praise God from the moment he rises to the moment he lies back down in the evening.

In today's verses, the psalmist hits on this truth. The name of the Lord is to be praised always. The Christian doesn't live in a compartmentalized fashion. He doesn't worship the Lord on Sundays, then live like the world for the rest of the week.

What are you currently doing to praise the Lord throughout your day? Maybe it's singing hymns or praise songs silently while you work, or maybe it's offering prayers of praise often.

If you find that you've fallen short, begin to shift your mindset from being someone who *goes* to church to being someone who *is* the church. That's not to say you won't also attend corporate worship, but that's just the start of your worship. Make praise as natural as breathing.

Father, I praise Your name this morning, and I'll praise it throughout the day.

OBEDIENT TO THE CALL

"Therefore, O King Agrippa, I was not disobedient to the heavenly vision, but declared first to those in Damascus, then in Jerusalem and throughout all the region of Judea, and also to the Gentiles, that they should repent and turn to God, performing deeds in keeping with their repentance."

ACTS 26:19–20 ESV

◆——◆——◆

During Paul's trial, he shared the story of his conversion to Christ. Jesus Himself appeared to Paul and appointed him as a servant and witness to the Gentiles to preach the Gospel to them so their eyes would be opened and they would turn from the power of Satan to God. He wanted King Agrippa to know that he was simply being obedient to Christ by telling any who would listen about the saving power of Jesus.

Paul mentioned that he started his Gospel declaration to people in Damascus, then transitioned to Jerusalem and throughout all the region of Judea, reaching Gentiles as well. In other words, he was unwavering as he shared the Gospel with various people groups. Do you have a similar heart to reach people who don't look or sound like you? Are you being a consistent and faithful witness? How could you do better?

Father, I'm inspired by Paul's courage to share the Gospel not only among so many people groups but also before kings. I'm resolved to be obedient to the call to do so as well.

FULLY COMMITTED

And he [King Amaziah] did what was right in the
eyes of the LORD, yet not with a whole heart.
2 CHRONICLES 25:2 ESV

King Amaziah started strong during his twenty-nine-year reign in Judah. He brought his father's killers to justice and built a mighty army, but then he fell into idolatry. After striking down the Edomites, he brought back the gods of the men of Seir and set them up as his gods and worshipped them. His whole heart hadn't been with God, and it led him astray.

His story is a common one. The hearts of humankind often find a false security in the things of this world. Today, Christian men wouldn't bring back false idols from battle, but they would possibly worship other idols—like power, wealth, or sex—all of which appeal to the flesh and make false promises.

One of the saddest stories that can be told about a man after his conversion is that he did what was right in the eyes of the Lord initially but then was led astray and worshipped idols. Don't allow that to be your story. Make a full commitment to the Lord and follow Him all the days of your life.

Lord, I want my story to be different—one that brings You glory from the day I became a Christian to the day I close my eyes in death and open them in glory.

STOP!

*Azariah the priest with eighty other courageous priests of the LORD followed
him in. They confronted King Uzziah and said, "It is not right for you,
Uzziah, to burn incense to the LORD. That is for the priests, the descendants
of Aaron, who have been consecrated to burn incense."*
2 CHRONICLES 26:17–18 NIV

During King Uzziah's fifty-two-year reign in Judah, he saw many successes,
and he went down in Judah's history as one of its good kings. But pride
got the better of him at one point and he entered the temple to burn incense
on the altar. Azariah and eighty other priests confronted him. Uzziah was
angered by their actions, but he caught leprosy as a result of his sin and spent
the rest of his life in an isolated house.

Azariah and the other priests are a model of what to do when a believer
sees a fellow believer entering into sin. They withstood Uzziah's wrath for his
own good, and ultimately their intervention spared his life.

If you've been in Uzziah's shoes, you know it wasn't an enjoyable situation.
But praise God for people who loved you enough to rescue you. And if you've
even been in Azariah's shoes, bless you for your concern for Christian brothers.

Christians need each other to stay on the narrow road.

*Father, thank You for surrounding us with other believers who
love us enough to confront us when we stray into sin.*

WHERE DO YOU START OVER?

"For our fathers have been unfaithful and have done what was evil in the sight of the LORD our God. They have forsaken him and have turned away their faces from the habitation of the LORD and turned their backs."
2 CHRONICLES 29:6 ESV

The worst had happened to the people of Judah. They had departed from the Lord and followed their own way, and they reaped the consequences of their choices as chaos and desolation enveloped them. Although it was surely common to revere their elders and to uphold the best memories of their ancestors, the only path for the people to start over was an honest assessment of the past. They couldn't overlook their sins and failures. It was time to come to terms with where things had gone wrong and how they could forge a new path.

If you're confronting your failures today, or the failures of your family's past, now is a good time to face the truth honestly. Don't try to hide the past or even the ways you've failed today. God already knows anyway! Even if you have to say hard things about your ancestors or your older family members, an honest assessment of your sins and history is essential for starting over.

Lord, help me to see my failures for what they are so that I can freely confess them and receive Your forgiveness.

WHY WE GATHER TOGETHER

For I long to visit you so I can bring you some spiritual gift that will help you grow strong in the Lord. When we get together, I want to encourage you in your faith, but I also want to be encouraged by yours.

ROMANS 1:11–12 NLT

◆━━━━◆━━━━◆

Although Paul had more experience and knowledge than the church in Rome, he didn't see himself as superior to the Roman believers. He visited them with the expectation that blessings would be shared in both directions. Paul's trip was completely for the benefit of the church he served. He brought them a spiritual gift that would help them rather than helping his own reputation in any way. In fact, Paul's desire to bless the Roman church led to an extremely dangerous trip that put his life in danger.

As you consider whom you can serve and the sacrifices your service may require, keep in mind that you will also find blessings and encouragement along the way. In fact, times of ministering to others could be some of the most restorative parts of each day. As you give of yourself to others, you will find them sharing God's goodness with you as well—provided you remain open to that possibility. The best reason to gather with others is to minister to each other as equals in the family of God.

Jesus, help me to serve others with humility so that I can receive the blessings they have for me.

DON'T LET ANYONE ELSE DEFINE GOD FOR YOU

And they shouted it with a loud voice in the language of Judah to the people of Jerusalem who were on the wall, to frighten and terrify them, in order that they might take the city. And they spoke of the God of Jerusalem as they spoke of the gods of the peoples of the earth, which are the work of men's hands.

2 CHRONICLES 32:18–19 ESV

◆———◆———◆

When the Assyrians invaded the nation of Judah, they slandered the Lord and reduced Him to a statue created by people. This invading army tried to strike fear into the people of Judah by speaking of their God in ways that would cause them to doubt Him in the middle of a crisis.

When life becomes challenging or doubts emerge, whom do you listen to? Do you seek the people who can strengthen your faith in God, or do you allow doubters or the enemies of God to plant ideas in your mind? While every crisis can prove disturbing and difficult to endure, your faith can stay unshakable if you remain confident in God's love for you and in His power to save. You won't know what deliverance will look like or how God will meet you in a difficult time, but the people you listen to when the odds look the worst may determine what your future looks like.

Lord, I trust that You can overcome my doubts and fears.

GOD'S PATIENCE ISN'T APATHY TOWARD SIN

Don't you see how wonderfully kind, tolerant, and patient God is with you? Does this mean nothing to you? Can't you see that his kindness is intended to turn you from your sin?

ROMANS 2:4 NLT

Although Paul had plenty of reasons to praise the Roman church, they were still in danger of misunderstanding some of the attributes of God's character. On other occasions, Paul's critics even misrepresented what he taught about God's patience, grace, and mercy. As he sought to share the goodness of God with this church, he also took care to share the bigger picture about God's patience.

It's possible that you grew up hearing about either God's wrath and anger or His patience and mercy. Both perspectives can misconstrue the aim of God to lead you toward holiness and spiritual health. You certainly need to obey what Jesus taught and live as if loving God and loving your neighbors are the two most important commandments. Obedience isn't optional. Yet God is patient and kind in leading you away from sin. It may be a process—a very messy, time-consuming process. In God's eyes, you are worth the wait, but the goal of patiently waiting is your transformation.

Holy Spirit, help me to see the areas of my life where I need to avail myself of Your mercy and patience so that I submit myself to Your redemptive power.

GOD USES WHAT WE REJECT

The stone the builders rejected has become the cornerstone;
the LORD has done this, and it is marvelous in our eyes.
PSALM 118:22–23 NIV

———◆———◆———◆———

Builders didn't choose stones haphazardly. They made deliberate choices based on long-held standards and specifications for a structure. Each stone was chosen based on years of experience and knowledge, with multiple workers having a hand in the construction process. If a faulty stone undermined the integrity of the building, the builder's reputation and future hopes of work would be ruined. Placing a rejected stone in the most important part of a building was a major risk indeed!

You may be surprised, then, to read the psalmist's declaration that a solid, unshakable foundation is the one made with a rejected cornerstone. Yet God specializes in taking the things and people we overlook or count out and using them for noble and essential purposes. God is most likely working in the people and the places you are most likely to overlook and count out. Even more striking, the results of God's work are marvelous and praiseworthy, revealing God's wisdom and power to all.

It will take courage to reject conventional wisdom and pursue God's influence in your life even as it draws you away from well-trod paths. Yet this is where you will find God's power and presence.

Lord, help me to see Your hand at work in the places I overlook.

LISTENING TO HARD TRUTHS

The LORD, the God of their fathers, sent persistently to them by his messengers, because he had compassion on his people and on his dwelling place. But they kept mocking the messengers of God, despising his words and scoffing at his prophets.
2 CHRONICLES 36:15–16 ESV

◆————◆————◆

God sent prophets to Judah who could help the people change their ways and find Him again. But they consistently chose to honor those who said what they wanted to hear rather than God's prophets, who spoke hard truths. God's prophets asked hard questions and challenged the status quo. Listening to the prophets was costly, challenging, and sometimes even put people at odds with each other. It was far easier to seek out false prophets giving the easy messages that reaffirmed what they already wanted to hear.

Is there anyone in your life right now who can speak a hard truth to you? A hard truth isn't the same as criticism. Rather, you need someone who can speak truthfully to you about your choices and the consequences you will face. Those who speak truthfully to you will have your best interests in mind and will share their words as a burden from God, not out of a personal agenda for more power and control in your life.

Lord, help me to listen to the hard truths I need to hear so that I can live in obedience to You.

THE BEST WAY TO STOP SINNING

Blessed are those whose ways are blameless, who walk according to the law of the LORD. Blessed are those who keep his statutes and seek him with all their heart—they do no wrong but follow his ways.

PSALM 119:1–3 NIV

The psalms often praise the value of living a blameless life. People who live that way know God's teachings and obey them consistently. Maintaining a commitment to God's direction is often thought of as a matter of willpower or desire, yet today's psalm offers another aspect of obedience that may be even more effective than human willpower.

If you want to leave sin behind, consider that the act of repentance is both a turning away from sin and a turning toward God. Repentance is a new direction in which a heart that was set upon sin finds a new desire: to be fully committed to seeking God.

When this daily pursuit of God occupies the majority of your "stray" thoughts, it opens you to the power of His Spirit working in your life. You no longer work at cross-purposes against God or struggle to choose between two warring desires. With a single desire in your heart to seek a God who loves you, you'll find that sin will become less of a temptation.

Father, help me to turn toward You so that I can pursue You and Your love wholeheartedly.

WHO ARE YOU SERVING?

Do not let any part of your body become an instrument of evil to serve sin.
Instead, give yourselves completely to God, for you were dead, but now
you have new life. So use your whole body as an instrument
to do what is right for the glory of God.
ROMANS 6:13 NLT

Although Paul needed to help the church in Rome sort out their beliefs about Jesus and the ways the Holy Spirit was manifest in their lives, he also had to address their practices. How would the Roman Christians live each day in light of salvation in Christ? Considering that they were no longer dead in their sins, they should live differently because of God's power in their lives.

Each decision you make is an opportunity to say yes to God and yield to His power in your life. . .or to offer yourself to the power of evil and sin in your life. Even if you have been saved by faith, your daily decisions matter a great deal in your relationship with God and your ability to glorify Him.

In fact, winning glory for God is a great test of your motives and the benefits of your decisions. Are you relying on God's power as you offer yourself to God's purposes in your life, or are you clinging to your own plans and desires?

Father, help me to give myself wholeheartedly to Your purposes today.

WHAT HAVE YOU SET YOUR HEART ON?

*For Ezra had set his heart to study the Law of the Lord,
and to do it and to teach his statutes and rules in Israel.*
Ezra 7:10 esv

◆━━━━━◆━━━━━◆

The direction of Ezra's life and the destiny of the people of Israel were determined in part by his heart's desire to study the law of the Lord, to obey it in his life, and to teach others to obey it too. In a time of uncertainty and loss, he found stability in God's unshakable message for his life.

The alternative to setting your heart toward something or setting a goal is living your life reacting to circumstances or seeking whatever feels good. Even when life becomes busy or overwhelming, having a "true north" can help you avoid mistakes, detours, and damage to your most important relationships.

While you may not have made a resolution to do something lately, is there something you are determined to do? Is there some change or long-term goal that drives you? Today's passage is an invitation to resolve to know what God asks of you and then follow through in doing it. What you resolve to do today can have a major impact on the direction of both your own life and the lives of many people you know.

*Lord, help me to see Your teachings with clarity
and to obey them with integrity.*

A SIMPLE TEST FOR YOUR SPIRITUAL STATE

*Those who are dominated by the sinful nature think about sinful things,
but those who are controlled by the Holy Spirit think about things that
please the Spirit. So letting your sinful nature control your mind leads to
death. But letting the Spirit control your mind leads to life and peace.*

ROMANS 8:5–6 NLT

❦

Although Paul digs into a number of weighty topics in his letter to the Roman church, he also gives his readers some helpful tips to evaluate their spiritual health. By examining their thoughts, they would find out just how much the Holy Spirit was influencing their thinking in comparison to their sinful nature. This self-examination offered immediate guidance for prayer so they could yield their lives to the Holy Spirit.

Take a moment to consider what you've thought about over the past day. Do you have a sense that your thoughts are dominated by good things that draw you near to God and help you love your friends, family, and colleagues? Or do you feel absorbed in your own desires, prone to flashes of anger, or preoccupied with the bitter seeds of envy or resentment? Reflection on your thoughts can offer valuable clues about the needs of your soul. You may need to spend more time in prayerful surrender to the Holy Spirit, asking God to work in your life and to guide your thoughts.

*Holy Spirit, help me to see the state of my thoughts with clarity,
and guide me toward Your purpose today.*

THE BEST WAY TO END YOUR DAY

Your decrees are the theme of my song wherever I lodge.
In the night, LORD, I remember your name, that I may keep
your law. This has been my practice: I obey your precepts.
PSALM 119:54–56 NIV

◆――――◆――――◆

The psalmist has kept the teachings of the Lord on his mind as a song and as his last thought each day so that he can remain obedient to God's law. By keeping the teachings of the Lord on his mind, he makes it that much easier to avoid temptation and willful sins. This practice became a life-giving habit that he freely passed along to others.

What fills your mind each day? What are you listening to, watching, reading, or pondering? However you answer that question, it's likely your answer will help determine whether it's easier to obey or disobey the teachings of scripture. Immersing yourself in examples of self-fulfillment, self-indulgence, and even hostility toward others will make it much harder to exhibit the humble self-sacrifice that Jesus modeled.

Filling your mind with songs about God's goodness, meditating on scripture before bedtime, or reading a book about scripture can be a useful way to fill your mind with God's direction. You can spend your days with scripture at the front of your thoughts, and your mind can drift off to sleep in harmony with God's teachings.

Jesus, help me to keep Your teachings at the front of my mind each day.

THE LORD IS ATTENTIVE TO CONFESSION

"Let your ear be attentive and your eyes open, to hear the prayer of your servant that I now pray before you day and night for the people of Israel your servants, confessing the sins of the people of Israel, which we have sinned against you. Even I and my father's house have sinned."

NEHEMIAH 1:6 ESV

Having lived in exile and then returning to the ruins of Jerusalem, Nehemiah knew that his people, his family, and even he himself had sinned greatly against the Lord. He fixed his mind on setting things right with God, asking the Lord to hear his daily prayers and confessions. He didn't try to cover up his wrongs or the wrongs of his ancestors. He faced the past with integrity and humility, creating an opportunity for restoration and a new beginning.

At your lowest point of failure and sin, the place to begin is always an honest and clear assessment of your wrongs and even the wrongs of your family. Sometimes patterns of sin can be modeled and passed down from one generation to the next. Like Nehemiah, you can bring your own failures and the failures of your family to God with the hope that God will listen and send help. Failure and sin never have to be the end for God's people. You can trust that God will honor your humility and honesty.

Lord, help me to see and to confess my sins.

WHERE WILL YOU FIND COMFORT?

May your unfailing love be my comfort, according to your promise to your servant. Let your compassion come to me that I may live, for your law is my delight. May the arrogant be put to shame for wronging me without cause; but I will meditate on your precepts.

PSALM 119:76–78 NIV

The psalmist faced the injustices and trouble of life with a focus on the precepts of the Lord and the promises of His unfailing love. While delighting in God's law, he asked Him for justice so that the arrogant would suffer the consequences of their behavior. He looked to God alone for his deliverance and restoration.

Conflict and trouble will certainly arise, and you will likely be wronged at times. Your response could be to hit back or to sit and stew on the offense. You could be consumed by anger and even meet an arrogant person on his own terms by building up your own self-image. Yet the unfailing and unwavering comfort of God's love is what will restore you through the highs and lows of life.

It's tempting to delight in the downfall of others, but today's psalm challenges you to delight in the Lord's law and precepts. Make these your go-to when you're discouraged or in the midst of conflict, and you'll find solid ground to stand on.

Lord, I trust that Your unfailing love can comfort me in difficult times.

HOW TO MAKE YOURSELF RIGHT WITH GOD

*If you openly declare that Jesus is Lord and believe in your heart
that God raised him from the dead, you will be saved. For it is
by believing in your heart that you are made right with God,
and it is by openly declaring your faith that you are saved.*

ROMANS 10:9–10 NLT

◆━━━◆━━━◆

The Roman Christians were surrounded by people who appeased different deities with certain behaviors or offerings. Keeping on the good side of an idol in those days was a matter of externals, regardless of what anyone thought. Sincerity or belief wasn't essential for pacifying an idol. Paul laid out a very different approach to Jesus, where the change begins in one's heart, with confessing and believing with sincerity.

Are you trying to win God's favor or to find a measure of assurance that you are right with Him? While your actions are important and obedience is certainly something Jesus expects, your starting point for any kind of assurance or faithful living is within. What you believe in your heart, what you think in your mind, and what you confess with your mouth will determine your direction in life.

Based on that foundation of confessing a sincere belief, you can ask for God's help in changing your life from the inside out, rather than making fragile attempts to change yourself from the outside in.

Jesus, You are Lord, and I need Your help to live faithfully today.

REPENT, BUT DON'T FORGET TO REJOICE

Then he said to them, "Go your way. Eat the fat and drink sweet wine and send portions to anyone who has nothing ready, for this day is holy to our Lord. And do not be grieved, for the joy of the LORD is your strength."
NEHEMIAH 8:10 ESV

◆ ◆ ◆

The people mourned when they heard the Law. They realized how far they had strayed from the Lord. They were rebuilding the ruins of Jerusalem after a previous generation's unfaithfulness, and it's likely that the consequences of disobedience had finally sunk in for them. Yet as they repented and mourned, Nehemiah urged them to celebrate their recommitment and to let the joy of God be their strength.

When you're starting over after a time of struggle and unfaithfulness, you may find that joy is a challenge. Guilt and shame can be paralyzing and discouraging. How can you recover and start over again? The answer is to repent and then rejoice. Guilt and shame won't help you move forward. Yet rejoicing in God's love and mercy will draw you to obedience and renewal. As you offer yourself to the Lord and live in reliance on His joy in your life, you'll find that obedience will be far easier than the heavy weight of guilt and shame that can give way to defeatism. In the Lord's joy, there is hope for tomorrow.

Lord, help me to remember Your love and mercy that bring joy.

SERVICE IS AN ACT OF WORSHIP

And so, dear brothers and sisters, I plead with you to give your bodies to God because of all he has done for you. Let them be a living and holy sacrifice— the kind he will find acceptable. This is truly the way to worship him.

ROMANS 12:1 NLT

Paul urges the Roman Christians to offer themselves in service to God and sacrifice their own plans and desires. While they could make any number of sacrifices in order to please God, the only sacrifice God desires as an act of worship is their sacrifice of themselves. Such a personal offering follows the same example Jesus set when He became a man and suffered death.

Consider all of the ways you try to win God's favor or capture His attention. Do you ever feel anxious or exhausted from the uncertainty of ever doing enough for God?

Paul's message today is both simple and costly, as he challenges you to offer yourself to God as an act of worship. This means asking God to guide you wherever He may take you. That will certainly prove challenging as you let go of things you consider important, but you will also gain intimacy with God that will surely overshadow what you leave behind.

Jesus, help me to offer myself to You for Your service.

WHAT IS GOD WAITING FOR?

My eyes fail, looking for your salvation, looking for your righteous promise.
Deal with your servant according to your love and teach me your decrees.
I am your servant; give me discernment that I may understand your statutes.
PSALM 119:123–125 NIV

While waiting for God's intervention, the psalmist placed himself fully at the Lord's mercy and resigned himself to trust in His love. Rather than relying on his own wisdom and insight, the psalmist asked the Lord to instruct him and to grant him discernment. In a time of waiting and uncertainty, he turned to God's unfailing promise to teach and to guide him personally.

There are a lot of sources of salvation to call upon these days, and you may find it helpful to consider whether you are waiting on God to lead you forward. Are you waiting for a financial, professional, or relational change that promises to lead you to a better place?

You don't know when or how the Lord will intervene in your life. His intervention is beyond your control. While you may be surrounded by people who cast doubt on this strategy, the best thing you can do in a time of waiting is to ask the Lord for wisdom and insight into His Word. You'll see examples of other people who have waited on God and find instruction to guide your path forward.

Lord, guide me and teach me as I wait on Your salvation.

ARE YOU GUARDING YOUR GATES?

Then I commanded the Levites that they should purify themselves and come and guard the gates, to keep the Sabbath day holy. Remember this also in my favor, O my God, and spare me according to the greatness of your steadfast love.

NEHEMIAH 13:22 ESV

When Nehemiah helped re-establish the city of Jerusalem, he found that many people continued to conduct business on the Sabbath rather than keeping it holy. He was forced to take the dramatic step of sending the Levites to guard the gates of the city to ensure that people actually observed the Sabbath. Although he was surely criticized for this "antibusiness" policy, he looked to God for approval and justification. The consequences of disobedience were all around him in the city's ruined walls.

Sometimes obedience to God's commands may require you to take drastic steps to guard against your worst inclinations. For instance, an alcoholic may remove all alcohol from his home just to limit the temptation. Taking action like Nehemiah may draw the unwanted attention of others, and it could even lead to criticism.

Temptation can turn into a downward spiral away from daily fellowship with God. Without a realistic understanding of the seriousness of sin, you won't take the necessary steps to guard your heart and your daily choices from the lure of sinful indulgence.

Lord, help me to make the sacrifices and changes necessary to obey Your Word.

THE STRONG
SUPPORT THE WEAK

*We who are strong must be considerate of those who are sensitive about
things like this. We must not just please ourselves. We should help others do
what is right and build them up in the Lord.*

ROMANS 15:1–2 NLT

D ifferent convictions and practices could have divided the Roman
church and driven some of its members to violate their consciences
by eating food that they considered wrong to eat. With Jewish dietary laws
and convictions over meat sacrificed to idols dividing churches, Paul urged
this congregation to put the well-being of one another ahead of any dispute.
Rather than trying to win an argument, those with a clear conscience should
try to help those who still struggled over what they ate.

You could say that this care for those with a sensitive conscience saves
you and your community from the weak becoming weaker while the strong
become stronger. It gives you a chance to seek the welfare of others, hoping
for the best when someone has a clear conscience. . .or keeping your thoughts
to yourself when someone can't enjoy the same freedoms as you. Rather than
winning an argument, you have an opportunity to build up a fellow believer
so that he won't live under guilt and condemnation. Having a clear conscience
is good, but having a stronger community is even better.

*Holy Spirit, show me how I can help those with a sensitive
conscience live with integrity in their convictions.*

DON'T WAIT TO DO
THE RIGHT THING

In those days, as Mordecai was sitting at the king's gate,
Bigthan and Teresh, two of the king's eunuchs, who guarded
the threshold, became angry and sought to lay hands on King
Ahasuerus. And this came to the knowledge of Mordecai, and he told
it to Queen Esther, and Esther told the king in the name of Mordecai.

ESTHER 2:21–22 ESV

Mordecai had every excuse to ignore what he had overheard. He was living in exile under the control of a king who had no attachment to his people. The king had taken his cousin into the harem regardless of her desires. It would have been understandable if Mordecai had said this wasn't his problem. Yet he remained committed to doing what was right, and that brought significant benefits to him and to his people.

You may not know how your actions today will play out into the future. It's impossible to see how one good deed can lead to one blessing after another. There is always a reward for obedience and a reason to seek the preservation of life, even if that person is your enemy. By seeking the welfare of all people, regardless of their allegiance to you, you are both obeying the command of Jesus to love your neighbors and creating opportunities for blessings in the days to come.

Father, help me to seek the welfare of all people, doing what
is right no matter what the circumstances may be.

DOES GOD HEAR YOUR PRAYERS?

May my cry come before you, LORD; give me understanding according to your word. May my supplication come before you; deliver me according to your promise. May my lips overflow with praise, for you teach me your decrees.

PSALM 119:169–171 NIV

◆   ◆   ◆

The writer of this psalm imagined his prayers rising up before the Lord, who heard his supplications and took action. As a result of God's actions, he would be able to praise Him with thanksgiving. This was a simple prayer—asking God to give him understanding. God will certainly respond to such a request, even if the details of this understanding may not be immediately apparent at first.

What are you praying about right now? Do you have similar confidence that your prayers are rising up to God and being noticed? Maybe you've had some doubts or fears that God has counted you out or that prayer just isn't working. You may imagine your prayers hitting the ceiling and stopping there.

Today's devotional is an invitation to seek understanding and wisdom so that you can live in obedience to God. Perhaps the most important place to start with prayer is the *content* of your prayers, looking to God for wisdom so that you can fulfill His desires and respond to Him in joy and gratitude.

Father, help me to pray with confidence that my prayers rise up before You.

HOW TO USE YOUR INFLUENCE TO HELP

For Mordecai the Jew was second in rank to King Ahasuerus, and he was great among the Jews and popular with the multitude of his brothers, for he sought the welfare of his people and spoke peace to all his people.

ESTHER 10:3 ESV

◆━━━━━━◆━━━━━━◆

The story of Esther and Mordecai doesn't specifically attribute any particular actions to God, but the goodness and selflessness of God's people are themes running throughout the story. They worked together to save God's people from an attack by putting their own lives on the line. When they gained power, they sought ways to ensure the welfare of their people and to bring about peace for them.

What kinds of opportunities do you have to serve or benefit others? Nothing may come to mind right now, and that's perfectly fine. Yet today's story is a reminder that you have influence, positions, and opportunities to bring about peace and justice for the people in your circles. You may not face the same kinds of risks that Esther and Mordecai faced, but you may have to inconvenience yourself for the sake of others in order to bring about good things for them.

Much like Mordecai, you may only need to remain vigilant for now, aware that someday you may be called upon to help others.

Lord, I trust You to guide me in using my influence for the benefit of others.

YOU DON'T HAVE TO BE CLEVER TO SERVE GOD

For Christ didn't send me to baptize, but to preach the Good News—and
not with clever speech, for fear that the cross of Christ would lose its power.
1 CORINTHIANS 1:17 NLT

W hat makes ministry effective today? It's easy to think that a great ministry requires excellent speaking skills, lots of money in the bank, and extremely talented people with extensive training and experience calling the shots. If sharing the Gospel with others is such a high calling, wouldn't we expect to rely on professionals to do it properly? While there's nothing wrong with training, education, or eloquence, these are not the determining factors for effective ministry. They don't make or break the way you serve others.

The power of God, displayed in Jesus on the cross and then shared through the Holy Spirit, undermines the systems and rules that many hold dear. The truth is you can accomplish great things through your weakness and inadequacy, because that's where you will find God's presence and power. If you can't think of anything clever to say, all the better! That only ensures that you will depend on the Holy Spirit to give you the words you need. . . when you need them most.

Jesus, help me to look at Your cross and Holy Spirit as the sources
of my ministry and my confidence in serving others.

THE SOURCE OF UNSHAKABLE FAITH

Those who trust in the LORD are like Mount Zion, which cannot be shaken but endures forever. As the mountains surround Jerusalem, so the LORD surrounds his people both now and forevermore.
PSALM 125:1–2 NIV

Consider the qualities of a mountain for a moment. Mountains are unmovable. Even if an earthquake caused the ground to tremble, the mountains would remain in place. A mountain can provide safety from floods, shelter from high winds, and even security during war. In the case of Jerusalem, the towering landscape around the city offered a feeling of being nestled in a secure fortress.

Whether or not you live near mountains that offer a sense of stability and security, you can certainly imagine what it would feel like to be surrounded by mountains. This is a picture of placing your faith in the Lord, of trusting that God is a constant, fixed, immovable source of strength in your life. If you don't trust in God right at this moment, now is the best time to confess your sins and to begin again with your faith in His mercy and unwavering support.

So many other sources of strength and support in your life will fail you, but with the power of God in your life, you have continual access to an advocate you can lean on in the unstable moments of life.

Lord, I trust in Your unshakable love for me.

WHAT TO DO WHEN YOU'RE READY TO GIVE UP

"Do not mortals have hard service on earth? Are not their days like those of hired laborers? Like a slave longing for the evening shadows, or a hired laborer waiting to be paid, so I have been allotted months of futility, and nights of misery have been assigned to me."

JOB 7:1–3 NIV

J ob was ready to give up, and he had every reason to feel that way. He had lost his livelihood, his servants, his children, and even his health. When his friends visited him, they only added to his wounds, leveling accusations against him and failing to bring any measure of comfort or consolation. What could Job do with so much stacked against him?

Perhaps Job's next step isn't quite obvious at first pass, but he correctly spoke the truth about his situation. He didn't try to dress things up or put a brave face on unbearable suffering.

Whatever you may be suffering now or in the future, you won't find God in delusions or tidy theological statements that aim to put a Band-Aid on a serious wound. You can tell God the truth about your disappointments, your longings, and even the perceived inequities of your life. Deliverance will come only when you first face your loss and oppression with honesty.

Help me, Lord, to be honest in my prayers about suffering and loss so that I can experience Your help.

FAITHFULNESS DOESN'T GUARANTEE PROSPERITY

*Even now we go hungry and thirsty, and we don't have enough
clothes to keep warm. We are often beaten and have no home.
We work wearily with our own hands to earn our living.
We bless those who curse us. We are patient with those who abuse us.*

1 CORINTHIANS 4:11–12 NLT

◆ ◆ ◆

I magine for a moment what faithfulness looks like. There may be no greater picture of faithful reliance on God than that of a preacher taking the Gospel to those who have never heard it before. It is an immensely costly and often dangerous undertaking, as was certainly the case with Paul and his missionary team. In fact, we read in his letter that hunger, thirst, exposure, homelessness, and physical attacks were among the adversity he faced.

How have you responded to seasons of adversity? You may be tempted to believe that adversity or even poverty means you've done something wrong.

Yet adversity and a lack of prosperity may actually mean you're doing the right thing. In other words, if you're taking flak, then you're over the target. Most importantly, God is present with you in times of suffering and adversity, an unshakable source of strength and hope, even when you feel like you can't go on much longer. When you feel as if everything is turning against you, that's the time to turn to God in faith rather than to second-guess His love for you.

*Holy Spirit, I trust that You will give me the words
and wisdom for the trials of life.*

GOD'S MERCY MAKES YOU WORTHY

If you, LORD, kept a record of sins, Lord, who could stand? But with you there is forgiveness, so that we can, with reverence, serve you.

PSALM 130:3–4 NIV

The psalmist made an honest assessment of himself, not believing he was better than warranted, and his final verdict rested entirely on God's mercy. Only with God's forgiveness could he hope to stand before Him and to serve others in His name. Rather than trying to justify himself, he saw matters for what they were.

What is your assessment of yourself today? Are you aware of your failures? Are you trying to put a brave face on your weaknesses? There's good news in today's scripture: a reminder that you only stand before God because of His mercy. Mercy isn't just an exception for the weak. It's the primary way that God interacts with people. If you're seeking God, then you need forgiveness.

While the Lord is seeking people who obey His commands, He is also well aware of the particular weaknesses you face. Mercy and obedience go together. You will always need God's support and kindness to overcome the temptations of life, but as you rely on Him, you will need to grow in your commitment to obedience. If you should fail, then God's forgiveness can lift you up again as you resolve to return to Him.

Lord, help me to approach You in humility and reverence, knowing that I can only serve You because of Your power at work in me.

GOD WILL BE WITH YOU AT THE END

"For I know that my Redeemer lives, and at the last he will stand upon the earth. And after my skin has been thus destroyed, yet in my flesh I shall see God, whom I shall see for myself, and my eyes shall behold, and not another. My heart faints within me!"

JOB 19:25–27 ESV

Gazing ahead to the dark, unknown hour of his death, Job took a hopeful look toward the Lord, who would one day redeem him even after so much suffering and loss. Although his friends accused him of sin and the evidence seemed to suggest he was cursed in some way, Job placed his faith and hope in God alone, trusting that one day he would be vindicated in His eyes and rewarded for his righteousness.

Perhaps looking forward to the hour of your death leaves you feeling unsettled, even fearful. Yet this hope for the future can make your faith unshakable, even when accusations, misunderstandings, or losses leave you with broken relationships and cause you to second-guess your decisions. God will save you from your sin and reward your goodness, regardless of what others say about you.

This hope to be seen by your Redeemer one day is the treasure in heaven that Jesus says you should store up.

Lord, I trust in the promise of Your forgiveness and redemption on the day I see You face-to-face.

BE HONEST ABOUT YOUR WEAKNESSES

Do not deprive each other of sexual relations, unless you both
agree to refrain from sexual intimacy for a limited time so
you can give yourselves more completely to prayer. Afterward,
you should come together again so that Satan won't be able
to tempt you because of your lack of self-control.
1 CORINTHIANS 7:5 NLT

Paul didn't hold back in his letter to the Corinthians. He knew what their weaknesses and limitations were, and sexual immorality and indulgence were quite high on the list. Although the Corinthians had many spiritual gifts and talented teachers, they also undermined their pursuit of God by their lack of self-control. Paul instructed that if married couples spent time apart for prayer, they should make plans to come together again before either spouse sinned.

Following Paul's example, go ahead and be honest about your weaknesses and limitations and the boundaries you need to put in place so you can focus on God's presence in your life. If you're struggling to make good choices or to act with restraint, consider ways you can avoid putting yourself in a difficult situation where temptation is overwhelming. Sometimes holiness and obedience are the result of a careful plan rather than brute willpower in the moment.

Holy Spirit, help me to see my weaknesses and to make better
plans so that I can live in obedience and holiness.

CAN YOU ACCEPT THE MYSTERIES OF GOD?

"By his wind the heavens were made fair; his hand pierced the fleeing serpent. Behold, these are but the outskirts of his ways, and how small a whisper do we hear of him! But the thunder of his power who can understand?"

JOB 26:13–14 ESV

Job felt the pain and suffering in his life with sharp clarity, and he wrestled with the mystery of his losses despite never sinning against God. As he turned his gaze outward to the rest of the world, he found more of the same: mysteries that gave only a dim idea of God's purpose and presence. That left him with a choice. Would he walk away from a God beyond his understanding, or would he hold on in faith that God's goodness would finally be revealed to him?

There's a good chance you're not suffering in the same ways as Job, but you surely have your own mysteries to ponder and moments of suffering and loss to endure. Can you always settle on a tidy explanation for the dark moments of life? More than likely you'll end up in the same place as Job. Yet his story of perseverance is a reminder that you can wait on the Lord, even beyond what you think you can bear, and find God—even if you don't find the answers you seek.

Lord, help me to endure suffering and trust in You despite the mysteries of life.

FREEDOM TO LIBERATE OTHERS

*It's true that we can't win God's approval by what we eat.
We don't lose anything if we don't eat it, and we don't gain
anything if we do. But you must be careful so that your freedom
does not cause others with a weaker conscience to stumble.*

1 CORINTHIANS 8:8–9 NLT

◆ ◆ ◆

Many in the Corinthian church knew that the false gods in their city were mere statues, and that freed them to eat food offered to these gods with a clear conscience. What harm could a statue do to them? Yet as these Christians enjoyed their freedom, they created a crisis for other Christians who remained convinced that false gods held power. These Christians risked violating their consciences because of what they saw fellow believers eat.

The solution wasn't necessarily to devise more rules for everyone. The simple path forward, according to Paul, is to remain aware of how your actions impact those around you. Even when you have freedom to act with a clear conscience, will you be creating challenges for someone else? It may be wise to limit yourself, often just for a limited time, so that others can be spared a crisis of conscience. Just as Christ laid down His freedom to liberate you, you have an opportunity to lay down your own freedoms to benefit others.

Jesus, help me to see the ways my actions impact my fellow believers.

AN UNSHAKABLE DEFENSE

*"If only someone would listen to me! Look, I will sign
my name to my defense. Let the Almighty answer me.
Let my accuser write out the charges against me."*

JOB 31:35 NLT

Every man faces moments when he must defend himself. Whether it's an attack on his reputation or a false accusation, a situation requiring self-defense can shake him to the core. For some, it's a constant frustration at work or in the home. Job defended himself when God allowed Satan to test him, and Paul did the same when the Corinthian church accused him of misusing his position (1 Corinthians 9:1–18).

Both men struggled with how and when to speak up—with the proper time and place for self-defense. Peter explained the best approach when he used Jesus' example: "He did not retaliate when he was insulted, nor threaten revenge when he suffered. He left his case in the hands of God, who always judges fairly" (1 Peter 2:23 NLT).

Some leadership materials might suggest immediate and intense intervention similar to the way Job responded (see Job 38 for God's response to Job's hasty defense). But Paul and Jesus demonstrated the wisdom in waiting and in knowing that a man's defense ultimately rests in God's hands—in the hands of the One "who alone does mighty miracles" (Psalm 136:4 NLT).

*Father, help me to listen to You and follow Your leading
whenever I feel the need to defend myself.*

TO WIN

*To the weak I became weak, to win the weak. . . . I do all this for
the sake of the gospel, that I may share in its blessings.*
1 CORINTHIANS 9:22–23 NIV

W eakness doesn't show up in most professional intelligence workshops.
It rarely appears in the self-improvement blogs. The fact is most
men would rather throw in the towel than admit their weaknesses. Becoming
"weak, to win the weak" doesn't make human sense.

Paul explained that to "share in" the blessings that come from telling
other men about Jesus, he needed to let his weaknesses encourage those who
needed help with their own. Paul knew, as do many deeply respected men,
that when influence is measured at the end of a man's life, it's the ability to
express and learn from weakness that helps a man "to win."

Opposite Paul, in the other corner of the ring, Job argued against his
weaknesses. Up against the ropes, he answered for God rather than admit he
didn't know why God was allowing the devastation in his life (Job 38:2). Job
felt alone in his insecurities. He could have profited from today's psalm, where
the writer reminds his audience that God remembers us "in our weakness"
(Psalm 136:23 NLT). You will never face this opponent alone.

So much of a man's ability to "win" people for Jesus is determined by
which corner he starts out in.

*Father, help me see the connection between sharing
my weaknesses and inviting people to Jesus.*

UNSHAKABLE WISDOM

Don't be concerned for your own good but for the good of others.
1 CORINTHIANS 10:24 NLT

❖───────❖───────❖

On this day in 1970, inspirational coach Vince Lombardi died. His statement, "Teamwork is what the Green Bay Packers were all about. They didn't do it for individual glory. They did it because they loved one another," echoes Paul's instruction in today's reading: "Don't be concerned for your own good but for the good of others." If inspirational quotes can motivate football teams, maybe Paul's words can inspire our concern for "the good of others."

Despite God's desire for selflessness in His followers, the opposite shows up throughout the Bible. For example, in Psalm 137:9 (NLT), the writer's caustic phrases (called "imprecations") express his desire for revenge. "Happy is the one who takes your babies and smashes them against the rocks!" makes sense when a man's friends and family have been slaughtered, but God wants His people to move past these raw emotions, no matter how justified.

Job felt justified when he attempted to explain the puzzle of his life by putting words in God's mouth. But like Paul and the psalmist, Job learned the significance behind God's question: "Who has put wisdom in the inward parts or given understanding to the mind?" (Job 38:36 ESV).

Accepting God's unshakable wisdom can help you move away from revenge and self-love to the rewarding life found in securing good things for others.

Father, please help me make concern for the good of others my motto.

UNSHAKABLE HUMILITY

"My ears had heard of you but now my eyes have seen you.
Therefore I despise myself and repent in dust and ashes."
JOB 42:5–6 NIV

J ob's success in business may have contributed to his need to "repent in dust and ashes," but his encounter with God's word helped him move beyond the seduction of success into a more accurate view of his limited understanding of God's purposes. After God's poetic intervention (Job 38–41), Job's understanding of God expanded from "my ears had heard of you" to "my eyes have seen you." He learned, the hard way, that there are better teachers than success.

The seduction of success frustrates the way people see God and the way they see each other. Paul confronted people who lacked the necessary humility to surrender their opinions. He ends his argument about head coverings with "If anyone wants to be contentious about this, we have no other practice" (1 Corinthians 11:16 NIV). Paul knew pride's seduction makes unity difficult.

The psalmist presents an answer for Job and the church that moves beyond the pride-infused classroom of success: "Though the LORD is great, he cares for the humble, but he keeps his distance from the proud" (Psalm 138:6 NLT). God's humble character is the best teacher.

Father, help me understand that I don't understand what You understand.
And help that understanding move me toward humility.

IN DIFFERENT WAYS AND TIMES

For everything there is a season,
a time for every activity under heaven.
ECCLESIASTES 3:1 NLT

◆   ◆   ◆

Labor Day became a federal holiday in 1894. Created by the labor movement, it celebrates the contributions of the working class.

Solomon wrote about labor: "So I saw that there is nothing better for people than to be happy in their work" (Ecclesiastes 3:22 NLT). He promoted the value of settling in and finding satisfaction in the efforts that consume most of every day. But Solomon also saw the importance of relaxation: "People should eat and drink and enjoy the fruits of their labor, for these are gifts from God" (3:13 NLT). His point is that there is a time for both, "a time for everything" (3:1 NIV).

Paul wrote that there are not only different times for things but also different ways to accomplish things: "There are different kinds of service, but we serve the same Lord. God works in different ways, but it is the same God who does the work in all of us" (1 Corinthians 12:5–6 NLT). Understanding the different ways and times can create unity and encourage the kind of wise living today's readings champion, the kind of living the psalmist celebrated: "You go before me and follow me. You place your hand of blessing on my head" (Psalm 139:5 NLT).

Father, help me appreciate the different times and ways You do things so that I might encourage and support the people who labor for You and rest in You.

UNSHAKABLE MOTIVES

And I saw that all toil and all achievement spring from one person's
envy of another. This too is meaningless, a chasing after the wind.
ECCLESIASTES 4:4 NIV

So much human motivation crawls from the carcass of envy. Instead of implementing new ideas for the right reasons, men find themselves constantly motivated by envy.

Solomon uses overstatement to share God's wisdom about the role that envy often plays in inspiring achievement, and he ends his counsel with "This too is meaningless" (Ecclesiastes 4:4 NIV). When a man manages his motivations, he can move away from envy to pure motives that encourage contentment and echo into eternity.

Paul wrote, "Love. . .does not envy, it does not boast, it is not proud. It does not dishonor others" (1 Corinthians 13:4–5 NIV). When you work because of love for God and others, your work encourages your soul and enters eternity.

David wrote, "Where can I go from your Spirit? Where can I flee from your presence? If I go up to the heavens, you are there; if I make my bed in the depths, you are there" (Psalm 139:7–8 NIV). Remember, God sees envy. But also remember that He is always nearby, ready to help you make every motive meaningful.

Father, help me escape envy by managing my motivations,
aligning them with Yours.

UNSHAKABLE UNDERSTANDING

Do not pay attention to every word people say, or you may hear
your servant cursing you—for you know in your heart that
many times you yourself have cursed others.
ECCLESIASTES 7:21–22 NIV

◆ ——— ◆ ——— ◆

Most of us have heard the expression "Hurt people hurt people." When sin entered the Garden of Eden, every human being suffered a separation from God and each other. That separation made us more than capable of cursing and slander.

Understanding that people will hurt you at some point promotes grace in every relationship, especially when you remember "you yourself have cursed others." People benefit when they learn to ask for forgiveness and when they apologize to the individuals with whom they've shared negative thoughts about other people. Pride makes it difficult to say, "What I said to you about so-and-so the other day was unkind. I've already asked for his forgiveness, but I need to ask for yours."

God certainly knows how it feels to be cursed. David wrote, "They speak of you with evil intent; your adversaries misuse your name" (Psalm 139:20 NIV). But David ends Psalm 139 with an unshakable understanding that benefits every man: "Search me, God, and know my heart; test me and know my anxious thoughts. See if there is any offensive way in me, and lead me in the way everlasting" (verses 23–24 NIV).

Father, help me extend grace to those who wrong me and to ask
forgiveness of those I wrong. Lead me in "the way everlasting."

UNSHAKABLE CALM

If a ruler's anger rises against you, do not leave your post;
calmness can lay great offenses to rest.
ECCLESIASTES 10:4 NIV

◆ ◆ ◆

Being the object of the anger of an employer, civic authority, or family member doesn't float most people's boats; it usually sinks them. But experiencing the impact of another person's anger is a regular part of life. Although Solomon's counsel to stay calm and to stay the course might negate only some of the anger, calmness at least inflates a life raft.

When Paul counseled against the disruption the gift of tongues brought to the churches, he reminded his readers, "For God is not a God of disorder but of peace" (1 Corinthians 14:33 NIV). God knows the benefits of peace in our assemblies; He knows the role calmness plays in laying "great offenses to rest."

Like Paul, David knew the angst produced when people stood against him, but he also knew the folly of taking revenge and retribution into his own hands. When you face another's anger, David's prayer can be your prayer too: "Rescue me, LORD, from evildoers; protect me from the violent, who devise evil plans in their hearts and stir up war every day" (Psalm 140:1–2 NIV). When the anger of an authority, an employer, a family member, or a friend "rises against you," choose to respond calmly, to pursue peace, and to pray.

Father, whenever I feel the angst brought on by the anger of others,
help me to choose calmness, peace, and prayer.

UNSHAKABLE CHARACTER

*Let him kiss me with the kisses of his mouth—for your love
is more delightful than wine. Pleasing is the fragrance of
your perfumes; your name is like perfume poured out.*
SONG OF SOLOMON 1:2–3 NIV

❖

Rare is the man who doesn't want to marry a woman who possesses this kind of passion for kissing. But just as rare is the man who understands what fuels this desire in a woman.

The Song's lyrics explain, "Your name is like perfume poured out." Since the concept behind the word *name* includes character, and since pouring perfume out is an extravagant act (see John 12:3), the young bride in the Song desires to be kissed because of her husband's intoxicating character. This is one of the reasons scripture warns against "bad company" that "corrupts good character" (1 Corinthians 15:33 NIV) and shows people how to develop the kind of outstanding character that makes a man kissable.

How does a man develop this kind of character? By obeying the One of whom the psalmist sang, "Surely the righteous will praise your name [character], and the upright will live in your presence" (Psalm 140:13 NIV).

Having a name that is kissable, "like perfume poured out," involves obeying God by studying His Word and taking time to read devotionals like this one. So keep up the good work. You're well on your way!

*Father, help me focus more time and energy on
developing my character than my career.*

UNSHAKABLE SEX

The mandrakes send out their fragrance, and at our door is every delicacy, both new and old, that I have stored up for you, my beloved.
SONG OF SOLOMON 7:13 NIV

❖ ❖ ❖

Most men secretly long for a marriage like the one described in today's reading. They long to experience the love of a wife who delights in offering "every delicacy, both new and old." As yesterday's entry explained, this won't happen unless a man's character becomes intoxicating.

Another way to develop tremendous character is to pray David's prayer in Psalm 141:4 (NIV): "Do not let my heart be drawn to what is evil so that I take part in wicked deeds along with those who are evildoers; do not let me eat their delicacies."

Paul echoed this idea from a positive perspective when he wrote, "Always give yourselves fully to the work of the Lord, because you know that your labor in the Lord is not in vain" (1 Corinthians 15:58 NIV). When men remember that their "labor in the Lord" requires daily sacrifices in their personal lives and marriages, they experience the intoxicating love God originally intended.

Your marriage can have an "every delicacy" quality when you resolve to obey God's Word and ask Him to help you trade the "delicacies" of those who mock God for the "delicacies" of a wife who serves Him.

Father, help me avoid malevolent men and their evil practices so that I can experience the delicacies of an intoxicating marriage.

UNSHAKABLE WORSHIP

*"Who asked you to parade through my courts with all your
ceremony? Stop bringing me your meaningless gifts. . . .
When you lift up your hands in prayer, I will not look.
Though you offer many prayers, I will not listen."*
ISAIAH 1:12–13, 15 NLT

◆━━━◆━━━◆

W hy isn't my life full of the happiness I see in so many others? Why
doesn't God answer my prayers too?" The emotions behind these
common queries betray dismal and dreary days—hundreds of mundane
moments that, when welded together, often produce confusion and even
depression.

In today's scripture, Isaiah presents one answer to both questions. He
explains that when the worship God's children "parade" in front of Him is
full of "meaningless gifts," He doesn't listen. Not to their worship and not
to their "many prayers" (1:15 NIV).

Often, the problem is in the motives that make worship lazy and self-
focused rather than engaging and God-focused. In contrast, the happiness
experienced in answered prayers usually follows the repentant heart of an
individual who worships with the meaning of the psalmist: "You are all I
really want in life" (Psalm 142:5 NLT).

This is why Paul admonished the Corinthians, "Be on your guard; stand
firm in the faith; be courageous; be strong. Do everything in love" (1 Corinthians
16:13–14 NIV). Love for God, not self, motivates meaningful worship.

*Father, help me see in Your Word and in others the devotion You want
to see in me. I long to worship You with an attitude that pleases
You and with prayers You are eager to hear.*

RIGHT LIVING

Tell the righteous it will be well with them,
for they will enjoy the fruit of their deeds.
Isaiah 3:10 niv

Who are the "righteous" Isaiah writes about in today's verse? Those who wake up and take captive their morning thoughts, who make thoughts about God—His purposes and provisions—their first breakfast.

Paul wrote about how this kind of right living was so necessary in his life that God had sometimes used the "sentence of death" to help him develop it: "Indeed, we felt we had received the sentence of death. But this happened that we might not rely on ourselves but on God, who raises the dead" (2 Corinthians 1:9 niv). Relying on God helps believers enjoy the fruit He created for every spirit-regulated social, intellectual, and emotional area of life. Paul knew that right living creates in people the optimal conditions for enjoying the "fruit of their deeds." This enjoyment is something God desires and produces for the righteous.

David, the shepherd and king, wrote about a fruit gifted through the righteousness of another, the righteousness of God. His lyrics "In your faithfulness and righteousness come to my relief" (Psalm 143:1 niv) bring to mind the underharvested fruit of divine rest that comes to those who rely "on God, who raises the dead." Although this rest is only one of the gifts of right living, it often multiplies all other enjoyments.

Father, help me enjoy the fruits of my deeds—
my righteous deeds, not the others.

CONSPIRACIES

The LORD has given me a strong warning not to think like
everyone else does. He said, "Don't call everything a conspiracy,
like they do, and don't live in dread of what frightens them.
Make the LORD of Heaven's Armies holy in your life."
ISAIAH 8:11–13 NLT

◆   ◆   ◆

Conspiracies are nothing new. Their power to consume time and energy is ancient. The Lord warned Isaiah not to become consumed by the newsworthy kinds of events surrounding him but instead to focus on Him.

Sometimes the negativity and suspicion encouraged by media organizations create the same kind of time-consuming and fear-inducing fervor today. It's easy to give in to fear, to become consumed by human ideas and events that seem so commanding—even when freedom and joy are waiting in the more powerful presence of God.

Paul struggled with the prevailing opinions and political pressures of his day as well, but he reminded the people of God that he and other disciples "depended on God's grace, not on our own human wisdom" (2 Corinthians 1:12 NLT). He had learned like David to replace panic and paranoia with trust: "Let me hear of your unfailing love each morning, for I am trusting you. Show me where to walk, for I give myself to you" (Psalm 143:8 NLT). You can too!

Father, help me avoid "thinking like everyone else does" so that I might
experience peace in the presence of the Lord of Heaven's Armies.

UNSHAKABLE EVIDENCE

*But thanks be to God, who always leads us as captives in Christ's
triumphal procession and uses us to spread the aroma of the knowledge
of him everywhere. For we are to God the pleasing aroma of Christ
among those who are being saved and those who are perishing.*
2 CORINTHIANS 2:14–15 NIV

P aul uses a smell metaphor to echo a sentiment often shouted by people who choose to see only hypocrisy in the church and say, "Those Christians are all the evidence I need." But Paul's meaning is antithetical: Christians who follow God as He "leads" *are* the evidence everyone needs.

Whether or not people believe in Jesus, believers are the "pleasing aroma of Christ" to them. They cannot miss the wonder in the way His followers live and love. Everywhere "the aroma of the knowledge of him" transforms the social stench into a satisfying scent.

Isaiah employed a different metaphor: "The people who walk in darkness will see a great light. For those who live in a land of deep darkness, a light will shine. You will enlarge the nation of Israel, and its people will rejoice" (Isaiah 9:2–3 NLT).

The metaphors of smell and light speak to the unshakable evidence of God's goodness in your life: "Yes, joyful are those who live like this! Joyful indeed are those whose God is the LORD" (Psalm 144:15 NLT).

*Father, help me to follow Your "triumphant" leadership so that the people
I work and live with will smell and see the unmistakable evidence of You.*

MOVING BEYOND THE OLD WAY

We are not like Moses, who would put a veil over his face to prevent the Israelites from seeing the end of what was passing away. But their minds were made dull, for to this day the same veil remains when the old covenant is read. It has not been removed, because only in Christ is it taken away.

2 CORINTHIANS 3:13–14 NIV

◆────────◆────────◆

First-century religious leaders found it difficult to transition from the old covenant to the new—even though the new was incomparably better.

Like Moses, who continued to wear a protective veil even after the glory of God's presence faded from his face, people find it difficult to move on. Things like reputation, accomplishments, and position can dull the good news of the Gospel.

Isaiah prophesied that the new covenant would cause people to say, "The LORD, the LORD himself, is my strength and my defense; he has become my salvation" (Isaiah 12:2 NIV).

Although Isaiah and the religious leaders knew that the old way of multiple sacrifices and human effort would be replaced by Jesus' sacrifice and effort, they still found it difficult to move away from what they had grown comfortable with. Do you?

Just as the "veil" could be removed "only in Christ," only Jesus can help you move beyond trusting in your own reputation, accomplishments, and position to trusting the One who is close to "all who call on him in truth" (Psalm 145:18 NIV).

Father, help me to move away from trusting in my own efforts.

UNSHAKABLE PLANS

*Therefore we do not lose heart. Though outwardly we are
wasting away, yet inwardly we are being renewed day by
day. For our light and momentary troubles are achieving for
us an eternal glory that far outweighs them all. So we fix our
eyes not on what is seen, but on what is unseen, since what is
seen is temporary, but what is unseen is eternal.*

2 CORINTHIANS 4:16–18 NIV

When Isaiah wrote, "The LORD Almighty has sworn, 'Surely, as I have planned, so it will be, and as I have purposed, so it will happen,' " his words encouraged the Old Testament believers (Isaiah 14:24 NIV).

Like Paul, Isaiah knew the discouragements that God's people face. The "wasting away" and "momentary troubles" make it easy to lose heart, to focus on what is "temporary"—the here and now. When you're discouraged or hurting, it's tempting to resort to human control, to trust human methods. This is partly why the psalmist wrote, "Do not put your trust in princes, in human beings, who cannot save" (146:3 NIV). Every time you trust only human beings and human methods, you diminish future blessing.

God's plans are unshakable. The troubles you experience serving Him always produce "an eternal glory that far outweighs them all." Remembering this truth can change the way you live and love, and it can encourage you to pray before you plan.

*Father, when I'm discouraged and begin to trust human methods,
help me to remember that only Your approved plans happen.*

UNSHAKABLE HONOR

*Are we commending ourselves to you again? No, we are giving you
a reason to be proud of us, so you can answer those who brag about
having a spectacular ministry rather than having a sincere heart.*
2 CORINTHIANS 5:12 NLT

Most men want to be honored at some point, to enjoy the satisfaction and pride that come with being recognized and remembered.

Paul certainly understood the power in this desire. Although he was often criticized for "commending" himself and the other apostles, Paul made it clear that honor comes less from the spectacular results of our labor than from the sincerity of our love. This is the real reason, he wrote, that people should be proud of each other.

Isaiah noticed a desire for human recognition and acclaim in Israel as well. He longed for the day people would discover that unshakable honor belongs to those who give God the credit instead of worshipping "what their own hands have made" (Isaiah 17:8 NLT). Like Paul, Isaiah listened every day to those who bragged about the things they'd done.

The psalmist reminded his readers, "The LORD supports the humble, but he brings the wicked down into the dust" (Psalm 147:6 NLT). Lasting honor comes less often to those who brag about the spectacular, and more often to those who sincerely honor God with their efforts.

Father, help me to understand the perpetual honor in sincerity.

A SIGNIFICANT DIFFERENCE

Do not be yoked together with unbelievers. For what do righteousness and wickedness have in common? Or what fellowship can light have with darkness? . . . For we are the temple of the living God.
2 CORINTHIANS 6:14, 16 NIV

❖ ❖ ❖

In celebrating the wisdom that comes from God's Word, the psalmist wrote, "He has done this for no other nation" (147:20 NIV).

Because the world doesn't value the wisdom of God, Paul warns against going into business or developing close relationships with unbelievers. There is a significant difference between those who are the "temple of the living God" and those who worship at the temples of consumption, hedonism, and distraction.

Far too many men have thought they could make such relationships work, only to discover the same pain and powerlessness Isaiah's audience expressed when they had gone into business and developed interdependencies with unbelievers: "See what has happened to those we relied on?" (Isaiah 20:6 NIV).

If you have already established a partnership with someone who doesn't share the same convictions you do, you don't necessarily need to sever it. Instead, you can work toward removing any arrangements that "yoke" you to the other party, arrangements like contracts and agreements that create financial dependency. Although believers won't always treat you better than unbelievers, you are better off following the Holy Spirit's counsel in Paul's letter to the Corinthians.

Father, help me carefully unyoke myself from unbelievers and enjoy the more secure fellowship of those who follow You.

HOLY MAINTENANCE

*But for those who are righteous, the way is not steep
and rough. You are a God who does what is right,
and you smooth out the path ahead of them.*
Isaiah 26:7 nlt

———◆———◆———◆———

When the asphalt is smooth, a car's undercarriage clears the pavement, the shocks have less work to do, and the road trip of life seems more satisfying.

While Isaiah explained that the "righteous" drive on the best roads, Paul reminds every motorist about the maintenance that makes the race enjoyable: "Because we have these promises, dear friends, let us cleanse ourselves from everything that can defile our body or spirit. And let us work toward complete holiness because we fear God" (2 Corinthians 7:1 nlt).

In a culture where the Christian experience is sometimes reduced to platitudes and personalized license plates, it's tempting to redefine evil so we can drive down any road we believe will make us happy. But Paul makes his meaning clear when he adds, "Let us work toward complete holiness because we fear God."

Most men know complete holiness means driving down only the roads that honor God and heading the opposite direction when temptation shows up. Complete holiness requires total rerouting and total restoration.

On the road to righteousness, you're never strapped into an underpowered vehicle. The psalmist said that God "has made his people strong, honoring his faithful ones" (Psalm 148:14 nlt).

---

*Father, help me to do the holy maintenance that will
help me follow Your road to righteousness.*

UNSHAKABLE WEALTH

I want to test the sincerity of your love by comparing it with the
earnestness of others. For you know the grace of our Lord Jesus
Christ, that though he was rich, yet for your sake he became
poor, so that you through his poverty might become rich.
2 Corinthians 8:8–9 niv

Ever had your sincerity tested? Paul told the Corinthians that becoming "rich" involved having an outside consultant compare one man's "earnestness" with another's.

Paul wanted to help the church benefit from Isaiah's prophecy: "See, I lay a stone in Zion, a tested stone, a precious cornerstone for a sure foundation; the one who relies on it will never be stricken with panic" (Isaiah 28:16 niv). He wanted them to build their ideas about lasting wealth on the solid rock of Jesus, and he knew that everyone needs help with that. Paul helped the men compare the sincerity of their love not only with the earnestness of other men but with the one man who ultimately matters. Though Jesus was infinitely rich, He chose poverty in order to create wealth for others. That kind of humility generates unshakable riches.

If you allow someone to help you compare your sincerity not only to that of others but especially to that of Jesus, you'll discover the kind of generosity and humility the psalmist celebrated: "For the Lord takes delight in his people; he crowns the humble with victory" (Psalm 149:4 niv).

Father, help me trust a mentor who can help me
stay focused on the riches that matter most.

UNWAVERING WORSHIP

*"These people say they are mine. They honor me with their lips,
but their hearts are far from me. And their worship of me
is nothing but man-made rules learned by rote."*
Isaiah 29:13 nlt

Hypocrisy hurts. It makes men believe they are passionately engaged in important work, when really their accomplishments are mostly ruins—monuments to rules taught by men.

God explained to Isaiah that people often find it easier to check off a list of man-made rules each day, to simply fall asleep thinking, *I used all the right religious words today.* David F. Miller summarized the problem with this way of thinking when he said, "Christianity is not a list of rules; it's a life of righteousness."

Paul continued Isaiah's insight when he explained to the church that meaningful worship engages more than the mouth—it becomes a man's entire way of life. Compassion touches the needy and disenfranchised where they live, and then it overflows and becomes worship: "This service that you perform is not only supplying the needs of the Lord's people but is also overflowing in many expressions of thanks to God" (2 Corinthians 9:12 niv).

Solomon wrote Proverbs to help men "live disciplined and successful lives, to help them do what is right, just, and fair" (Proverbs 1:3 nlt). It's that kind of righteousness, justice, and equity that makes worship more than lip service.

*Father, help me examine any lists I've created so that my living can
move beyond the rules of men into meaningful worship.*

UNSHAKABLE LEADERSHIP

*See, a king will reign in righteousness and rulers will rule with
justice. Each one will be like a shelter from the wind and
a refuge from the storm, like streams of water in the desert
and the shadow of a great rock in a thirsty land.*

Isaiah 32:1–2 niv

The kind of leadership God wants His people to experience recognizes human needs. Isaiah's prophecy about leaders who protect their followers from the "wind" and the "storm" and meet needs like "streams of water in the desert" can be realized now.

Paul reminded the church that although "we live in the world, we do not wage war as the world does" (2 Corinthians 10:3 niv). The management methods God endorses surpass and ultimately supplant the world's. Throughout history, God has spoken against egotistical leaders who put themselves before their followers and said things like "Let's swallow them alive, like the grave, and whole, like those who go down to the pit; we will get all sorts of valuable things and fill our houses with plunder" (Proverbs 1:12–13 niv).

You can be the kind of leader who champions equity, who provides real and metaphorical shelter, protection, water, and shade for your employees or coworkers—the kind of leader who helps with housing and legal assistance, who intervenes for others like the "shadow of a great rock in a thirsty land."

Father, help me be the kind of leader You desire, a leader who meets needs.

RELENTLESS MISERY

*"Since you disregard all my advice and do not accept my
rebuke, I in turn will laugh when disaster strikes you;
I will mock when calamity overtakes you."*
PROVERBS 1:25–26 NIV

When people disregard wisdom's advice, a relentless misery follows. No matter where they go, the evidence of their disregard eventually catches up.

Paul explained that those who prefer their own ideas and disdain instruction are easier marks for charlatans—those who pretend to have another's best interests at heart: "You happily put up with whatever anyone tells you, even if they preach a different Jesus than the one we preach, or a different kind of Spirit than the one you received, or a different kind of gospel than the one you believed" (2 Corinthians 11:4 NLT). Deception is not the only misery that follows the immature.

Isaiah explained that the fool who disregards wisdom's advice will not have a part in God's future: "A great road will go through that once deserted land. It will be named the Highway of Holiness. Evil-minded people will never travel on it. It will be only for those who walk in God's ways; fools will never walk there" (Isaiah 35:8 NLT).

Reading the scriptures in this book and accepting the Spirit's rebuke will help you avoid wisdom's mockery and the manipulations of false preachers—and also will help you keep traveling the Highway of Holiness.

*Father, help me follow wisdom's advice and accept the Spirit's rebuke.
Help me avoid relentless misery.*

UNSHAKABLE HOPE

The LORD will save me, and we will sing with stringed instruments
all the days of our lives in the temple of the LORD.
ISAIAH 38:20 NIV

In today's passage, King Hezekiah's enemies had gathered, his personal and professional affairs were a mess, and he was dying. No medicines or treatments, no counsel or consult, held any hope.

Hezekiah made the usual request men make at times like this: he asked God for help. But his preface to the request was unusual: "Remember, LORD, how I have walked before you faithfully and with wholehearted devotion and have done what is good in your eyes" (38:3 NIV). How many other Old Testament kings could use such a strategy? Could you?

The next time you're feeling like Hezekiah, remember that taking the time to study scripture and read devotions like these makes you more, not less, like him—like someone who has "done what is good" in God's eyes.

And if God doesn't fix your situation, remember what Jesus told Paul: "My grace is sufficient for you, for my power is made perfect in weakness" (2 Corinthians 12:9 NIV). Sometimes God will answer the way He did for Hezekiah, sometimes the way He did for Paul. Either way, you can find strength in these words: "Whoever listens to me will live in safety and be at ease, without fear of harm" (Proverbs 1:33 NIV). Keep reading and listening!

Father, help me to experience the hope that comes from hearing You!

MANAGING MANIPULATION

*Some of you admit I was not a burden to you. But others still
think I was sneaky and took advantage of you by trickery.*
2 CORINTHIANS 12:16 NLT

◆———————◆———————◆

Have you ever been deceived? Maybe a car salesperson sold you a lemon
without a recipe for lemonade, or an excavation company buried you
under hidden fees.

Some people raised under Machiavelli's principle "the end justifies the
means" believe that the only thing that matters is that they get ahead, no
matter who they leave behind. Ideas like these intensify manipulation.

Hezekiah found himself exploited by the king of Babylon, who "sent
Hezekiah letters and a gift, because he had heard of his illness" but also used
the opportunity to spy on the riches in the treasury (Isaiah 39:1 NIV). This
"trickery" severely cost the nation when Babylon eventually took the treasures.

The Corinthians called Paul "sneaky" and claimed he took advantage of
them. Paul defended himself with facts and sarcasm, but the passage elevates
the concern over exploitation.

How can anyone manage all the manipulation?

Solomon shared the solution: "Wisdom will save you from the ways of
wicked men. . .who are devious in their ways" (Proverbs 2:12, 15 NIV). As you
continue studying the book of Proverbs, you'll find that most schemes can be
avoided through the practice of self-control. It would have helped Hezekiah
and the church in Corinth. It, and the other wisdom principles in Proverbs,
will help you too.

Father, give me wisdom to manage any manipulation I encounter.

UNSHAKABLE HISTORY

Who will hear these lessons from the past and see the ruin
that awaits you in the future?
ISAIAH 42:23 NLT

I saiah prophesied about the human inability to learn from the past—the tendency to repeat poor decisions and to rely on human reasoning that so often leads to personal and financial ruin. He knew it didn't have to be this way.

Paul wrote to the church in Galatia about the same frustration: "I am shocked that you are turning away so soon from God, who called you to himself through the loving mercy of Christ. You are following a different way that pretends to be the Good News but is not the Good News at all. You are being fooled by those who deliberately twist the truth concerning Christ" (Galatians 1:6–7 NLT). The Galatians had begun adding to their faith a historically failed philosophy within Gnosticism that said truth is whatever you make it. Contemporary Christianity suffers from similar ideas.

One of the best ways to avoid personal failure is to study the social and individual failures in the Bible's historical records. Those stories can help you "follow the steps of the good, and stay on the paths of the righteous" (Proverbs 2:20 NLT).

Father, help me to understand the relationship between history and my life
so that I can "hear these lessons from the past" and see better days.

UNSHAKABLE MEMORIES

"Forget the former things; do not dwell on the past. See, I am doing
a new thing! Now it springs up; do you not perceive it?"
ISAIAH 43:18–19 NIV

❖

Ever faced criticism that created deep emotional conflict?
When Paul faced criticism about the direction of the church, instead of focusing on the history that built it, he moved past the "former things" and honored the "new thing" God was doing. Like Paul, if you gently and respectfully do the same when people try to do things like add requirements to the Gospel, you'll experience the joy in watching the "new" as it "springs up" all around you.

Perhaps the best memories to stick with during times of conflict appear in two of today's scripture readings. First, Paul's memory: "I have been crucified with Christ and I no longer live, but Christ lives in me. The life I now live in the body, I live by faith in the Son of God, who loved me and gave himself for me" (Galatians 2:20 NIV). When you remember your co-crucifixion, you'll find little joy in being right or in protecting the provisions of the past.

Second, the memory Solomon recommends relates to wisdom: "My child, never forget the things I have taught you. Store my commands in your heart. If you do this, you will live many years, and your life will be satisfying" (Proverbs 3:1–2 NLT).

Father, give me unshakable memories of my
co-crucifixion with Christ and of Your wisdom.

UNSHAKABLE WINS

*"I am the LORD, the Maker of all things. . .who overthrows
the learning of the wise and turns it into nonsense."*
ISAIAH 44:24–25 NIV

O n this day in 1940, a fan at the University of California's Memorial Stadium ran onto the field thinking he could help his team stop Michigan's Tom Harmon from scoring, but he failed to tackle Harmon, who scored on the play.

Paul wrote that the Galatian believers thought their human efforts could help God out. "How foolish can you be? After starting your new lives in the Spirit, why are you now trying to become perfect by your own human effort?" (Galatians 3:3 NLT). They thought they could win for God by requiring believers to practice aspects of Old Testament law.

Dreaming of stardom, most men feel they can improve employment situations, family dynamics, and relational conflicts with their own cunning and intelligence. But Isaiah cautions that God "overthrows the learning of the wise and turns it into nonsense." Those who try to improve the score by relying on their own effort usually miss the tackle and end up fighting sleepless nights and the fears that come with misdirected efforts. Been there?

Paul, Isaiah, and Solomon show that listening to your coach, to "the Maker of all things," means that "you can go to bed without fear; you will lie down and sleep soundly" (Proverbs 3:24 NLT). That's a win!

Father, help me to listen rather than trust my own efforts.

UNBORROWED CLOTHES

"I am the LORD your God, who teaches you what is best for you,
who directs you in the way you should go."
ISAIAH 48:17 NIV

When Shakespeare's Macbeth said, "Why do you dress me in borrowed robes?" he was struggling with an identity he wasn't sure belonged to him.

This is a constant theme in literature: Does clothing really make the man? Paul used the same metaphor sixteen hundred years earlier to explain that in Jesus, they do: "For all of you who were baptized into Christ have clothed yourselves with Christ" (Galatians 3:27 NIV). His are not borrowed clothes—and they determine the identity of every man who wears them.

Unlike Macbeth, who murders to assume his new identity, believers possess counsel like "Do not withhold good from those to whom it is due, when it is in your power to act. Do not say to your neighbor, 'Come back tomorrow and I'll give it to you'—when you already have it with you" (Proverbs 3:27–28 NIV). The fruit of the Spirit listed in Galatians 5:22–23 sum up the kinds of actions and attitudes Christians wear. They're what secure God's blessing: "If only you had paid attention to my commands, your peace would have been like a river, your well-being like the waves of the sea" (Isaiah 48:18 NIV). The continual waves of well-being God wants to give you are a result of the clothes you wear—the unborrowed clothes of Jesus Christ.

Father, help me wear the clothes that show the identity You have given me.

UNSHAKABLE LOVE

"Can a mother forget the baby at her breast and have no compassion on the child she has borne? Though she may forget, I will not forget you!"
Isaiah 49:15 niv

The Beatles' "Eleanor Rigby," Ray Charles's "Lonely Avenue," and Lauren Daigle's "You Say" express the universal experience of loneliness. Although men often find it difficult to admit, at some point everyone feels forgotten.

Sometimes loneliness results when people choose self-centered friends who can't "sleep till they make someone stumble" (Proverbs 4:16 niv). Wisdom warns that these "friends" intensify loneliness. Others begin to feel forgotten when they trade their relationship with God for religious traditions. Paul warned the Galatians about this: "But now that you know God—or rather are known by God—how is it that you are turning back?" (Galatians 4:9–10 niv). He cautioned them that religion never feels the same as relationship.

If you are struggling with loneliness, maybe it's time to find better friends and to start hanging out with the people least like you at church, people who are more concerned about another's success and relationship with God than about their own religious piety.

Finally, whenever you feel people have forgotten you, remember God never does. His memory of you is permanent—for as He put it, "I will not forget you! See, I have engraved you on the palms of my hands" (Isaiah 49:15–16 niv).

Father, thank You for the unshakable love You demonstrated on the cross when You chiseled my name into Your hands.

DISTRACTED DRIVING

Let your eyes look straight ahead;
fix your gaze directly before you.
PROVERBS 4:25 NIV

◆　◆　◆

Have you ever been a passenger in a car driven by a distracted driver? While his hands are busy with a cell phone or the radio or whatever, yours are white-knuckle-gripping the armrests. While he's looking anywhere except the road, you see every potential accident ahead of you.

According to the National Highway Traffic Safety Administration, distracted drivers killed 2,841 people in 2018 alone. In addition to the deaths of the drivers, these casualties also included 605 passengers, 400 pedestrians, and 77 bicyclists.

When driving, you have to be aware of your surroundings. If you aren't looking where you're going, you endanger yourself and everyone around you.

The same is true of your relationship with God. You may start your day in devotions and prayer, then get distracted by the concerns of the day. Soon you're looking anywhere except where God wants your attention to be. Instead of being an example of God's love, you are like a car sporting a Jesus fish decal whose driver is cutting off other drivers on the highway.

How can you be more mindful? Set an alarm to remind you to pray. Fast from a food or activity, and then when you find yourself wanting to do that thing, check in with God. Whatever you do, do it intentionally with your eyes fixed on God.

God, keep my eyes from distractions.

DOUGHNUTS

"Why spend your money on food that does not give you strength?
Why pay for food that does you no good? Listen to me, and
you will eat what is good. You will enjoy the finest food."
ISAIAH 55:2 NLT

On June 1, 2018, competitive eating champion Joey Chestnut set the record for eating Hostess Donettes when he downed 257 of the miniature doughnuts in six minutes.

Doughnuts are delicious. They come in a variety of flavors and fillings, but they all share one thing in common: they have almost no nutritional value. Eating one can leave you feeling like you have a hole in *your* middle as soon as you finish eating it. Even after eating 257 Hostess Donettes, Joey Chestnut probably could have eaten a few more.

Empty calories won't satisfy your hunger, and empty worship won't satisfy your soul.

Isaiah 55 is a universal invitation by God to join in a feast designed to satisfy your cravings. "Is anyone thirsty?" asks God in Isaiah 55:1 (NLT). "Come and drink—even if you have no money! Come, take your choice of wine or milk—it's all free!"

Are you trying to fill up on your own achievements? You've been invited to the feast of worshipping God. Come, listen to His wisdom, partake in His goodness, fill up on His mercy. Take delight in the God who satisfies perfectly.

God, knock the doughnut out of my hand and feed me from Your Word!

SEE A NEED, FILL A NEED

*So then, as we have opportunity, let us do good to everyone,
and especially to those who are of the household of faith.*
GALATIANS 6:10 ESV

———◆———

I t's easier at harvesttime to see what's been planted than it is a week after
the seeds went in the ground.

In Galatians 6:7–9 (ESV), Paul says, "Do not be deceived: God is not
mocked, for whatever one sows, that will he also reap. For the one who sows
to his own flesh will from the flesh reap corruption, but the one who sows to
the Spirit will from the Spirit reap eternal life. And let us not grow weary of
doing good, for in due season we will reap, if we do not give up."

Are you growing the fruit of the Spirit or sowing seeds of corruption?
Harvesttime will tell, but by then it will be too late. What can you do right now?

Take a deep breath. Let it out. Take another. Good! You're alive. You have
the opportunity to sow some good seeds.

Look around. Does someone from your church need a hand with a project?
Could your kids use some individual attention? Did your wife ask you to do
something a while back?

Ask the Spirit to reveal good deeds for others that would give God glory,
then do those things until harvesttime comes.

Lord, may my actions for others give You glory.

LENDING MONEY

*My son, if you have put up security for your neighbor, if you have
shaken hands in pledge for a stranger, you have been trapped by
what you said, ensnared by the words of your mouth. So do this, my
son, to free yourself, since you have fallen into your neighbor's hands:
Go—to the point of exhaustion—and give your neighbor no rest!*
PROVERBS 6:1–3 NIV

◆━━━◆━━━◆

In a 2019 survey by Bankrate.com, 60 percent of respondents said they had lent cash to help out a friend or family member, 37 percent said they lost money on the deal, and 21 percent said the relationship with the borrower was harmed by the incident.

Lending money—whether to a loved one or a stranger—can be a trap waiting to spring. The Bible says it is unwise to enter into loan agreements without due consideration. In most cases, it would be better to treat any transfer of cash as a gift rather than a loan. Don't give more than you can afford to lose, and don't plan on getting anything back in return. Look at the situation as a chance to show generosity.

Psalm 37:21 (NIV) says, "The wicked borrow and do not repay, but the righteous give generously." If you've already loaned out money you can't afford to lose, either make plans for your anticipated loss or don't sleep—and don't let your borrower sleep—until your loan has been repaid.

Lord, help me be wise with my finances.

MADE FOR GOOD WORKS

For we are his workmanship, created in Christ Jesus unto good works,
which God hath before ordained that we should walk in them.
EPHESIANS 2:10 KJV

———◆———◆———◆———

God does good work. He made the heavens and the earth, light and darkness, the sun and the moon, and everything living beneath them. After making each thing, He declared it to be good. Then on the final day of creation, God made man and woman in His own image. Genesis 1:31 (KJV) says, "And God saw every thing that he had made, and, behold, it was very good. And the evening and the morning were the sixth day."

You are God's handiwork, crafted in His image to reflect His goodness to the world. When sin entered the picture, the reflection needed to be redeemed before it could be seen. Just as God created humans, Jesus created the way for humanity to be right with God again. Why? So we could fulfill our original purpose.

Since you have been made in God's image, and He is the original doer of good works, you have been made for good works too. When your relationship with Him is right, your good works make it possible for others to see His reflection living in you.

The works are not the way to the relationship but the result of it. Can people see God's image reflected in your works?

Father God, make me ready to do good works.

NATURAL CONSEQUENCES

*"I will send them great trouble—all the things they
feared. For when I called, they did not answer. When I
spoke, they did not listen. They deliberately sinned before
my very eyes and chose to do what they know I despise."*
ISAIAH 66:4 NLT

T he Rolling Stones famously sang that you can't always get what you
want. But what if they got it wrong? What if you got exactly what you
wanted, but you just wanted the wrong things? Paul expressed this tension
between a person's natural and supernatural desires in Romans 7:15 (NLT):
"I don't really understand myself, for I want to do what is right, but I don't
do it. Instead, I do what I hate."

People are naturally selfish. They don't want to be told what to do. And
while God gave humanity guidelines for how to live and thrive, He also gave
people the ability to make their own choices.

When people choose selfishly, God gives them the natural consequences
of their actions. Injustice isn't part of God's character. If you commit a crime,
you do the time. God is willing to give you what you *want*, but He knows
that what you *need* is Him.

Fortunately, God didn't leave you to your natural inclinations. He gave
you the Holy Spirit so you could choose His happiness over your own. When
you do, you'll find that His happiness means your happiness too.

Lord, help me choose what You want to give me.

GET READY

"But you, dress yourself for work; arise, and say to them
everything that I command you. Do not be dismayed
by them, lest I dismay you before them."

JEREMIAH 1:17 ESV

◆ ◆ ◆

When God called the prophet Jeremiah into His service, he had some hesitations. Jeremiah 1:4–7 (ESV) says, "Now the word of the LORD came to me, saying, 'Before I formed you in the womb I knew you, and before you were born I consecrated you; I appointed you a prophet to the nations.' Then I said, 'Ah, Lord GOD! Behold, I do not know how to speak, for I am only a youth.' But the LORD said to me, 'Do not say, "I am only a youth"; for to all to whom I send you, you shall go, and whatever I command you, you shall speak.' "

Jeremiah didn't feel prepared to do God's work, but God called him anyway. If you don't feel up to the task of being God's representative to this generation, listen to what God said in Jeremiah 1:17 (today's verse).

God isn't setting you up for failure. He's paving the way for your success. But in order to succeed, you need to get ready. Dress yourself in righteous deeds (see Revelation 19:8). Rise up for action at God's call. Tune in to God's Word. And don't let the world get you down, because Jesus has overcome the world (see John 16:33).

Lord, make me ready to do Your will.

GOOD HUMOR

Obscene stories, foolish talk, and coarse jokes—these are not for you.
Instead, let there be thankfulness to God.
EPHESIANS 5:4 NLT

◆――◆――◆

Laughter is good for the body. According to an article from the Mayo Clinic, laughter can provide short-term benefits—stimulating organs with oxygen-rich air, increasing the endorphins released by the brain, activating and relieving your stress response, and soothing tension in the muscles—and long-term benefits—improving your immune system, relieving pain, and improving your mood.

Proverbs 17:22 (NLT) says, "A cheerful heart is good medicine, but a broken spirit saps a person's strength." God gave humor to be a blessing for His people, but like other blessings, it has been twisted by sin and must be approached with wisdom. Not all humor is appropriate. But where do you draw the line?

Paul writes in Ephesians 5:4 that obscenity, folly, and coarse jokes are no laughing matter. A few verses earlier in Ephesians 4:29 (NLT), he says, "Don't use foul or abusive language. Let everything you say be good and helpful, so that your words will be an encouragement to those who hear them."

If your words or jokes aren't encouraging to others or thankful to God, stop talking. Humor that disparages an individual or a group of people isn't humorous. And don't let your desire to be funny overshadow your responsibility to reflect God's character to the world.

Lord, may my sense of humor be a source of joy to You.

FALSE TRUTHS

"A horrible and shocking thing has happened in the land:
The prophets prophesy lies, the priests rule by their own authority,
and my people love it this way. But what will you do in the end?"
JEREMIAH 5:30–31 NIV

❖ ❖ ❖

Fake news isn't a new problem. The prophet Jeremiah often spoke against rival prophets who told lies to keep their influence in the kingdom. The sad truth is that people believe what they want to believe, even when their belief runs counter to the truth.

Why? Affirming things believed by your chosen group provides you with a sense of belonging. There's safety in numbers, and group members often choose each other over truth.

If acceptance isn't your main motivator, maybe it's comfort. When truths require you to confront past actions in a new light or commit to doing things differently in the future, it's easier to simply disregard the truth.

The book of Jeremiah sounds like the world today. False truths spread rapidly through social media. People listen to certain sources not to learn but to have their beliefs echoed back to them. They love thinking they are right, regardless of the truth.

Jeremiah 5:31 ends with this question from God: "But what will you do in the end?"

In the end, only God's truth matters. Are you listening to it or to an echo chamber of your choice?

God, teach me Your truths so I can recognize the world's falsehoods.

RICHES OF THE NEW WORLD

Choose my instruction instead of silver, knowledge rather
than choice gold, for wisdom is more precious than rubies,
and nothing you desire can compare with her.
PROVERBS 8:10–11 NIV

◆———◆———◆

In 1492, Columbus sailed the ocean blue. He sought a quicker passage to Asia than the route around the south of Africa. Convinced he could simply sail west, the Italian explorer miscalculated the earth's diameter and ended up among the West Indies of North America.

For months, Columbus sailed from island to island in the Caribbean in a fruitless search for gold, silver, and spices to bring to his sponsors in Spain.

When Columbus returned to the New World in 1493, he subjugated the indigenous people and forced them to mine their land for gold. But as they didn't find much, Columbus sent the indigenous peoples themselves to Europe to work as slaves.

Columbus's legacy of exploration has been marred by his atrocities against the indigenous peoples he encountered. Although he professed to be a man of faith, Columbus's desire for gold and other riches of the New World led him into infamy.

Had he searched for wisdom as diligently as earthly goods, the world would be a different place. Europeans would have encountered America eventually, but the rise of the transatlantic slave trade wouldn't have happened as it did.

As you explore this world for yourself, are you searching for wisdom or something less precious?

Lord, be more precious to me than all else.

THE PRIVILEGE OF SUFFERING

*For you have been given not only the privilege of trusting
in Christ but also the privilege of suffering for him.*
PHILIPPIANS 1:29 NLT

❖ ❖ ❖

There are many levels of suffering: from getting an elbow in the gut all the way up to stepping on a Lego brick. Some suffering is accidentally self-inflicted (e.g., the Lego brick), while other kinds happen because of other people.

When suffering is a result of sin, it's an opportunity for believers to learn their lesson, repent, and avoid future sinful situations. But when suffering is a result of standing up for Christ, of refusing to sin, it's a privilege.

By suffering for Jesus' sake, you get to experience an aspect of His life on earth. Also, persecution for your faith is evidence your faith is real.

Matthew 5:10–12 (NLT) says, "God blesses those who are persecuted for doing right, for the Kingdom of Heaven is theirs. God blesses you when people mock you and persecute you and lie about you and say all sorts of evil things against you because you are my followers. Be happy about it! Be very glad! For a great reward awaits you in heaven. And remember, the ancient prophets were persecuted in the same way."

You may not feel like your suffering is a privilege when you're in the midst of it, but ultimately it will end in a great reward.

*Lord, thank You for allowing me to experience
Your life in joy and in suffering.*

SPORTS SUPERSTITIONS

Every man is stupid and without knowledge;
every goldsmith is put to shame by his idols, for his
images are false, and there is no breath in them.
JEREMIAH 10:14 ESV

◆━━◆━━◆

The world of sports is rife with superstition.

In the 1991 French Open, Andre Agassi realized too late that he had forgotten to pack underwear for his match, so he played without them. When he won, he attributed his good fortune to his missing item of clothing, and he kept competing commando-style all the way to his fourth Grand Slam title.

Basketball superstar Michael Jordan wore his University of North Carolina shorts under his uniform every time he played. Baseball Hall of Famer Wade Boggs ate chicken before every game. And Patrick Roy, the legendary NHL goaltender, talked to his goalposts constantly.

There are some people who accept these superstitions and say, "If it works, don't mess with it." But modern sports superstitions are no different than ancient idol worship practices.

Only God has the power to change the world. Putting faith in anything less—lucky shorts, chicken dinners, one-way conversations with inanimate objects—is modern idol worship.

Don't hope for good luck. Pray for God's blessing. Better still, have faith that He'll take care of you, whether what you're going through feels like a blessing or not. After all, God didn't promise you'd win games but that He'd win the final battle and invite you to His victory feast.

Lord, You are the only source of blessings.

TOWARD PERFECTION

*Brothers and sisters, I do not consider myself yet to have
taken hold of it. But one thing I do: Forgetting what is
behind and straining toward what is ahead. . .*
PHILIPPIANS 3:13 NIV

Practice makes perfect. Well, closer to perfect anyway. Perfection isn't available on this side of heaven, though its direction is within your grasp.

When Paul wrote to the church at Philippi, he encouraged them to follow his example of moving in the right direction. Philippians 3:12–14 (NIV) says, "Not that I have already obtained all this, or have already arrived at my goal, but I press on to take hold of that for which Christ Jesus took hold of me. Brothers and sisters, I do not consider myself yet to have taken hold of it. But one thing I do: Forgetting what is behind and straining toward what is ahead, I press on toward the goal to win the prize for which God has called me heavenward in Christ Jesus."

The best way to move consistently forward is to stop looking behind. Forget your past failures. Forget your past victories too. Focus on the path in front of you, and keep walking toward perfection. Remember, you're not walking alone. The Holy Spirit, the seal of your salvation, empowers you and walks beside you through this imperfect world until you come to rest eternally in perfection in the next.

God, keep me walking with Your Spirit in the right direction.

CORRECTION

Do not rebuke mockers or they will hate you;
rebuke the wise and they will love you.
PROVERBS 9:8 NIV

✦ ✦ ✦

Everyone makes mistakes. How you deal with your mistakes shows the world whether you are a wise man or the other sort. Specifically, it matters how you handle someone bringing your mistake to light.

Being corrected is never easy. You may feel ashamed for blowing it. Shame could lead to anger or denial. You may want to cover up your mistake, ignoring it rather than dealing with it. Maybe you'd even blame someone else in an effort not to feel stupid.

Or maybe it wasn't a mistake at all. If you are caught up in sin, being corrected for your intentional misdeeds can result in greater shame, more violent anger, and deeper denial.

Proverbs 28:13 (NIV) says, "Whoever conceals their sins does not prosper, but the one who confesses and renounces them finds mercy." Humbly admitting you were wrong, seeking forgiveness for your failure, and making restitution for your wrongdoing are the three steps to dealing with correction like a wise man.

God knows you'll fail, but He doesn't want you to be stuck in your failure. "For though the righteous fall seven times, they rise again, but the wicked stumble when calamity strikes" (Proverbs 24:16 NIV).

Rise up with humility and move on in grace.

God, help me to be corrected like a wise man,
not scoff at my mistakes like a fool.

HEALING SUNLIGHT

He has delivered us from the domain of darkness and
transferred us to the kingdom of his beloved Son,
in whom we have redemption, the forgiveness of sins.
COLOSSIANS 1:13–14 ESV

◆   ◆   ◆

Sunlight kills bacteria. This bit of household wisdom was scientifically verified by a group of researchers led by Ashkaan Fahimipour at the University of Oregon in a 2018 study published in the journal *Microbiome*.[*]

Researchers placed household dust in three dollhouse-size rooms—one that sat in darkness, one exposed to sunlight, one exposed to ultraviolet light—for ninety days before analyzing the samples for bacteria. The sample that sat in darkness had twice the amount of bacteria as the sunlit and UV-exposed samples.

The healing influence of sunlight has long been known. In fact, the Bible is full of examples where God's presence and healing are associated with light. Here are two examples:

"Again Jesus spoke to them, saying, 'I am the light of the world. Whoever follows me will not walk in darkness, but will have the light of life' " (John 8:12 ESV).

"But if we walk in the light, as he is in the light, we have fellowship with one another, and the blood of Jesus his Son cleanses us from all sin" (1 John 1:7 ESV).

If you want to be spiritually healthy, live your life in the light of the Savior. Don't walk any longer in the darkness of sin.

Lord, You've delivered me from darkness. Help me live in Your light.

[*] Ashkaan K. Fahimipour, Erica M. Hartmann, Andrew Siemens, et al., "Daylight Exposure Modulates Bacterial Communities Associated with Household Dust," *Microbiome* 6, no. 175 (October 18, 2018), https://doi.org/10.1186/s40168-018-0559-4.

THE POTTER'S WORK

And the vessel that he was making from clay was spoiled in
the hand of the potter; so he made it over, reworking it into
another vessel as it seemed good to the potter to make it.
JEREMIAH 18:4 AMPC

Making pottery requires clay, a potter's wheel, and patience. To make clay, a potter takes dirt, mixes it with water, and pours it into an empty vessel, allowing heavy stones and other impurities to drop to the bottom of the mix. He pours the purified mixture into a cloth bag so the water can run out, leaving the clay behind.

Once the clay is free of impurities and has reached the proper moisture level, it is repeatedly slammed onto a surface to remove any air bubbles. The potter then begins to work the clay between his hands in preparation for turning it on the wheel. Finally, the potter gently shapes the clay with the wheel into whatever he needs. The clay doesn't get to decide what to be.

Isaiah 64:8 (AMPC) says, "Yet, O Lord, You are our Father; we are the clay, and You our Potter, and we all are the work of Your hand."

There will be uncomfortable times in life when God is refining you, helping you work out impurities. You may feel slammed or squeezed, but God is simply preparing you for a specific purpose. Trust the Potter. Let Him shape you as He sees fit.

Lord, help me trust You always.

HARD WORK AND VINEGAR

As vinegar to the teeth and smoke to the eyes,
so are sluggards to those who send them.
PROVERBS 10:26 NIV

Vinegar has been used medicinally for centuries. Hippocrates—who lived around 420 BC and for whom the Hippocratic oath is named—used vinegar to treat wounds. Although vinegar does have some antimicrobial properties, modern medicine advises against this practice, as there are far more effective ways to kill germs and treat wounds.

Vinegar was also formerly used to whiten teeth. It's true, teeth can appear whiter after using a vinegar mouthwash, but since vinegar is so acidic, it actually eats away at the enamel of the teeth. This leaves teeth vulnerable to cavities and infections.

Vinegar's effect on teeth makes it an apt comparison to a lazy person's effect on an organization or business. Employers who hire a lazy man may see some immediate improvement in morale, but when work starts piling up, the lazy man's presence will weaken the integrity of the organization like a cavity, allowing infections to grow.

At the proper time, levity in an organization is a great thing—just like vinegar can be a great thing when properly used. Good workers work hard according to their deadlines, and then they have the freedom to enjoy some socialization.

If you are tempted toward laziness, remember the One you are ultimately working for: the Lord (see Colossians 3:23–24).

Lord, may I know when to work hard and when to take it easy.

GET DRESSED

Above all, clothe yourselves with love,
which binds us all together in perfect harmony.
COLOSSIANS 3:14 NLT

Polonius from Shakespeare's *Hamlet* advised his son Laertes to pay attention to how he dressed because he knew people often judged a man by his clothes: "Costly thy habit as thy purse can buy, but not express'd in fancy; rich, not gaudy; for the apparel oft proclaims the man."

While Polonius is portrayed as something of an old fool, his folk wisdom has descended into modern sayings like "Clothes make the man."

There is actually biblical support for this idea.

In Colossians 3:12–14 (NLT), Paul writes, "Since God chose you to be the holy people he loves, you must clothe yourselves with tenderhearted mercy, kindness, humility, gentleness, and patience. Make allowance for each other's faults, and forgive anyone who offends you. Remember, the Lord forgave you, so you must forgive others. Above all, clothe yourselves with love, which binds us all together in perfect harmony."

Paul's message to his fellow believers was clear: Dress for success by putting on God's attributes. When you wear the clothes of Christ—mercy, kindness, humility, gentleness, patience, forgiveness, and love—you'll show the world what it means to be in perfect harmony with God Almighty.

Clothes *don't* make the man, but dressing in God's apparel can show the world what does—God's love.

Lord, help me be intentional about dressing in Your righteousness today.

PRIDE

When pride cometh, then cometh shame:
but with the lowly is wisdom.
PROVERBS 11:2 KJV

◆———◆———◆

Pride, in the sense of putting yourself on a pedestal, is sometimes seen as the opposite of shame. If you are proud of something, you want people to see it. If you are ashamed of something, you want to hide it away. But pride is not shame's opposite; it is its precursor.

Pride isn't just the condition before a person's fall; it is the condition of man's original fall from grace. In their pride, Adam and Eve ate of the forbidden fruit, ignoring God's command and listening to their own desires. This act shifted humanity's gaze from God to themselves.

C. S. Lewis, in his masterpiece *Mere Christianity*, says, "In God you come up against something which is in every respect immeasurably superior to yourself. Unless you know God as that—and, therefore, know yourself as nothing in comparison—you do not know God at all. As long as you are proud you cannot know God. A proud man is always looking down on things and people: and, of course, as long as you are looking down, you cannot see something that is above you."

The solution to pride is a proper understanding of your position in the world. This is called humility. When you humble yourself in your own eyes, you are able to turn your eyes back to God.

God, keep my eyes on You, not on me.

IMITATION

*You became imitators of us and of the Lord, for you
welcomed the message in the midst of severe suffering
with the joy given by the Holy Spirit.*
1 Thessalonians 1:6 NIV

I mitation, it is said, is the highest form of flattery. While flattery is typically used to manipulate people, imitation need not be so selfishly motivated. Indeed, it is when imitation is not the goal but the natural result of a godly lifestyle that it is most pleasing to God and most effective in reaching others.

When Paul wrote to the church in Thessalonica, he encouraged his fellow believers to be imitators of him and of Jesus in a very specific way. First Thessalonians 1:6 (NIV) says the church "welcomed the message in the midst of severe suffering with the joy given by the Holy Spirit."

As Paul had joy in his suffering, the church had joy in theirs. They held fast to the truth of Jesus' resurrection, knowing the suffering they experienced in the world was temporary and the glory afterward was everlasting. Since their joy didn't come from the world, the world couldn't take it away.

The church's example became a convincing testimony to the reality of Jesus' resurrection. Paul writes, "And so you became a model to all the believers in Macedonia and Achaia" (1 Thessalonians 1:7 NIV).

Instead of avoiding suffering, embrace the joy of the Holy Spirit.

Jesus, help me imitate You. Fill me with joy even while I suffer.

FALSE HOPE

"Go, tell Hananiah, 'Thus says the LORD: You have broken wooden bars, but you have made in their place bars of iron.'"
JEREMIAH 28:13 ESV

Everyone wants to believe everything is going to be all right. And it will be. . .eventually. But nothing will be perfect until God calls His children eternally home. Thinking things will be all right before then is both foolish and dangerous.

The prophet Jeremiah regularly had bad news for God's chosen people. In one symbolic act, God told Jeremiah to make for himself a yoke to put around his neck like a farm animal. Jeremiah explained that the yoke was an example of how Nebuchadnezzar of Babylon was going to put God's people in bondage.

A rival—and false—prophet named Hananiah took the yoke off Jeremiah's neck, broke it, and declared God would remove the threat of Nebuchadnezzar in the same way within two years. Hananiah's declaration was much more hopeful than Jeremiah's, but that didn't make it true.

Hananiah encouraged people with false hope. He didn't tell people to turn toward God in their distress. He told them the distress was unfounded.

When life isn't going the way you want it to, well-meaning friends may tell you everything will be all right soon, whereas real friends will encourage you to depend on God regardless of your circumstances and pray alongside you come what may.

Lord, help me not to ignore troubles but to rely on You alone.

UNASHAMED

*For you yourselves know perfectly well that the day
of the [return of the] Lord will come [as unexpectedly
and suddenly] as a thief in the night.*
1 Thessalonians 5:2 ampc

How many movies have you seen where a group of teenagers throws a party and the parents come home early? This trope is a common device to heighten tension in a film. It works because people can relate to the feeling of nervousness that comes with doing something they shouldn't.

Everyone's greatest fear while doing something bad is being found out. It goes all the way back to Adam and Eve, who—after eating the forbidden fruit—were afraid of having their sin uncovered: "They heard the sound of the Lord God walking in the garden in the cool of the day, and Adam and his wife hid themselves from the presence of the Lord God among the trees of the garden" (Genesis 3:8 ampc).

The solution to that nervous feeling isn't covering up, but being naked and unashamed. When you have nothing to hide from God or others, you can live without fear. It won't matter exactly when Jesus returns, because you will be found doing the right thing when He does.

As Paul wrote, "For you are all sons of light and sons of the day; we do not belong either to the night or to darkness" (1 Thessalonians 5:5 ampc).

Jesus, may I be found living in the light when You return.

THE NEW COVENANT

"This is the covenant I will make with the people of Israel after that time," declares the LORD. "I will put my law in their minds and write it on their hearts. I will be their God, and they will be my people."

JEREMIAH 31:33 NIV

In the first covenant, God chose the nation of Israel and set it aside for a special relationship with Him. He gave the people laws to live by, sacrifices to atone for their sins, and land where they could live. But the Israelites broke the covenant to bits.

They violated the written laws. They offered sacrifices to other gods. The land they were promised was conquered so God's people would turn back to Him for help. God kept His covenant faithfully, but His people broke it all the same.

Then the prophet Jeremiah announced a new covenant. The old covenant was written on breakable tablets and scrolls, but God's new covenant would be written directly on a person's heart.

The promise of a new covenant came to fruition in the atoning grace of Jesus' sacrifice and resurrection. The Holy Spirit, who visited Israel in the past, now takes up residence in the hearts of believers. God expanded the new covenant beyond the nation of Israel to every nation on earth.

God has called you to be part of this unbreakable covenant. Are you committed to Him? He is committed to you.

Lord, thank You for making me part of Your new covenant!

STAND FIRM

So then, brothers and sisters, stand firm and hold fast to the teachings
we passed on to you, whether by word of mouth or by letter.
2 THESSALONIANS 2:15 NIV

The church of Thessalonica wanted answers. When was Christ coming back? How would they know it was really Him? What if they missed His return?

When faced with big questions, people are apt to believe sources that sound plausible, even if they aren't true. That's where the trouble starts. When people form opinions based on things they've heard but haven't verified, they are less likely to believe the truth when it does come along.

This is the problem Paul addresses in 2 Thessalonians 2:1–2 (NIV): "Concerning the coming of our Lord Jesus Christ and our being gathered to him, we ask you, brothers and sisters, not to become easily unsettled or alarmed by the teaching allegedly from us—whether by a prophecy or by word of mouth or by letter—asserting that the day of the Lord has already come."

Instead of being shaken by fearful lies or rumors, Paul wanted the people to cling to the truths they knew, to test rumors against the traditions Paul had taught them.

When you hear something troubling from people you know or see something questionable on social media, you should definitely ask questions, but you should also test the answers against what you know to be true. A man of unshakable faith stands fast on the truth.

God, help me to be firm in my faith and test rumors against Your Word.

FOOLISH TALK

The wise don't make a show of their knowledge,
but fools broadcast their foolishness.
PROVERBS 12:23 NLT

◆————◆————◆

I magine you are in a classroom. The teacher asks the class to name the twentieth US president. The name Chester A. Arthur springs to mind, accompanied by an image of a stately gentleman with a mustache and muttonchops. You are about to raise your hand to answer when the teacher calls on your neighbor.

"James A. Garfield," he says. And he's right. Arthur was Garfield's vice president. He became the twenty-first president when Garfield was assassinated. Sometimes it's better to be quiet even when you think you're right.

It's one thing to be wrong about trivial facts. It's another to be proven wrong about things that matter—or to make a fool of yourself. Proverbs 12:23 (today's verse) isn't telling you never to speak up when you have knowledge. It's saying never to show off. There's nothing wrong with knowing it all if you don't act like a know-it-all.

When you broadcast foolishness—either by speaking foolishly or communicating in a foolish way—people are less likely to listen to you. Then when you want to tell people about God, your audience will tune you out.

It's better to be silent most of the time so people listen to you when you have something important to say.

God, may I know when to speak up and when to stay silent.

SURRENDERING YOUR RIGHTS

*Then the officials said to the king, "This man should be put
to death. He is discouraging the soldiers who are left in this city,
as well as all the people, by the things he is saying to them.
This man is not seeking the good of these people but their ruin."*
JEREMIAH 38:4 NIV

The prophet Jeremiah, never the most optimistic of people, had more bad news for the Israelites: "This is what the LORD says: 'Whoever stays in this city will die by the sword, famine or plague, but whoever goes over to the Babylonians will live. They will escape with their lives; they will live.' And this is what the LORD says: 'This city will certainly be given into the hands of the army of the king of Babylon, who will capture it' " (Jeremiah 38:2–3 NIV).

No one wants to be told they have to surrender to the enemy. The idea of surrender goes against one's sense of freedom, and not fighting seems to point to a lack of faith. But faith isn't doing what seems right—it's doing what God says and trusting that He has a plan.

Jeremiah wasn't advocating for a Babylonian takeover; he was telling the Israelites to surrender to God.

If you are in a similar situation, forget your individual freedoms. Stop fighting. Surrender to God's will. Trust Him and He can show His power through you, even when you're somewhere you never thought you'd be.

Lord, I surrender to You.

LOSING BY WINNING

Wealth gained hastily will dwindle, but whoever
gathers little by little will increase it.
PROVERBS 13:11 ESV

◆―――◆―――◆

In 1988 William "Bud" Post III bought a lottery ticket and won $16.2 million. He told newspapers he had less than three dollars in his bank account at the time.

In the first few months, Bud blew through his winnings in a series of sibling-related business expenditures and extravagant purchases—including a twin-engine plane, even though he lacked the pilot's license needed to fly it.

Before long, Bud was estranged from his family and fighting in court over claims against his fortune. In spite of his winnings, Bud soon found himself in debt. Then, after he fired a gun over a debt collector's head, he found himself in jail.

"Everybody dreams of winning money, but nobody realizes the nightmares that come out of the woodwork, or the problems," he once said.

The lottery isn't a good way to make money, not only because so few people actually win, but because people who play are not likely to make wise decisions with the money if they do.

The key to money management is the willingness to earn money by honest work and the commitment to use it as God intended—giving generously to others as God has generously provided for you. Jesus said, "Seek the Kingdom of God above all else, and live righteously, and he will give you everything you need" (Matthew 6:33 NLT).

God, make me wise with my finances.

SPIRITUAL EXERCISE

Have nothing to do with godless myths and old wives' tales;
rather, train yourself to be godly. For physical training is of
some value, but godliness has value for all things, holding
promise for both the present life and the life to come.
1 TIMOTHY 4:7–8 NIV

◆   ◆   ◆

In 2016 Eddie Hall deadlifted 1,100 pounds at Europe's Strongest Man competition. Jamaican sprinter Usain Bolt set the world record in the 100-meter sprint at 9.58 seconds in 2009. Jan Železný, the Czech javelin thrower, holds the record for the five best throws ever, the top of which was set in 1996 at 98.48 meters.

Physical feats of strength like these require a lifetime of exercise and training. And while the Bible does praise physical fitness (see 1 Corinthians 6:19–20), it is of comparably lesser importance than someone's spiritual fitness.

While they live, these athletes can lift more, run faster, and throw farther than anyone else in the world, but when they die, their strength no longer benefits them.

Compare that with spiritual exercise—loving your neighbor, giving to the poor, defending the powerless, spreading the Gospel. Paul says in 1 Timothy 4:8 (NIV), "Godliness has value for all things, holding promise for both the present life and the life to come."

When you train in godliness, the benefits start now and last beyond death as you show people the way to have life everlasting.

Lord, help me work out my spiritual muscles.

DISCIPLINE AND SELF-DISCIPLINE

*He who spares his rod [of discipline] hates his son, but he who
loves him disciplines diligently and punishes him early.*

PROVERBS 13:24 AMPC

◆———◆———◆

Most four-year-olds lack the self-discipline to choose good attitudes when they don't get what they want, to obey all the rules set down by their parents, or to prioritize tasks by importance rather than by entertainment value. (Many adults also lack self-discipline in these areas.)

When children's lack of self-discipline results in misbehavior, parents need to step in and lovingly correct them. This doesn't mean hitting them with a literal rod—or spanking or hitting them in general—and it definitely doesn't mean punishing them while you are upset. Loving disciplinary measures are carefully implemented so kids change their attitudes in addition to their behavior.

If parents shirk their duties in disciplining their children, their kids may think rules don't apply to them. They will grow up to be fools who hate any kind of discipline, including self-discipline.

The goal of parenting is to raise kids who not only follow God's rules but do it for the best reasons. Whether or not you have kids, you have an opportunity to model self-discipline to others. Show by example how to choose good attitudes, obey authority, and prioritize well. Teach others to know God so He can help them succeed, just as He helps you.

*Father, give me the self-discipline I need
so I can discipline wisely when needed.*

SAFE FROM PREDATORS

But as for you, O man of God, flee these things. Pursue righteousness, godliness, faith, love, steadfastness, gentleness.
1 TIMOTHY 6:11 ESV

❖ ❖ ❖

The hippopotamus is a surprising animal. Bull hippos can weigh up to 6,000 pounds and run up to 30 miles per hour on land—faster than Usain Bolt, the world's fastest human. According to BBC News, it's the world's deadliest large land mammal, killing an estimated five hundred people per year in Africa. The majority of these attacks happen along rivers where people get their fresh water for the day.

But the hippopotamus is not the only deadly animal to inhabit Africa's rivers. Crocodiles kill more humans than hippos do. So if you find yourself along an African riverbank and a hippopotamus charges at you, pay attention to where you look for safety. A man being chased by one predator would be wise not to run into a different predator's mouth.

The apostle Paul said something similar in a letter to Timothy. "But those who desire to be rich fall into temptation, into a snare, into many senseless and harmful desires that plunge people into ruin and destruction" (1 Timothy 6:9 ESV).

It isn't enough to flee the temptation to be rich and the desires that accompany it. You must run toward the attributes of God to be safe—"Pursue righteousness, godliness, faith, love, steadfastness, gentleness" (1 Timothy 6:11 ESV).

God, be my goal and my strength.

TRICK-OR-TREAT

Only simpletons believe everything they're told!
The prudent carefully consider their steps.
PROVERBS 14:15 NLT

In late September 1982, seven people in the Chicago area were poisoned with cyanide-laced Tylenol. The murders led to a nationwide recall of Tylenol—an estimated 31 million bottles, with a retail value of over $100 million. The incident led to industry-wide changes in food and drug packaging, but it also had unintended consequences for Halloween celebrations.

With the increased anxiety raised by the poisonings, rumors ran amok in the 1980s regarding poisoned candy and apples with hidden razor blades being given to trick-or-treaters. Almost all of these rumors proved to be hoaxes, but fear still lingers in some communities about the dangers of Halloween.

The trick to trick-or-treating safely is the same as with the rest of life's potential dangers: prudence. Test everything against what you know to be true.

First Thessalonians 5:20–21 (NLT) says, "Do not scoff at prophecies, but test everything that is said. Hold on to what is good."

Fear is a terrible guide. Whether you're afraid of bad things happening—like razor blades hiding in apples—or of something being too good to be true—like God blessing some new endeavor—fear will kill more opportunities than it saves.

Give your fears to God. He will help you test them one by one. Trust Him to give you wisdom. "Fearing people is a dangerous trap, but trusting the LORD means safety" (Proverbs 29:25 NLT).

Lord, replace my fears with prudent wisdom.

LIKE A GOOD SOLDIER

Join with me in suffering, like a good soldier of Christ Jesus.
2 Timothy 2:3 niv

Militarily speaking, a good soldier is the courageous one who *expects* hardship and suffering to be a part of the job. A good soldier doesn't shrink away from suffering but instead willfully joins his brothers in arms in enduring hardship.

The apostle Paul lived in a time and place where being a Christian often meant intense suffering. Many believers in those days suffered persecution—even death—because they openly followed Jesus Christ. That is why Paul encouraged a young preacher named Timothy to "join with me in suffering."

Here in the West, Christians don't face much suffering for their faith. But in some parts of the world, believers often are treated just as badly as Christians were in the first century. So the question you must ask yourself is *Am I willing to suffer for following Jesus?*

If you can honestly answer yes, then you are more likely to stand steadfast should persecution and suffering become a part of your life of faith.

Lord Jesus, You told Your followers that trouble and hardship would come to those who follow You faithfully. I accept suffering as part of my life as a Christian and ask You to give me the strength, courage, and wisdom I need to live unshakably for You.

GOD'S INSTRUCTION BOOK

All Scripture is inspired by God and is useful to teach us what is true and to make us realize what is wrong in our lives. It corrects us when we are wrong and teaches us to do what is right.
2 TIMOTHY 3:16 NLT

❖

If you were to write a short review or synopsis of the Bible, it wouldn't be as good as the one the apostle Paul wrote in today's scripture verse. Paul wanted his young protégé, a pastor named Timothy, to understand just how important Bible reading is for the Christian man. Paul wrote that the Bible is:

- *Inspired by God.* This means that the Holy Spirit gave the men who wrote the books of the Bible the words that God Himself wanted us to read. That makes the Bible the most trustworthy book ever written.

- *Useful for teaching Christians truth.* Every word of the Bible, without exception, is God's truth.

- *Useful for helping you see what is wrong in your life.* The Bible gives you instructions for making course corrections in your life of faith.

- *The Book that corrects you and teaches you to do what is right.* When you have questions about how God wants you to live, you will find answers in the Bible.

Father in heaven, thank You for providing me with all I need to know about living unshakably for You through Your written Word. Give me a hunger for Your Word and the empowerment I need to do what it says.

WORTHLESS, LYING IDOLS

*Idols are worthless; they are ridiculous lies! On the day of reckoning
they will all be destroyed. But the God of Israel is no idol!*
JEREMIAH 51:18–19 NLT

In 1 Corinthians 10:14 (NIV), the apostle Paul instructs the Christians living in Corinth, "My dear friends, flee from idolatry." Today's scripture verse tells you why you should make every effort to avoid idolatry—which in the biblical sense means the pursuit of any worldly thing to find fulfillment in life.

When most people hear the word *idol*, their minds go to statues or other man-made items that people in the past bowed down to and worshipped. But we have our own idols today, including material wealth, power, social status, sex, and countless other things. And when men pursue those things over God, those things are "worthless" and "ridiculous lies."

Today's verse ends with these words: "But the God of Israel is no idol!" That means the Lord is everything that worldly idols are not. He is of infinitely more value than anything you can pursue in this world to find peace and meaning in life. And it means that God Himself is eternal truth.

Man-made idols will one day be destroyed. But your God will live forever.

*Precious Lord, nothing this world has to offer compares with You.
May I always look to You alone as my source of complete satisfaction and
rid my life of anything and everything that could become an idol.*

TRUE CONTENTMENT

Better a little with the fear of the LORD
than great wealth with turmoil.
PROVERBS 15:16 NIV

———◆———◆———◆———

The first-century Roman philosopher Seneca once wisely observed, "For many men, the acquisition of wealth does not end their troubles, it only changes them." Since the days of Seneca, many men—including some very godly men—have made similar observations.

Today's proverb is one of many that presents readers with a dichotomy— this one between a life of true contentment in knowing and honoring God and a life of great material wealth but without true peace. This verse challenges its readers to consider which life they want to pursue.

The Bible does not condemn working hard to acquire material wealth. Instead, it enjoins godly men to make sure they pursue first the things that will last beyond this life.

Having much material wealth could lead you into a life of trouble and turmoil. But living a life that honors God will spare you from much trouble and lead you to true peace and contentment. Knowing your options, which life do you want to pursue?

Father, I want to live a life that pleases You in every way.
That means I need to be careful not to put my focus on worldly
wealth but instead to love and serve You with everything
I am and have. When I do that, I'm a truly rich man.

NEW MERCIES EVERY DAY

It is of the LORD's mercies that we are not consumed, because his compassions fail not. They are new every morning: great is thy faithfulness.

LAMENTATIONS 3:22–23 KJV

Humanly speaking, the sight of the smoldering ruins of the great city of Jerusalem didn't offer much in the way of hope. God had executed His judgment on His people, and now the city was left in utter desolation. But as the prophet Jeremiah, who had foretold what had happened, looked at the results of the Babylonian attack on the city, he found hope. . .in the same God who had just poured out His wrath.

Jeremiah's heart was broken over what he saw, yet he still was able to write the words in today's scripture passage. He saw much suffering and devastation, but he still remembered God's tender compassion and faithfulness.

When you are going through difficult times, do you find yourself complaining and dwelling on your present situation, or do you turn to your loving, compassionate heavenly Father and thank Him from your heart for His goodness and for His acts of compassion toward you?

Gracious, merciful God, thank You that I can wake up every morning aware of Your goodness, mercy, and love toward me. That is an amazing way for me to start each and every day.

RECEIVE DISCIPLINE HUMBLY

Those who disregard discipline despise themselves,
but the one who heeds correction gains understanding.
PROVERBS 15:32 NIV

◆━━━━━◆━━━━━◆

Many talented athletes have failed to live up to their potential because they couldn't receive instruction and discipline. In the sports world, they are labeled as "uncoachable"—and the result is short or disappointing careers.

Today's verse warns that failing to receive discipline (or "instruction" in some Bible versions) is the same as hating oneself. These are people who hurt themselves as well as those to whom they are close.

All men need discipline, instruction, and correction if they are to live unshakably in this world. God has ordained different means to instruct and correct you when you need it. Those means include man-to-man relationships and your relationship with God Himself.

If you're like most men, you don't enjoy being corrected or disciplined. But God has said that you gain wisdom when you heed correction. So humble yourself and submit to God's discipline. He loves you and always has your very best interests in mind!

Loving heavenly Father, thank You for loving me enough to correct me when I need it. Help me to listen when You speak and to remain humble enough to allow You to make changes that need to be made in me.

SPEAK FEARLESSLY

*"And you, son of man, do not be afraid of them or their words.
Do not be afraid, though briers and thorns are all around you
and you live among scorpions. Do not be afraid of what they say
or be terrified by them, though they are a rebellious people."*

EZEKIEL 2:6 NIV

God had given Ezekiel a difficult assignment. He would speak to a rebellious people, and most of them would refuse to listen to him. God warned the prophet that their rejection would feel like briers, thorns, and scorpion stings. Yet He told Ezekiel not to give in to despair or fear but to continue speaking God's messages.

Ezekiel is one of many men in the Bible who faced opposition—sometimes violent opposition—when he spoke the words God told him to speak. Yet he stood up, unshaken and without fear, and obeyed his God.

While you may not face the kind of opposition Ezekiel and other men of God faced, there still may be times when you feel some fear or trepidation when God asks you to speak His truth. But God will tell you the same thing He told Ezekiel: *Don't be afraid! Speak up!*

Lord, I live in a rebellious world filled with rebellious people. It seems like very few want to hear Your truth or respond to Your love. Please give me opportunities to speak Your truth and the courage I need to speak it.

THE VALUE OF WISDOM

How much better to get wisdom than gold,
to get insight rather than silver!
PROVERBS 16:16 NIV

◆　　◆　　◆

Most men, at some point in their lives, have found themselves fretting over money. They wonder if they'll have enough to meet their and their family's needs. Men seem naturally inclined to seek out ways to earn money. But what about the wisdom they need to live victorious, powerful lives of faith?

The apostle James wrote that when you lack wisdom, "you should ask God, who gives generously to all without finding fault, and it will be given to you. But when you ask, you must believe and not doubt, because the one who doubts is like a wave of the sea, blown and tossed by the wind" (James 1:5–6 NIV).

It's important for you to work and earn money so you can care for your needs and the needs of your family. But even more important is growing in wisdom so that you can live and speak in ways that please God and truly benefit other people.

So seek wisdom—seek God and ask for wisdom with diligence and passion. He wants you to have it!

Father in heaven, thank You for Your willingness to give me the
wisdom I need to live a life that pleases You. Help me not just to walk
in that wisdom but to always remember how precious that gift really is.

ONE OF US

Therefore, it was necessary for him to be made in every respect like us, his brothers and sisters, so that he could be our merciful and faithful High Priest before God. Then he could offer a sacrifice that would take away the sins of the people.

HEBREWS 2:17 NLT

<hr/>

You've probably heard it said that when Jesus was on earth, He was wholly God *and* wholly human. That's not an easy bit of theology to fully understand, but today's scripture verse explains why it's so important—why it is absolutely *essential*.

Hebrews 2:17 says that there was no other way for God to provide a sacrifice that could be effective in taking away your sins—and the sins of all humankind. In order to be our representative before God, Jesus—God Himself in human form—had to come to earth and live as one of us.

The apostle Paul described this act of eternal, divine love this way: "He [Jesus] made himself nothing by taking the very nature of a servant, being made in human likeness. And being found in appearance as a man, he humbled himself by becoming obedient to death—even death on a cross!" (Philippians 2:7–8 NIV).

Meditating on the amazing truth that God became one of us can help you live unshakably in His profound love.

<hr/>

Jesus, thank You for coming to earth and becoming fully human in order to give Yourself up so that I could be forgiven for my sin.

A LOVING ATTITUDE

Whoever gloats over disaster will not go unpunished.
PROVERBS 17:5 NIV

The German word *schadenfreude* (which literally means "harm-joy") refers to the feeling of satisfaction, joy, or pleasure one can feel over the failures, troubles, or humiliations of another person.

Today's scripture verse warns that God does not approve when His people gloat over another person's disaster. In fact, it warns that He will punish those who hold this kind of attitude in their heart.

Jesus once told His followers that instead of wishing ill on their enemies or rivals, they should love them and pray for them: "You have heard that it was said, 'Love your neighbor and hate your enemy.' But I tell you, love your enemies and pray for those who persecute you, that you may be children of your Father in heaven" (Matthew 5:43–45 NIV).

Feeling a sense of joy over someone else's troubles is both unloving and uncaring. But loving and praying for anyone and everyone you know who is going through difficult times is a demonstration of the kind of love God has shown you.

Father in heaven, I confess that I have in the past taken pleasure in the failures and humiliations of other people. Forgive me, Lord. Help me never to feel a sense of satisfaction when an enemy or rival fails. Remind me instead to pray for those who suffer because of trouble or failure.

YOUR PERFECT HIGH PRIEST

This High Priest of ours understands our weaknesses, for he faced all of the same testings we do, yet he did not sin. So let us come boldly to the throne of our gracious God. There we will receive his mercy, and we will find grace to help us when we need it most.
HEBREWS 4:15–16 NLT

In Old Testament times, the Jewish priests served as intermediaries between God and humans. They performed ceremonial offerings so that people could have forgiveness for their sins—if only temporarily. The high priest was the supreme leader of the other priests and of all Israelites.

The priesthood and the system of sacrifices in the Old Testament were imperfect. . .and temporary. The New Testament teaches that Jesus' onetime sacrifice on the cross replaced the priesthood and the sacrifices for good. Now Jesus, who lived a life of sinless perfection here on earth, is your perfect High Priest. Because of that, you can confidently approach the throne of God when you need His grace and mercy, both of which Jesus has made freely available.

Knowing that Jesus is your perfect High Priest, you can live unshakably in your life of faith in Him.

Lord Jesus, thank You for understanding my weaknesses and for giving me the privilege of coming boldly and confidently to my heavenly Father when I need His help. Thank You, Father, for providing all I need to live unshakably for You.

YOUR BEST FRIEND

A friend loves at all times, and a brother
is born for a time of adversity.
PROVERBS 17:17 NIV

◆━━━━◆━━━━◆

What comes to your mind when you think of the word *friend*? Someone who loves you unconditionally, even when you're at your worst? Someone who wants to spend time with you, just because? Someone who is willing to sacrifice of himself for you? Someone who speaks gentle words of encouragement—or firm words that challenge or correct you?

You may not have thought of it this way, but Jesus is that kind of friend—and so much more. Jesus is the friend who sacrificed everything for you when He died on a wooden cross so that you could be forgiven for your sins and then live forever with Him in heaven. At this very moment, your friend Jesus intercedes with God on your behalf. And He did all those things not because He *had* to, but because He and His Father in heaven *wanted* to.

To paraphrase the old hymn, what a friend you have in Jesus!

Today, take the time to thank Jesus for being not just your Lord and Savior but also the best friend you will ever have.

Lord, I want to have true friends—the kind of friends who love
me unconditionally and who can encourage me to remain unshaken in
the most difficult of times. Thank You for being that kind of friend.

JESUS PRAYS FOR YOU!

Therefore he is able, once and forever, to save those who come to God through him. He lives forever to intercede with God on their behalf.

HEBREWS 7:25 NLT

Just knowing that a good, godly friend is praying for you—in other words, interceding with God on your behalf—can be a tremendous source of comfort and encouragement, can't it?

But today's scripture verse takes that comfort and encouragement to a whole different level when it promises that the best Friend you'll ever have intercedes for you at all times. Wow!

The apostle Paul wrote of the wonderful truth that Jesus Himself intercedes for you: "Who will bring any charge against those whom God has chosen? It is God who justifies. Who then is the one who condemns? No one. Christ Jesus who died—more than that, who was raised to life—is at the right hand of God and is also interceding for us" (Romans 8:33–34 NIV).

Knowing that Jesus—the King of kings and Lord of lords—actually takes time to stand before God on your behalf can encourage you to stand steadfast in your walk of faith.

Lord Jesus, I am always encouraged when I know that a good friend is praying for me. But knowing that You pray for me gives me absolute assurance that my Father in heaven will give me what I need to persevere in living for You.

SPEAK WISELY

The mouths of fools are their undoing,
and their lips are a snare to their very lives.
PROVERBS 18:7 NIV

◆————◆————◆

Are you the kind of guy who prides himself on being someone who "tells it like it is" (in other words, a bigmouth), or do you most often think before speaking your mind, knowing that saying something unwise or unkind could harm your witness for Jesus and/or hurt another person?

The Bible has much to say about the words you should speak—as well as the kind of speech you should avoid. A good summary of what God says on this subject is to only speak words that glorify God and help build others up.

The apostle Paul gave some solid advice for the kinds of words you should speak (and not speak) when he wrote, "Do not let any unwholesome talk come out of your mouths, but only what is helpful for building others up according to their needs, that it may benefit those who listen" (Ephesians 4:29 NIV).

So before you speak, ask yourself, *Does what I'm about to say glorify God and build others up?* If the answer is no, then hold your tongue.

Lord, I never want to speak foolishly, but I'm far from
perfect in that area of my life. Forgive me when I say things
I shouldn't. Guard my mouth so that I speak only words that
glorify You and are helpful to my brothers and sisters in Christ.

LOST CAUSES?

"Do you think that I like to see wicked people die?
says the Sovereign LORD. Of course not! I want them
to turn from their wicked ways and live."
EZEKIEL 18:23 NLT

<hr />

Have you ever found yourself, even if only a little bit, secretly condemning certain people—or groups of people—as beyond God's reach, as headed to hell with no hope of a course correction?

From a purely natural perspective, it can be hard to understand how God could save those we consider the vilest of sinners. But God has been doing just that from the very beginning. More times than we can possibly know, God has miraculously saved those you might consider beyond reach.

Also, He is giving humans time to turn to Him so that they can live forever with Him. The apostle Peter put it like this: "The Lord is not slow in keeping his promise, as some understand slowness. Instead he is patient with you, not wanting anyone to perish, but everyone to come to repentance" (2 Peter 3:9 NIV).

So let God be God and pray that He does the same kind of miracle in others as He did when He saved you.

<hr />

Loving Father, sometimes when I think about sinful people,
I forget that You want them to turn away from their sin and
toward You. Remind me daily to pray for the people I know who
need Jesus. Never allow me to think of anyone as a "lost cause."

GO TO CHURCH!

And let us not neglect our meeting together, as some
people do, but encourage one another, especially now
that the day of his return is drawing near.
HEBREWS 10:25 NLT

You've probably heard at least one of your Christian brothers say something like, "I don't need to go to church to be a Christian!" Maybe you've thought or said something like that yourself.

But that's not sound thinking. Not at all!

Consider this: The phrase "one another" appears dozens of times in the New Testament alone. Christians are enjoined to be devoted to one another, to live in harmony with one another, to love one another, to accept one another, and to greet one another—and that's just in the book of Romans!

It's probably safe to say that no one has figured out how to do those "one anothers" without meeting together regularly.

God has designed the Christian faith so that we need one another, and not just so we can spend quality time with like-minded people. We are to hold one another accountable, encourage one another, and pray for one another.

So don't neglect to meet together regularly with other believers.

Lord, You desire that those You've saved spend time with one another
so they can be strengthened and encouraged. Never let me forget how
important it is that I get myself to church regularly so that I can
worship and fellowship with fellow brothers and sisters in Christ.

THE PRIVILEGE OF INTERCESSION

*"I looked for someone among them who would build up the
wall and stand before me in the gap on behalf of the land so I
would not have to destroy it, but I found no one."*
EZEKIEL 22:30 NIV

D o you ever find yourself grieving over the current state of our world, or perhaps desiring that someone you love (a friend or family member) turn to Jesus for salvation? If your answer to either of these questions is yes, then it may be that God is calling you to a special kind of prayer called "intercession."

For the Christian man, any bad or discouraging news he sees around him, as well as the spiritual needs he sees in others, gives him the opportunity to engage in what is called intercessory prayer. That's the kind of prayer in which someone "stands in the gap" before God and pleads for His mercy and intervention on behalf of another—including friends, family members, government leadership. . .the list goes on and on.

God has given each of us an amazing responsibility—and privilege: to be men of prayer, men who come to Him and plead fervently with Him on behalf of others. Who or what can you begin praying for today?

*Father in heaven, I believe that You still seek men of prayer to
"stand in the gap" and pray to You on behalf of individuals
and my nation. Lord, I want to be one of those men.*

BLIND FAITH?

It was by faith that Abraham obeyed when God called him to leave home and go to another land that God would give him as his inheritance. He went without knowing where he was going.
HEBREWS 11:8 NLT

Christians hold up the patriarch Abraham as a great example of faith and obedience. The writer of the book of Hebrews tells us why he is worthy of such acclaim. In today's verse, Abraham is lauded as a man who left his home and followed God to the place the Lord promised would be his inheritance.

Amazingly, Abraham left his home *without knowing where he was going*. But the most important part of the early part of Abraham's story isn't where he was going but whom he was following: the God who would make Abraham a blessing to the whole world.

Your obedience to God isn't based on a blind faith. It's based on knowing who He really is—an all-powerful, all-knowing, all-loving Creator and heavenly Father who always has your best and His glory in mind when He tells you what He wants you to do and where He wants you to go.

Heavenly Father, my faith in You is not a blind faith. It's a faith that follows You and obeys You because I know You are more than worthy of my trust. Thank You for being who You are—100 percent worthy of my love, my trust, and my obedience.

GOT FAITH?

By faith these people overthrew kingdoms, ruled with justice, and received what God had promised them. They shut the mouths of lions, quenched the flames of fire, and escaped death by the edge of the sword. Their weakness was turned to strength.

HEBREWS 11:33–34 NLT

When you find yourself feeling discouraged, or when you just want to have your faith strengthened, just crack open your Bible and take a little time to read Hebrews 11—the Bible's "Faith Hall of Fame." This chapter includes many accounts of Old Testament men and women who accomplished amazing things and received God's promises, and for one reason: they believed God and took Him at His word.

The writer of the book of Hebrews included accounts of imperfect human beings (if you want examples of how imperfect these people of faith are, just look up the stories of men like Abraham, Samson, and David) who received great things from God. . .just because they believed His promises.

Seeing how a perfect God responded to the faith of imperfect men can be a great source of encouragement and strength for the man who needs both to live unshakably.

Lord, Your written Word has taught me that there is but one way for me to receive all You have already promised me, and that's to believe You when You make me a promise. Thank You for keeping all Your promises, even to an imperfect man like me.

WHY ME?

Endure hardship as discipline; God is treating you as his children. For what children are not disciplined by their father? If you are not disciplined—and everyone undergoes discipline— then you are not legitimate, not true sons and daughters at all.
HEBREWS 12:7–8 NIV

◆━━━◆━━━◆

When you're going through difficulties in this life (and everyone does), it can be tempting to believe that God is punishing you for some sin you've overlooked. Eventually, that line of thinking can lead you to wonder, *Why me? What have I done?*

Instead of allowing your mind to be dominated with *Why me?* when you're going through hardship or suffering, try this: focus in on the biblical truth that God is your perfect and loving heavenly Father who wants you to learn more and more about Him and to live the way He wants you to live more and more each day.

Today's scripture verse says that hardship is often God's means to discipline and teach and correct you—not to punish you. His discipline shows you how much He loves you—not that He is angry with you.

Lord God, thank You for the privilege of calling You "Father." Thank You also that as my Father in heaven, You discipline me when I need it. While I may not enjoy when Your hand of discipline is on me, I know it's further proof that You love me.

AVOID DRUNKENNESS

Wine is a mocker and beer a brawler;
whoever is led astray by them is not wise.
PROVERBS 20:1 NIV

◆━━━━◆━━━━◆

The consumption of alcoholic drink is a matter of sometimes intense debate in today's Christian community. Some believe that Christians should abstain completely, while others believe that God allows His people to drink in moderation.

No matter where you fall in that debate, it's important to understand that the Bible doesn't forbid the consumption of wine and other alcoholic drink but repeatedly condemns drunkenness as sin.

Today's scripture verse offers strong counsel against being "led astray" by alcoholic drink. Sadly, many are led astray, leading to ruined lives, ruined careers, ruined relationships, and a ruined witness for Jesus. These aren't the marks of a man living a steadfast life of faith, are they?

If you want to live unshakably in all areas of your life—especially your life of faith—then you'll need to use wisdom when it comes to the consumption of alcoholic beverages. As today's verse warns, the abuse of alcohol will always lead you to places God doesn't intend for you to go. Consequently, it isn't an unwise decision to abstain completely.

Lord, Your written Word tells me it's not wise to engage in the excessive consumption of alcohol. I've seen examples of how true that is! May I never dishonor You (or harm my family or friends) through excessive drinking.

KEEPING MONEY IN ITS PLACE

*Keep your lives free from the love of money and be
content with what you have, because God has said,
"Never will I leave you; never will I forsake you."*
HEBREWS 13:5 NIV

Many who think they know the Bible will tell you that it says, "Money is the root of all evil." But that is one of the most common misquotes of what the Bible really says. In reality, the apostle Paul wrote, "For the *love of money* is a root of all kinds of evil" (1 Timothy 6:10 NIV, italics added).

The writer of the book of Hebrews doesn't address the love of money as the root of all kinds of evil but instead encourages his readers to keep themselves free from the love of money and to be content with what they have. The reason? Because God has promised always to be with them and to provide for them.

Remembering that God has promised to care for you and provide for you can keep you from the love of—and worries over—money. That will help you keep money in its place—and to live an unshakable life of faith.

*Father, I want to glorify You in my financial life. As I work to provide
for myself and my family, help me to be content with what You've
provided me, knowing that You'll never fail to give me what I need.*

HEARING AND DOING

Do not merely listen to the word,
and so deceive yourselves. Do what it says.
JAMES 1:22 NIV

◆   ◆   ◆

If you're a father, you've no doubt felt the frustration that comes when you tell your young child to do something. . .only to later find it undone. Your child's inaction isn't necessarily the behavior of a rebellious or disrespectful kid. More likely it's a symptom of immaturity. In other words, it's a stage the child will likely grow out of.

In today's verse, the apostle James calls his readers to a new level of spiritual maturity—a level at which the Christian reads and understands the commands God has given him in the Bible. . .and then consistently obeys them.

You can only live an unshakable life of faith when you make it your priority to read and study the Bible and then do what it says. God didn't give you His written Word simply so you can enjoy some good literature. He gave it to you to encourage you, bless you, and strengthen you in your life of faith. When you obey what God says in the Bible, you put yourself in a position to receive everything He has promised you.

Father, I'm usually good at hearing what You say to me in Your written Word. It's the doing part where I too often fail. Forgive me, and help me to be a faithful doer when it comes to what scripture says to me.

THANKFUL EVERY DAY

*"You are my sheep, the sheep of my pasture,
and I am your God, declares the Sovereign LORD."*
EZEKIEL 34:31 NIV

◆ ◆ ◆

For several decades after the end of the Revolutionary War, many Americans celebrated a day of thanksgiving. The date of this celebration depended on, among other things, which state you lived in. But on December 26, 1941, President Franklin D. Roosevelt signed a joint resolution of Congress establishing the fourth Thursday in November as the national Thanksgiving Day.

For the Christian, Thanksgiving should be more than a gathering of family for a huge feast—and a few football games. It should be a day that reminds him to express his gratitude for God's blessings, favor, and protection.

Today's verse, though it was written hundreds of years before Jesus came to earth, is a reminder of the most important thing for which we can give thanks every day. It shows us how much God, the heavenly Shepherd, values His people and how committed He is to caring for them.

As you offer thanks to God today and every day, why not start with, "Thank You, Lord, that You are my God!"

Loving heavenly Father, thank You for being my God and for caring for me in every way. May You always bring me back to You when I wander even the shortest distance from You.

WISDOM FROM HEAVEN

But the wisdom that comes from heaven is first of all pure;
then peace-loving, considerate, submissive, full of mercy
and good fruit, impartial and sincere. Peacemakers who
sow in peace reap a harvest of righteousness.
JAMES 3:17–18 NIV

◆━━━━━◆━━━━━◆

In today's scripture passage, the apostle James makes a stark contrast between godly wisdom, which he calls "wisdom that comes from heaven," and worldly wisdom, which he calls "earthly, unspiritual, demonic" (James 3:15 NIV).

This wisdom from above produces results very similar to what the apostle Paul called the "fruit of the Spirit": "But the fruit of the Spirit is love, joy, peace, forbearance, kindness, goodness, faithfulness, gentleness and self-control. Against such things there is no law" (Galatians 5:22–23 NIV).

James says that wisdom from heaven is marked by peacefulness, gentleness, consideration for the good of others, and mercy. It is pure in its motivation and filled with love for God and for others.

You'll find yourself living unshakably as you grow and mature in wisdom from heaven. You can start today by asking God to give you the kind of wisdom that helps you to live in a way that glorifies Him, brings you closer to Him, and helps you be a blessing to those He has placed in your life.

Lord, the wisdom that comes from You is far and away
higher and better than the world's wisdom. May I live
unshakably in Your wisdom today and every day.

SUBMIT YOUR PLANS TO GOD

Now listen, you who say, "Today or tomorrow we will go to this or that city, spend a year there, carry on business and make money." Why, you do not even know what will happen tomorrow. What is your life? You are a mist that appears for a little while and then vanishes.

JAMES 4:13–14 NIV

◆━━━━◆━━━━◆

Nowhere in the Bible are you discouraged from planning for the future. But God's written Word includes many passages encouraging Christian men to submit all their planning to God. For example, King Solomon wrote, "Commit to the LORD whatever you do, and he will establish your plans" (Proverbs 16:3 NIV).

In today's scripture passage, the apostle James gave a New Testament voice to Solomon's words. James wanted to remind his readers that they should always make plans with an eye toward their own limitations (you can't know what will happen beyond today) and toward the will of God (who knows all things—even what will happen in the future).

That's why the apostle followed today's scripture passage with this sound advice: "Instead, you ought to say, 'If it is the Lord's will, we will live and do this or that' " (James 4:15 NIV).

Father in heaven, help me always to remember that my life here on earth is fleeting compared with eternity. Remind me that only You know what will happen in my life beyond this very moment.

WATCH AND LISTEN

He said to me, "Son of man, watch and listen. Pay close attention to everything I show you. You have been brought here so I can show you many things. Then you will return to the people of Israel and tell them everything you have seen."
EZEKIEL 40:4 NLT

◆――――◆――――◆

The apostle Peter once wrote this about preparation: "Always be prepared to give an answer to everyone who asks you to give the reason for the hope that you have" (1 Peter 3:15 NIV).

That's great advice, but you might be asking, "How can I prepare myself to tell others about Jesus?" Ezekiel provides a good clue. Before an angel of the Lord showed the prophet a vision of the rebuilt temple in Jerusalem, he told Ezekiel to pay close attention to what he was about to see and hear— and then tell the people of Israel everything he had seen and heard.

Obviously, Ezekiel needed to pay close attention to what God would show him and tell him. In the same way, you should commit yourself to paying close attention to what God teaches you in your times of prayer and Bible reading. When you do that, you'll be prepared when you meet someone who needs to hear about Jesus.

Lord Jesus, help me to watch and listen as You show me Your truths in the Bible. Teach me and prepare me to share my faith with those who need You.

A GOOD REPUTATION

A good name is more desirable than great riches;
to be esteemed is better than silver or gold.
PROVERBS 22:1 NIV

I t's probably safe to say that you can think of examples of men who have accomplished great things—and made huge amounts of money—but who didn't have the best of reputations when it came to their personal behavior. In the worlds of athletics, business, entertainment, and more, many men have sacrificed their good names as they achieved great success.

Today's scripture verse indicates it's never a good idea to pursue worldly riches at the expense of a good reputation. In fact, it says that having a good name is better than having all the riches in the world while being saddled with a bad reputation

Being unshakable in your life of faith means zealously guarding your reputation. And zealously guarding your reputation means being unshakably committed to living, speaking, and thinking in ways that glorify God. Doing those things doesn't guarantee that everyone will think and speak well of you. But it will ensure that no one will have a legitimate reason to look down on you for anything you've said or done.

Lord, I want to have a good reputation in all my dealings and relationships.
But more than that, I want to be worthy of that good reputation.
Build in me good character so that others will see You in me.

AN AMAZING MIRACLE

For you have been born again, but not to a life that will
quickly end. Your new life will last forever because
it comes from the eternal, living word of God.
1 PETER 1:23 NLT

✦

While He was on earth, Jesus performed some amazing miracles through the power of God. He walked on water, calmed storms just by speaking to them, raised people from the dead, and healed the sick and disabled. But His greatest miracles were yet to come—and they're still happening today.

Have you ever thought of someone being "born again" as a miracle? If not, then consider this: When someone comes to faith in Jesus, what was once dead is made alive—alive *forever*. That's God miraculously doing what no man could ever do on his own. And it's what happened to you when you turned to God and accepted His free gift of eternal life through Jesus Christ.

Just as you could never make yourself right with God through your own works of righteousness, you can never repay Him for the miracle of eternal life. What you can do, however, is express your gratitude through speaking words of praise and gratitude and living in a way that glorifies Him.

Father, knowing that I will live forever with You in heaven
thrills me and encourages me to live an unshakable life of faith
for as long as I'm here on earth. Thank You!

GOD'S SPECIAL POSSESSION

But you are a chosen people, a royal priesthood, a holy nation,
God's special possession, that you may declare the praises of him
who called you out of darkness into his wonderful light.
1 PETER 2:9 NIV

◆ ◆ ◆

As you read through the Old Testament, you see the account of God's chosen nation—Israel—and how the Israelites so often turned away from the God who loved them. But you also read about how God never stopped loving His wayward people. For example, He said, "When Israel was a child, I loved him, and out of Egypt I called my son" (Hosea 11:1 NIV).

God wanted His people to understand how special they were to Him. And He wants you to know how valuable you are to Him today.

Today's scripture verse tells you how special and important you—and every other Christian—are to God. But your specialness isn't based on who you are or what you've done. It's based solely on the fact that you are His "special possession" whom He so lovingly called "out of darkness into his wonderful light."

Knowing that you are God's special possession can help you to live unshakably for Him—today and every day.

Heavenly Father, thank You for calling me Your "special possession." I know
there is nothing special about me except that You have brought me out of
darkness and into the light through Jesus' sacrifice on the cross.

WELL DONE

*What kind of glory [is there in it] if, when you do wrong
and are punished for it, you take it patiently? But if you bear
patiently with suffering [which results] when you do right and
that is undeserved, it is acceptable and pleasing to God.*

1 Peter 2:20 AMPC

◆——◆——◆

Imagine you're eight years old and you do something your mom told you not to do. You get in trouble and spend some quality moments in time-out. Would anyone call you brave? Would people say you did the right thing by doing the wrong thing? Would your grandchildren years later call you a hero?

This is likely a story you wouldn't share—except in pointing out what *not* to do. You've lived through course corrections in life and you'll probably live through them again.

But what about those times when you suffer for doing the right thing? History often celebrates those kinds of stories, but living through them is no fun.

God knows of your unshakable moments when you suffer for taking a stand. He notices when no one else will. He's the One who can tell you, "Well done."

Father, if I suffer negative consequences for breaking Your law, then I am no different than anyone else. If I suffer for doing the right thing, that's when I see proof that I am following where You're leading me.

A RESPECTFUL CHALLENGE

*Daniel resolved that he would not defile himself with the king's food,
or with the wine that he drank. Therefore he asked the chief of
the eunuchs to allow him not to defile himself.*

DANIEL 1:8 ESV

D aniel likely wasn't even twenty years of age when he was taken prisoner
and carted off to Babylon. That's part of what makes his step into the
unshaken so impressive. He respectfully challenged the order of the vanquishing
king, who wanted some of his prisoners to eat a rich and expensive diet. It
sounded generous and welcoming, but Daniel knew God's menu for His
people, and the food the king offered didn't line up with what God approved.

Has it become easy for you to match your decisions with the cultural
environment in which you find yourself? Have the opinions of others become
more important than God's rules? Have you sacrificed God's best in an effort
to avoid confrontation?

You can take a step in an unshaken direction by pre-deciding how you
will respond in situations where your values are challenged. If you determine
your actions ahead of time, your final choice will reflect God's heart.

*God, I don't have to be a man who makes continual mistakes in order to learn
that following You is a good choice. I can start early and stay close to You.
I don't have to be old to be wise. I don't have to sin to know it's a bad choice.*

NO FRESH REBELLION

Be sober, be vigilant; because your adversary the devil, as a roaring lion,
walketh about, seeking whom he may devour. . . . But the God of all grace,
who hath called us unto his eternal glory by Christ Jesus, after that ye have
suffered a while, make you perfect, stablish, strengthen, settle you.
1 Peter 5:8, 10 kjv

❖

Take the attacks of the devil seriously. Stand guard. God's adversary is scheming. He waits for an opportunity to pounce. He's hungry for fresh rebellion. He thinks he can find that in you. But will you cooperate? If so, why?

God's plan is different. He sent you a personal invitation with eternal benefits. He said the devil would be an effective hunter, and He said you would endure suffering. But the unshakable will find new strength and profound peace in Jesus. In Him is a great place to be.

This life you lead doesn't place God last on the list. The key to standing in a shaken world is knowing who you stand for and why you choose to obey Him and believing that what He promised is exactly what He will deliver.

Father, You've done everything necessary to give me life and to rescue me
from sin, but I can choose to reject or follow. As I follow You, make me
new as I walk through the struggle that leads me home.

DISSECTING GOD'S WORD

My son, give me your heart and let your eyes delight in my ways.
PROVERBS 23:26 NIV

◆━━━━━◆━━━━━◆

Remember back in school when your science teacher said it was time to go through the dissection portion of class? Often the unfortunate subject was a frog, but it might have been a different creature. The dissection elicited repulsed looks from some class members, but you learned there was more to a frog than warts and skin.

You can do that with God's Word. Let's do this first dissection together.

King Solomon wrote Proverbs 23:26. It's possible he wrote it from his own wisdom and for his own son. It's also possible it was presented as a word from God for His people.

My son: This refers to a younger family member who has much to learn.

Give me your heart: The decision to accept instruction should not be coerced.

Let your eyes delight in my ways: The older and wiser knows more than the younger and inexperienced. This is not only a teachable moment but something that can and should be looked forward to.

Delight in God's ways—stand unshakable.

God, I could live detached from You. I could live like an outcast from Your family and find Your ways laughable. But that's not how You want me to act. That's not how You want me to live. Help me delight in Your ways.

FOOLISH AND SHAKEN

*So they brought in the gold goblets that had been taken from the temple
of God in Jerusalem, and the king and his nobles, his wives and his
concubines drank from them. As they drank the wine, they praised
the gods of gold and silver, of bronze, iron, wood and stone.*
DANIEL 5:3–4 NIV

❖ ◆ ❖

Sometimes being shaken begins with thinking you *can't* be shaken. It may
come after a personal victory and usually involves believing you're skilled
enough and strong enough to manage a crisis without help. It is believing
you're wise—but ultimately acting foolishly.

Belshazzar was a king who believed that no nation was stronger than
his, that no one had a greater chance of winning a war, and that no one could
defeat him or stop his plans. He hadn't met God. . .and he needed to.

The king took holy objects that had been in God's temple and used them
to throw a party. Those vessels were supposed to be returned to the temple,
not used for a party. The king assumed he was stronger and wiser. *He wasn't.*

You will always be shaken when you assume you might know more than
God—about anything.

*Father, place a fence across the path to arrogance. Keep me from believing
that I know more than You. Place stop signs on the way to pride.
Keep me focused on You and the plans You have for me.*

PEOPLE ARE STUBBORN

*The Lord isn't really being slow about his promise, as some
people think. No, he is being patient for your sake. He does not
want anyone to be destroyed, but wants everyone to repent.*

2 PETER 3:9 NLT

❖

People's sin doesn't cause God to shake, quiver, or worry. He gave us a choice, and He knew that every person who ever lives would disobey Him. He could say, "Enough is enough!" and destroy everything. He could make people obey every law He spoke. Yet God chooses to love, forgive, accept, and offer new life. His plan is to give everyone the greatest chance to live unshaken.

God is patient because people are stubborn. While many people refuse His offer, He still extends life and hope. Jesus has promised to return—*and He will*—but there are still people who need to hear His story, experience His love, and follow His plan.

God has every reason to destroy, but for now He waits. He wants to see Christians live their faith boldly and share His story of rescue faithfully. . .while He waits patiently so that more people have the chance to become part of His family.

*God, thanks for being patient with me. Help me be patient with others.
Let me not think of Your return as being late but rather see Your patience
as a sign of Your grace. You are not slow, but I can be impatient.*

NO GUESSES OR LIES

Don't talk about your neighbors behind their backs—
no slander or gossip, please.
PROVERBS 24:28 MSG

H ave you ever wondered why it's so easy to talk about other people when they aren't around? You can say what you think and there's no one to defend the other person. You could be totally wrong, but when you say what you think, there will probably be someone who takes *what you imagine* as truth. But when you don't know if something is true, then you shouldn't share it as if it is.

Slander is saying something about someone you *know* is not true, and gossip is sharing something you're not sure is true. Both are signs of weakness that show that you didn't have the boldness to seek the truth before sharing something that could be a lie. *Love doesn't do that.*

Being unshakable means always telling the truth. Gossip and slander are not only guesses or lies, but they try to minimize others and elevate the status of the one sharing the stories.

Love puts a blanket over gossip because it is more interested in helping others than pointing out faults that may not even be true.

Father, help me to hold my tongue when I'm tempted to speak ill of another person. When I do speak, let my words always be truthful and loving.

THE INDICATOR

I set my face to the Lord God to seek Him by prayer
and supplications, with fasting and sackcloth and ashes.
DANIEL 9:3 AMPC

◆ ◆ ◆

Daniel knew that the prophecies speaking of the length of the Babylonian captivity meant that the people who had been captives for nearly seventy years would one day go home. He had been a captive himself and longed for his people to go home. Daniel took the time to pray, speaking of the day his people would go free. His prayer was engaging—a powerful example of a prayer of the unshaken.

At the end of the prayer? God was ready to let Daniel see what would happen in the future. God wanted Daniel to write down what he saw for others to read. What Daniel saw was very different from anything he had seen before. Daniel was ready, and God shared what the prophet never could have known on his own.

You might not hear from God directly, but prayer is an indicator that you take your relationship with Him seriously, that you're learning to be bold in approaching Him with respect, and that you believe He has the ability to answer your prayer.

God, there's so much I don't know and so much You can teach me.
If You're willing, I'm ready to listen. Help me learn what I can
at this stage in my faith walk. Then teach me more.

CHOOSE LOVE

*This is the message that you have heard from
the beginning, that we should love one another.*
1 JOHN 3:11 ESV

Unshaken people know they're loved, and they love other people. Love dislodges fear and sends it packing. God has done that for you so you can do it for other people. The love you share should shine a bright light on the God who loved enough to rescue every willing person.

God the Father and Jesus the Son would both emphasize love as the primary command and greatest relationship tool the world can ever know. This love isn't a *feeling* first. It involves *doing*. It's giving something to someone who may not deserve it but who needs it more than most. It comes from a heart that longs to see others through the eyes of the God who created them and His Son who died for them. They're precious in His sight and should be precious to you too.

Love is for the messy, the left behind, and those whom society has labeled misfits. It honors the outcast because God came to save everyone—*including the outcast*.

God created you to be bold enough to choose love over anything else.

*Father, You make a big deal about showing love to others. This love is a
blend of kindness and compassion that pays attention to the soul behind the
skin tone, the heart behind the street address, and the life behind the pain.*

GHOST TOWN

He that hath no rule over his own spirit is like a
city that is broken down, and without walls.
PROVERBS 25:28 KJV

◆———————◆———————◆

If you expect to live whatever way you want after accepting Jesus' offer of rescue, then you need to read the verse above at least one more time. You might *want* to live unshaken, but when you refuse to follow God on an adventure that includes denying self, loving others, and giving help when help is needed, then your spirit exists in an environment that Proverbs 25:28 describes as a run-down city with no walls. It's a ghost town. It's ancient ruins. It's a story told in hushed tones.

If you're the mayor of a personal ghost town with a desolate spirit, then maybe you've decided you don't need to repair what has been broken. Or you might encounter others who are in this place of personal ruin.

When you find yourself shaken, you will need God's help. Often He chooses to bring someone who is currently unshaken to help you through a season when you have given up on yourself. And sometimes you'll need to be this kind of friend yourself.

God, You don't experience the desolation of the shaken, but You know how to fix it. You must feel sad when I allow my spirit to continue on in a broken state. Help me care enough to seek You for the repairs my life may need.

RETROFITTED JAWS

"Let us acknowledge the LORD; let us press on to acknowledge him.
As surely as the sun rises, he will appear; he will come to us like
the winter rains, like the spring rains that water the earth."
HOSEA 6:3 NIV

This is a brilliant verse tucked into a story of how God corrected His people following their prolonged rebellion. Every sin you could name was being committed by people who took God for granted and felt as if following was optional and obeying was a suggestion.

This verse can provide great encouragement to those who need new shoes to walk in God's direction, a new mind to remember His plan, and a new heart that stores His wisdom.

Following the Lord once again would take commitment. Those who had walked away would need to return. People who had stopped honoring God would need to retrofit their jaws to move their mouth in worship.

Maybe this kind of recommitment is just what you need. If not today, then sometime in the past or in the future when the embers of love and hope run cold.

When you are intentional about acknowledging God, then He returns with a refreshing spiritual rain that allows growth to resume.

Father, You are God. If I haven't recognized You as the greatest who ever will be, please help my mouth form the words that acknowledge that fact. Help my heart mean it. Bring me back to the place where You restore. I need You.

TRUTH AND FAITHFULNESS

*It has given me great joy to find some of your children walking
in the truth, just as the Father commanded us.*

2 JOHN 1:4 NIV

You can read about a lot of people in the Old Testament who didn't follow God faithfully. It seems as if you can't go more than a chapter or two without reading about an unfaithful king, a rebellious people, or a God-inspired course correction. At the same time, though, you can read about faithful followers in the Old Testament and New Testament alike.

Tucked away in the New Testament book of 2 John is a verse that indicates that some followers of Jesus encouraged the apostle John by walking in the truth in a world with no shortage of lies.

This is important because God can take a small group of unshaken followers and ignite a flame that blazes far beyond their reach. Because God leads, He loves to see people follow Him. Even when His followers seem few, God can use their lives to introduce those who seek to a God who can be found.

God can redeem people, forgive their sins, and give them purpose. The world could use more examples of those who are faithful and unshaken.

---

*God, this isn't a time for me to be sleepy. Give me the courage to rise
to the occasion and share Your love. I don't want to be afraid or give up.
May it be said at the end of my life that I was faithful—to You.*

HYPOCRISY

*People may cover their hatred with pleasant words, but they're
deceiving you. They pretend to be kind, but don't believe them.
Their hearts are full of many evils. While their hatred may be
concealed by trickery, their wrongdoing will be exposed in public.*
PROVERBS 26:24–26 NLT

◆────◆────◆

Standing unshaken means turning your back on hypocrisy. You come to
God as a hypocrite, but then He works to remove the hypocrisy. God
doesn't want you to put a mask on hatred when hatred exists. He doesn't
want His family to just appear kind when their preference is really rudeness.
Looking like God does not require a degree in acting.

In your interactions with others, you may be tempted to give a godly-
sounding response if it benefits you—even when you don't really believe what
you're saying. But such a response is deceptive.

Hypocrisy is dangerous because while you say one thing, people will detect
something else in you—and they may even call you out for your dishonesty.

God has given you a soul and He's given you a story. Share the real you
and allow that unique story to mean more than any story you wish were true
about you.

*Father, I was honest when I said I needed rescue, but it can be easy to
think I need to brag about how faithful and trustworthy I am. Help me
speak truth about how I'm doing in my relationship with You. I don't
want to conceal bad behavior. I want to live honestly as I seek You.*

GENERATIONAL STORIES TO SHARE

Attention, elder statesmen! Listen closely, everyone, whoever and wherever you are! Have you ever heard of anything like this? Has anything like this ever happened before—ever? Make sure you tell your children, and your children tell their children, and their children their children. Don't let this message die out.

JOEL 1:2–3 MSG

◆   ◆   ◆

Because God can take bad situations and ultimately cause good to prevail, even the bad stories that were touched by His grace can and should be shared.

God started talking to the oldest men first and said that the history they were living was to be shared with all future generations. Many had lived through a dark moment in history. The stories they shared could betray the struggle with trust they once faced. Some had not followed God and then lived through difficult times as a result. Who wants to share these kinds of stories? Remember—God had touched this story, so sharing it was important.

The cautionary tale of your own sin, the story of God's faithfulness, and the message given to a people who would be restored are all stories worth sharing. Don't let the message die out.

God, there are stories I don't want to tell because they prove I have been shaken. But some of those same stories can make You famous to people I talk to. Help those who hear my stories to recall Your goodness, faithfulness, and love—not my bad decision-making, faithlessness, and jealousy.

THE BLESSING STORY

Blessed (happy, to be envied) is the man who reads aloud [in the assemblies] the word of this prophecy; and blessed (happy, to be envied) are those who hear [it read] and who keep themselves true to the things which are written in it [heeding them and laying them to heart], for the time [for them to be fulfilled] is near.

REVELATION 1:3 AMPC

◆ ◆ ◆

Shaken people don't want to admit their sin, and they certainly don't want to talk about truths that frighten them. Yet what might cause fear in the book of Revelation should instill a sense of hope instead. Unshaken people recognize the difference between fear and hope, and it changes their response.

Revelation describes the chaos and pain of earth's last days. When earth is the only home you've known, thinking it will come to an end can be frightening. The easiest choice is to avoid the subject altogether. But right at the beginning of the book, you are told that's a bad idea.

If you take a step further, you learn that those who hear the story will be blessed. One more step? Those who set themselves apart to be faithful to God's final story will be blessed.

Father, the best part of Your final story is not that this current world will pass away, but that a new life in Your presence will begin. This final story is a blessing to those who read it, hear it, and pay attention to what ultimately is great news.

THE PURSUIT OF JUSTICE

Evil men do not understand justice, but those who seek
the LORD understand it completely.
PROVERBS 28:5 ESV

◆——————◆——————◆

E vil men could be described as those who selfishly choose their own way
and don't care about the needs of others around them. They see injustice,
but it's not an issue as long as it doesn't affect them. These people are as prone
to being shaken as anyone—and they often have a secret fear that they have
made the wrong choice when it comes to God.

Those who seek the Lord, in contrast, see injustice and want to help in
ways that go beyond sympathy. Justice is God's best for people, but injustice
denies God's best from extending to certain people. Evil men are comfortable
with injustice. God seekers should not be.

You might have a tendency to dismiss injustice as something people deserve
for all kinds of reasons. You could say, "What can you expect? You know where
they come from." Prejudice can pronounce a difference between what is just
and unjust in a way that God never intended. But those who seek the Lord
not only understand justice but understand that it should be for everyone.

God, I should want justice for everyone. The oppression of others
should move me to action. Yet sometimes I'm more concerned about
justice for me and forget that others need it too. Give me a heart
large enough to care for everyone—because You created everyone.

PASSION IN THE PURSUIT

Be watchful, and strengthen the things which remain, that are ready to die:
for I have not found thy works perfect before God.
REVELATION 3:2 KJV

◆━━━◆━━━◆

Today's verse was a wake-up call for the church in Sardis. The people had played the hypocrite by acting the part of faithful followers, but they couldn't recognize that their faith was on life support. They started their journey with God but abandoned it for something less amazing. Jesus was telling them that they were shaken, scattered, and existing without really living.

This verse has been applicable to Christians down through the centuries. The shaken want to please God, but they also want to do their own thing. They begin to look at their faith as something they can check off their to-do list, but there are so many other things they want to do. They set aside their faith walk for whatever seems shiny and new. They might even see their choices as God blessing them with things they enjoy. They are playacting—and don't realize that's what they're doing. Yet when their actions are matched against God's commands, they are shown to be lacking.

You don't have to settle for a halfhearted walk with no passion in the pursuit. Don't follow at a distance. Get close to the Father, choose authenticity, and love honesty.

Father, give me a life that follows Your lead, does what You love, and adjusts to Your plan. Help me stand unshaken, honest, and willing.

THE GOD WHO. . .

[God said,] "I will restore David's fallen shelter—I will repair its broken walls and restore its ruins—and will rebuild it as it used to be."
AMOS 9:11 NIV

◆―――◆―――◆

Today's scripture uses three related words: *repair*, *restore*, *rebuild*. In this Old Testament setting, God was pointing to an even more powerful and unshakable future. God was going to bring redemption and rebirth to those who responded to Him.

God will prove to you over and over again that He is completely unshakable. Pay attention long enough and you can say, "God has never let me down." And that knowledge can move you from shakable to unshaken.

When you want to be unflinching, trust will be important. Trust God, and your own opinions will not waver as much as they used to. Why? Because the God who repairs, restores, rebuilds, redeems, and instigates rebirth changes those who respond.

God can make something new from an old life. He takes what's broken and, like a master potter, makes the unusable useful. This is good news that strengthens weak hearts, expands limited thinking, and renews a right spirit in those who trust Him.

―――――――――――――

God, sometimes I just need to be reminded that You have done so much for me. I don't restore myself—You do. I don't redeem my life—You do. I don't build a future—You do. You are beyond awesome.

THE RECIPIENT

Then I looked and heard the voice of many angels, numbering thousands upon thousands, and ten thousand times ten thousand. They encircled the throne and the living creatures and the elders. In a loud voice they were saying: "Worthy is the Lamb, who was slain, to receive power and wealth and wisdom and strength and honor and glory and praise!"

REVELATION 5:11–12 NIV

Angels have often been thought of as God's messengers. They brought Mary news about Jesus and came to many other people whose stories are recorded in scripture. Angels could do their job because they are unshaken.

It's unclear if angels knew that Jesus would die for the sins of humanity. They must have struggled to manage their thoughts when Jesus took His last breath from the cross, but when John experienced a vision of heaven, he witnessed many thousands of angels worshipping Jesus. They were unshaken when they recalled what Jesus did. He was a lamb slain for humanity's sin. He is worthy to take hold of power and strength. He is the recipient of honor, glory, and blessings.

No conditions. No exclusions. No disclaimers.

Father, You are unshaken, Jesus is unshaken, and the angels send the message that I should be unshaken. Tens of thousands of angels showed great trust in Your Son. Help me to be a participant in their worship. Help me to honor You, give glory to Your Son, and bless Your Spirit who works in my life.

COMPARE, CONTRAST, CONSIDER

Mockers can get a whole town agitated,
but the wise will calm anger.
Proverbs 29:8 nlt

◆———————◆———————◆

U ncontrolled anger is a mark of the shaken. Shaken people inspire other people to shake and then quake. Worry and anxiety are the great stealers of confidence. Believing you're a victim creates trust issues.

Today's verse points out two things to do (actually, *not* do) when you want to become or stay unshaken: don't mock and don't stay angry. If you haven't used the word *mock* in a while, here's a short list of related words: belittle, despise, disdain, insult, ridicule, scorn, trash-talk. This kind of personality "can get a whole town agitated."

The unshaken, on the other hand, will speak words that calm and offer hope. It's the difference between shaken and unshaken, between a setting sun and a rising sun, between a fearful outlook and a confident outlook.

You have come face-to-face with examples of what an unshaken life looks like, and you've also met people who are easily shaken. Compare their stories. Contrast the outcomes. Consider why it is important to God that His people live unshaken.

God, it's easy to think I've been dealt a bad hand. I can even come to
the place where I think You don't care. At these times I may be tempted
to mock You, insult others, and cause trouble. Help me to remember that
allowing myself to become shaken will always affect others.

SHAKEN BUT TRANSFORMED

"I will transform the battered into a company of the elite. I will make a strong nation out of the long lost, a showcase exhibit of God's rule in action, as I rule from Mount Zion, from here to eternity."
MICAH 4:7 MSG

G rab hold of good news. Keep it close. Brand it on your heart's doorframe. God was speaking to the shaken of Israel when He promised to "transform the battered" and "make a strong nation out of the long lost." Now, replace "battered" and "long lost" with *shaken.* There's a connection to be made.

This is a fantastic reminder that being shaken doesn't have to be a permanent condition and that being lost can mean being found. God can showcase your transformation. Sometimes the person who needs to be convinced that God can do this is *you.*

Come to Jesus quaking and discover an unshakable future. You can even learn how to live through a shaking and still stand unshakable. It's not a trick—it's trust. Not in yourself, but in God.

Be transformed. Change your thinking. Gain freedom from all that shakes your world. Contentment arrives with this new unshakable life.

Father, I'm intrigued by the idea that You can transform the timid. I love the notion that You can reclaim the prodigal, bring him home, and give him strength. This is me at times. I know I can be transformed to be unshaken, but I also know I'm not able to do it on my own.

UNSHAKEN THROUGH CHALLENGES

Where there is no vision [no redemptive revelation of God], the people perish; but he who keeps the law [of God, which includes that of man]—blessed (happy, fortunate, and enviable) is he.

PROVERBS 29:18 AMPC

W ithout God, your best life is like trying to read a map in the dark or walking with your eyes closed. Your best life without God is completely unproductive. You can't even tell if your step has led you anywhere important.

People wither in darkness. They shake like a leaf in winter winds. They want to make up their mind but can't decide. They have no confidence, joy, or contentment. They dream of something different—something better and hope-filled. God makes the offer that fulfills their deepest desires.

To live unshaken is a blessing. It starts and ends with following God into the great unknown. The reason you worry is because you wonder how to handle the challenges that will certainly come your way. But to live unshaken means you stand with the God who can lead you through those challenges—the ones you can't handle and the ones you don't know how to handle.

God, if I think about all the things that could happen to me— and then believe those things will happen—then I'm about as far away from unshaken as I can be. Give me Your vision for my future and allow me to really live.

BIG ENOUGH FOR ALL

"Look among the nations, and see; wonder and be astounded. For I am doing a work in your days that you would not believe if told."

Habakkuk 1:5 esv

◆━━━◆━━━◆

You can become stronger in your faith just by paying attention to what God is doing. Miracles are happening—even if those miracles are for others. The problem is that you can become jealous of the good things happening for other people and then become shaken.

God isn't working just in your life. He didn't send His Son only for you. His love is big enough for all. That's why it makes sense to be joyful with those who are happy and to express sorrow with those who are sad.

You weren't created to be selfish, petty, or envious. Your world can, and should, expand to include others. That means more than just saying other people are important; it's allowing your heart to connect with their world. Feel what they feel, walk a mile in their shoes, and discover a changed heart. This heart doesn't compare miracles and it doesn't feel shortchanged.

God is at work in this world, and especially at this time of year we celebrate this good news.

Father, when I'm guilty of not paying attention to what You do in my world, give me eyes to see the miracles around me and thank You for them. May they leave me both astounded and unshaken.

SAVED

*I will undo all that afflict thee: and I will save her that halteth,
and gather her that was driven out; and I will get them praise
and fame in every land where they have been put to shame.*
ZEPHANIAH 3:19 KJV

◆————◆————◆

I t's Christmas Eve and this verse may seem out of place on this day. Where
are the bells, lights, and trees? Where's the caroling, the shopping, the
merriment?

You might be tempted to read something into this verse that isn't there.
God was telling the people of Judah that He could turn things around for
them. Sin wasn't the end of their story. It certainly wasn't the end of His love
for them. Even then He had a plan that is described in places like the first
two chapters of Luke (a great read on a day like today).

The verse above hints at a time when God would save and gather and
make His name famous. That would come with Jesus. God would replace His
people's tendency to quiver with bold confidence in His glorious name. The
shepherds were told not to fear or be terrified but rather to take hope because
a baby was born. That baby would grow up to become the Savior of the world.

---

*God, the unshaken can rejoice because the peace on earth the
angels spoke of was a gift Jesus left for me and all who follow.
That's how You undo all that afflicts me.*

ALL NATIONS

*"This is what the Lord Almighty says: 'In a little while I will once
more shake the heavens and the earth, the sea and the dry land.
I will shake all nations, and what is desired by all nations will come,
and I will fill this house with glory,' says the Lord Almighty."*
HAGGAI 2:6–7 NIV

G ood news. There was a time when God did the shaking so you would never need to be shaken.

The prophet Haggai recorded God's words: "I will once more shake the heavens and the earth." Then, "I will shake all nations." Followed by, "What is desired by all nations will come." The One who came? *Jesus.*

He shook the preconceived ideas people had about Him. He shook the rug of humanity and exposed sin and the need for a Savior. He shook all nations so all people would seek rescue.

The answer to all the shaking arrived as a baby who grew and learned to speak. He used His words to point people to God's answer to their great need. He died and rose again so people could be left unshaken.

*Father, thank You for making it possible for me to stand with
You unshaken by Your purposeful shaking. Thank You for Your Son
and for the rescue He brought. I celebrate His birth. You shook
all nations, and people from all nations noticed You.*

A NEW TAKE ON OLD PRAISE

"Great and marvelous are your deeds, Lord God Almighty. Just and true are your ways, King of the nations. Who will not fear you, Lord, and bring glory to your name? For you alone are holy. All nations will come and worship before you, for your righteous acts have been revealed."

REVELATION 15:3–4 NIV

What a wondrous display of marvelous works! You are God. You are Lord. You are mighty. Your ways are fair. Your words are true. Your kingdom is filled with saints. Who can refuse to respect You? Who would refuse to think of Your name as glorious? Holy describes You. People from all places will not hold back their hearts from worshipping You. Your final decisions are perfect, and You fulfill Your every promise."

This is a new take on an old praise from the passage above. Did it make you feel fresh strength? Did your spirit gain courage? Honoring God has this effect on you. It brings clarity to your thinking and purpose to your choices.

The shaken become settled when they pray and praise God. The alternative is to fixate on problems while overlooking His solutions.

God, I can't understand why You love me the way You do, but I'm grateful. I can't explain why You forgive, but I need it. I can't list all the ways my life is better for knowing You, but I will tell others about a good God with good plans for shaken people.

THE CONCEPT OF INTRODUCTION

*"Do not oppress widows, orphans, foreigners, and the poor.
And do not scheme against each other."*
ZECHARIAH 7:10 NLT

◆━━━━◆━━━━◆

You've been shaken, but you don't have to shake other people. God doesn't want you to. He asks you to bear with others in the shaken state they're in—not to add to their struggle.

Shaken people shake others. That's unhelpful; it doesn't show love. Passing your insecurities on to another leaves you both in a pit. Don't make things difficult for those who have no one to help. Don't make plots that are designed to hurt others. *Just don't.*

So what's the opposite response? Introduce others to the concept of being unshaken. Help however you can, knowing that everyone struggles. Love them and leave your insecurities with God. If you see someone in a self-imposed pit, lend a hand and help them out. Pray before you ever criticize. Ask God to help you help others.

Today's verse came from the same writer who penned, "Judge fairly, and show mercy and kindness to one another" (verse 9 NLT). This is living unshaken. It's just what God has always wanted for you.

Father, sometimes when I want to feel better about myself, I feel like I have to criticize someone else for being less than perfect. But because everyone sins, no one is worse than me—and no one is better. Help me to be kind instead of critical. People need You—and they need to see kindness in me.

SOUL-SEEPING ACID

If you're dumb enough to call attention to yourself by offending people and making rude gestures, don't be surprised if someone bloodies your nose. Churned milk turns into butter; riled emotions turn into fist fights.
PROVERBS 30:32–33 MSG

◆　◆　◆

The word *violence* conjures up all kinds of images. Your mind is probably entertaining some right now. There's no need for examples because your perspective delivers a more personal experience.

Violence is a natural reaction to a personal shaking. Someone says or does something that seems disrespectful or rude. It hurts and you respond in anger, yet a defensive response can open the door to violence—and violence gives birth to more violence. A rude response generally results in someone willing to play the rudeness game.

Staying away from the bait of violence requires pure bravery. Taking the bait causes an acid to seep into your soul that screams, "Injustice!" and believes that you cannot overlook a wrong. It believes that forgiveness doesn't hold someone accountable. This bitterness often leads to violence.

Stop offending people and stop letting their offenses toward you dictate your response. Resolve to be unflinching.

God, Your Son could have been justified in exhibiting violence against those who came to destroy His life, yet some of His final words were "Forgive them." Help me to remember that a violent response exposes a wound in my soul or in the souls of others. Bring healing, Lord. Everyone could use that.

FIND HIM HERE

*I will pour out upon the house of David and upon the inhabitants of
Jerusalem the Spirit of grace or unmerited favor and supplication.
And they shall look [earnestly] upon Me Whom they have pierced,
and they shall mourn for Him as one mourns for his only son, and shall
be in bitterness for Him as one who is in bitterness for his firstborn.*
ZECHARIAH 12:10 AMPC

The story of Jesus is mentioned in multiple Old Testament passages. Even details of His death are visible to those who pay attention to the pages of scripture. You'll find Him here. The Son of God hanging on a tree, pierced, wounded, and mourned. *But He didn't stay dead.*

What was God's plan? He would pour out a grace and favor you can't earn and a reconciliation between you and Him you could never pay for. The story of Jesus and the redemption He brings is a story for the shaken. Every word is true.

God knows that every person who will ever live will be shaken, which is why He offers the remedy. He is the source of strength, power, bravery, courage, and steady endurance.

*Father, I know what it's like to be afraid, even when I refuse to admit it.
You know what it is to grieve over loss. When I'm shaken, You're steadfast
and You invite me to learn from You. I accept Your invitation.*

SALVATION, GLORY, POWER

"Hallelujah! Salvation and glory and power belong to our God."
REVELATION 19:1 ESV

◆────────◆────────◆

A re you surprised to encounter words of praise in a book of the Bible dedicated to describing the end of time? This wasn't the first instance of praise. It wouldn't be the last. But it said something about the God who creates and chooses to re-create. He has established an earth and a new earth, humans and new-life Christians, an old covenant and then a new.

Look at today's scripture verse and locate three words that point to a strengthening God: *salvation*, *glory*, *power*. God is something you aren't. Somehow, He sees the shaken and loves them enough to show compassion, offer forgiveness, and instill confidence in those who can see only trouble and don't realize that trouble has been overcome by Jesus, the very One who was sent with salvation, glory, and power.

This book includes 365 daily writings about God's unshakable nature, about the shaken nature of mankind, and about the remedy for timidity. Revisit these words anytime, and if you took advantage of the Bible reading program, then you encountered full stories of how God deals with the fearful. It involves changed hearts, minds, and spirits.

God, never let me forget that I serve You. In Your name are salvation, glory, and power. Your love for me makes those attributes an ally in my struggles. I need the kind of help only You offer.

BE THAT ONE

Behold, I will send my messenger, and he shall prepare the
way before me: and the LORD, whom ye seek, shall suddenly
come to his temple, even the messenger of the covenant, whom
ye delight in: behold, he shall come, saith the LORD of hosts.

MALACHI 3:1 KJV

◆———◆———◆

I f this book were a vaccination offered to provide protection against fear and indecision, then consider this New Year's Eve thought a booster shot.

Today's verse points directly to John the Baptist, who would be sent to prepare the way for the coming of Jesus. John would proclaim the arrival of Jesus, and this servant's life would be marked by hardship and persecution. Yet John would live unshaken.

How did he do that? The answer might be that he discovered his purpose and used it to give him energy to live beyond the trouble he encountered. Unshaken people understand that God has a good plan and wants to give opportunities to those who are ready for fresh adventure in the new year. Is that you?

Father, there's living and dying. You're there for all the in
between and beyond. John knew that You're not fragile. He knew
You would rescue. He knew his job was to make Jesus known.
Give me the heart of the unshaken. It takes a purpose that's bigger
than my own. May I be willing to let You work in me.

CONTRIBUTORS

Ed Cyzewski is the author of *Reconnect: Spiritual Restoration from Digital Distraction* and *Flee, Be Silent, Pray: Ancient Prayers for Anxious Christians* and is the coauthor of *Unfollowers: Unlikely Lessons on Faith from Those Who Doubted Jesus*. He writes about prayer and imperfectly following Jesus at www.edcyzewski.com. Ed's devotions are found in January and August.

Glenn A. Hascall is an accomplished writer with credits in more than a hundred books. He is a broadcast veteran and voice actor and is actively involved in writing and producing audio drama. Glenn's devotions are found in February and December.

Matt Koceich is a husband, father, and public school teacher. Matt and his family live in Texas. Matt's devotions appear in April.

Josh Mosey is a writer and conference speaker with fifteen years of experience in retail book selling. Josh is the author of *Dare to Be a Brave Boy, 3-Minute Prayers for Boys,* and *Men of Valor* (with Bob Evenhouse), among other titles. He lives in Michigan with his amazing family. Josh's devotions appear in March and October.

David Sanford's speaking engagements have ranged everywhere from the Billy Graham Center at the Cove (NC) to UC Berkeley (CA). His book and Bible projects have been published by Zondervan, Tyndale House, Thomas Nelson, Doubleday, and Amazon. His professional biography is summarized at www.linkedin.com/in/drsanford. His personal biography features his wife of thirty-eight years, Renée, their five children, and their fourteen grandchildren (including one in heaven). David's devotions are found in May.

Tracy M. Sumner is a freelance author, writer, and editor in Beaverton, Oregon. An avid outdoorsman, he enjoys fly-fishing on world-class Oregon waters. Tracy's devotions are found in June and November.

Marty Trammell, PhD, is a Professor of English/Communication at Corban University and the Worship and Family Pastor at Perrydale Church in Amity, Oregon. Marty has coauthored *Love Lock*, *Spiritual Fitness*, *Redeeming Relationships*, and *Communication Matters*. Marty codirects redeemingrelationships.com and enjoys hiking, camping, and leading couples' retreats with his wife, Linda. Marty's devotions are found in September.

Lee Warren is published in such varied venues as *Discipleship Journal*, *Sports Spectrum*, Yahoo! Sports, Crosswalk.com, and ChristianityToday.com. He is also the author of *Finishing Well: Living with the End in Mind* (a devotional), as well as several Christmas novellas in the Mercy Inn series. Lee makes his home in Omaha, Nebraska. Lee's devotions are found in July.

READ THRU THE BIBLE IN A YEAR PLAN

1-Jan	Gen. 1-2	Matt. 1	Ps. 1
2-Jan	Gen. 3-4	Matt. 2	Ps. 2
3-Jan	Gen. 5-7	Matt. 3	Ps. 3
4-Jan	Gen. 8-10	Matt. 4	Ps. 4
5-Jan	Gen. 11-13	Matt. 5:1-20	Ps. 5
6-Jan	Gen. 14-16	Matt. 5:21-48	Ps. 6
7-Jan	Gen. 17-18	Matt. 6:1-18	Ps. 7
8-Jan	Gen. 19-20	Matt. 6:19-34	Ps. 8
9-Jan	Gen. 21-23	Matt. 7:1-11	Ps. 9:1-8
10-Jan	Gen. 24	Matt. 7:12-29	Ps. 9:9-20
11-Jan	Gen. 25-26	Matt. 8:1-17	Ps. 10:1-11
12-Jan	Gen. 27:1-28:9	Matt. 8:18-34	Ps. 10:12-18
13-Jan	Gen. 28:10-29:35	Matt. 9	Ps. 11
14-Jan	Gen. 30:1-31:21	Matt. 10:1-15	Ps. 12
15-Jan	Gen. 31:22-32:21	Matt. 10:16-36	Ps. 13
16-Jan	Gen. 32:22-34:31	Matt. 10:37-11:6	Ps. 14
17-Jan	Gen. 35-36	Matt. 11:7-24	Ps. 15
18-Jan	Gen. 37-38	Matt. 11:25-30	Ps. 16
19-Jan	Gen. 39-40	Matt. 12:1-29	Ps. 17
20-Jan	Gen. 41	Matt. 12:30-50	Ps. 18:1-15
21-Jan	Gen. 42-43	Matt. 13:1-9	Ps. 18:16-29
22-Jan	Gen. 44-45	Matt. 13:10-23	Ps. 18:30-50
23-Jan	Gen. 46:1-47:26	Matt. 13:24-43	Ps. 19
24-Jan	Gen. 47:27-49:28	Matt. 13:44-58	Ps. 20
25-Jan	Gen. 49:29-Exod. 1:22	Matt. 14	Ps. 21
26-Jan	Exod. 2-3	Matt. 15:1-28	Ps. 22:1-21
27-Jan	Exod. 4:1-5:21	Matt. 15:29-16:12	Ps. 22:22-31
28-Jan	Exod. 5:22-7:24	Matt. 16:13-28	Ps. 23
29-Jan	Exod. 7:25-9:35	Matt. 17:1-9	Ps. 24
30-Jan	Exod. 10-11	Matt. 17:10-27	Ps. 25
31-Jan	Exod. 12	Matt. 18:1-20	Ps. 26
1-Feb	Exod. 13-14	Matt. 18:21-35	Ps. 27
2-Feb	Exod. 15-16	Matt. 19:1-15	Ps. 28
3-Feb	Exod. 17-19	Matt. 19:16-30	Ps. 29
4-Feb	Exod. 20-21	Matt. 20:1-19	Ps. 30
5-Feb	Exod. 22-23	Matt. 20:20-34	Ps. 31:1-8
6-Feb	Exod. 24-25	Matt. 21:1-27	Ps. 31:9-18
7-Feb	Exod 26-27	Matt. 21:28-46	Ps. 31:19-24
8-Feb	Exod. 28	Matt. 22	Ps. 32
9-Feb	Exod. 29	Matt. 23:1-36	Ps. 33:1-12
10-Feb	Exod. 30-31	Matt. 23:37-24:28	Ps. 33:13-22
11-Feb	Exod. 32-33	Matt. 24:29-51	Ps. 34:1-7
12-Feb	Exod. 34:1-35:29	Matt. 25:1-13	Ps. 34:8-22
13-Feb	Exod. 35:30-37:29	Matt. 25:14-30	Ps. 35:1-8
14-Feb	Exod. 38-39	Matt. 25:31-46	Ps. 35:9-17
15-Feb	Exod. 40	Matt. 26:1-35	Ps. 35:18-28
16-Feb	Lev. 1-3	Matt. 26:36-68	Ps. 36:1-6
17-Feb	Lev. 4:1-5:13	Matt. 26:69-27:26	Ps. 36:7-12
18-Feb	Lev. 5:14 -7:21	Matt. 27:27-50	Ps. 37:1-6
19-Feb	Lev. 7:22-8:36	Matt. 27:51-66	Ps. 37:7-26
20-Feb	Lev. 9-10	Matt. 28	Ps. 37:27-40
21-Feb	Lev. 11-12	Mark 1:1-28	Ps. 38
22-Feb	Lev. 13	Mark 1:29-39	Ps. 39
23-Feb	Lev. 14	Mark 1:40-2:12	Ps. 40:1-8
24-Feb	Lev. 15	Mark 2:13-3:35	Ps. 40:9-17
25-Feb	Lev. 16-17	Mark 4:1-20	Ps. 41:1-4
26-Feb	Lev. 18-19	Mark 4:21-41	Ps. 41:5-13
27-Feb	Lev. 20	Mark 5	Ps. 42-43
28-Feb	Lev. 21-22	Mark 6:1-13	Ps. 44

1-Mar	Lev. 23-24	Mark 6:14-29	Ps. 45:1-5
2-Mar	Lev. 25	Mark 6:30-56	Ps. 45:6-12
3-Mar	Lev. 26	Mark 7	Ps. 45:13-17
4-Mar	Lev. 27	Mark 8	Ps. 46
5-Mar	Num. 1-2	Mark 9:1-13	Ps. 47
6-Mar	Num. 3	Mark 9:14-50	Ps. 48:1-8
7-Mar	Num. 4	Mark 10:1-34	Ps. 48:9-14
8-Mar	Num. 5:1-6:21	Mark 10:35-52	Ps. 49:1-9
9-Mar	Num. 6:22-7:47	Mark 11	Ps. 49:10-20
10-Mar	Num. 7:48-8:4	Mark 12:1-27	Ps. 50:1-15
11-Mar	Num. 8:5-9:23	Mark 12:28-44	Ps. 50:16-23
12-Mar	Num. 10-11	Mark 13:1-8	Ps. 51:1-9
13-Mar	Num. 12-13	Mark 13:9-37	Ps. 51:10-19
14-Mar	Num. 14	Mark 14:1-31	Ps. 52
15-Mar	Num. 15	Mark 14:32-72	Ps. 53
16-Mar	Num. 16	Mark 15:1-32	Ps. 54
17-Mar	Num. 17-18	Mark 15:33-47	Ps. 55
18-Mar	Num. 19-20	Mark 16	Ps. 56:1-7
19-Mar	Num. 21:1-22:20	Luke 1:1-25	Ps. 56:8-13
20-Mar	Num. 22:21-23:30	Luke 1:26-56	Ps. 57
21-Mar	Num. 24-25	Luke 1:57-2:20	Ps. 58
22-Mar	Num. 26:1-27:11	Luke 2:21-38	Ps. 59:1-8
23-Mar	Num. 27:12-29:11	Luke 2:39-52	Ps. 59:9-17
24-Mar	Num. 29:12-30:16	Luke 3	Ps. 60:1-5
25-Mar	Num. 31	Luke 4	Ps. 60:6-12
26-Mar	Num. 32-33	Luke 5:1-16	Ps. 61
27-Mar	Num. 34-36	Luke 5:17-32	Ps. 62:1-6
28-Mar	Deut. 1:1-2:25	Luke 5:33-6:11	Ps. 62:7-12
29-Mar	Deut. 2:26-4:14	Luke 6:12-35	Ps. 63:1-5
30-Mar	Deut. 4:15-5:22	Luke 6:36-49	Ps. 63:6-11
31-Mar	Deut. 5:23-7:26	Luke 7:1-17	Ps. 64:1-5
1-Apr	Deut. 8-9	Luke 7:18-35	Ps. 64:6-10
2-Apr	Deut. 10-11	Luke 7:36-8:3	Ps. 65:1-8
3-Apr	Deut. 12-13	Luke 8:4-21	Ps. 65:9-13
4-Apr	Deut. 14:1-16:8	Luke 8:22-39	Ps. 66:1-7
5-Apr	Deut. 16:9-18:22	Luke 8:40-56	Ps. 66:8-15
6-Apr	Deut. 19:1-21:9	Luke 9:1-22	Ps. 66:16-20
7-Apr	Deut. 21:10-23:8	Luke 9:23-42	Ps. 67
8-Apr	Deut. 23:9-25:19	Luke 9:43-62	Ps. 68:1-6
9-Apr	Deut. 26:1-28:14	Luke 10:1-20	Ps. 68:7-14
10-Apr	Deut. 28:15-68	Luke 10:21-37	Ps. 68:15-19
11-Apr	Deut. 29-30	Luke 10:38-11:23	Ps. 68:20-27
12-Apr	Deut. 31:1-32:22	Luke 11:24-36	Ps. 68:28-35
13-Apr	Deut. 32:23-33:29	Luke 11:37-54	Ps. 69:1-9
14-Apr	Deut. 34-Josh. 2	Luke 12:1-15	Ps. 69:10-17
15-Apr	Josh. 3:1-5:12	Luke 12:16-40	Ps. 69:18-28
16-Apr	Josh. 5:13-7:26	Luke 12:41-48	Ps. 69:29-36
17-Apr	Josh. 8-9	Luke 12:49-59	Ps. 70
18-Apr	Josh. 10:1-11:15	Luke 13:1-21	Ps. 71:1-6
19-Apr	Josh. 11:16-13:33	Luke 13:22-35	Ps. 71:7-16
20-Apr	Josh. 14-16	Luke 14:1-15	Ps. 71:17-21
21-Apr	Josh. 17:1-19:16	Luke 14:16-35	Ps. 71:22-24
22-Apr	Josh. 19:17-21:42	Luke 15:1-10	Ps. 72:1-11
23-Apr	Josh. 21:43-22:34	Luke 15:11-32	Ps. 72:12-20
24-Apr	Josh. 23-24	Luke 16:1-18	Ps. 73:1-9
25-Apr	Judg. 1-2	Luke 16:19-17:10	Ps. 73:10-20
26-Apr	Judg. 3-4	Luke 17:11-37	Ps. 73:21-28
27-Apr	Judg. 5:1-6:24	Luke 18:1-17	Ps. 74:1-3
28-Apr	Judg. 6:25-7:25	Luke 18:18-43	Ps. 74:4-11
29-Apr	Judg. 8:1-9:23	Luke 19:1-28	Ps. 74:12-17
30-Apr	Judg. 9:24-10:18	Luke 19:29-48	Ps. 74:18-23
1-May	Judg. 11:1-12:7	Luke 20:1-26	Ps. 75:1-7
2-May	Judg. 12:8-14:20	Luke 20:27-47	Ps. 75:8-10
3-May	Judg. 15-16	Luke 21:1-19	Ps. 76:1-7

11-Nov	Ezek. 11-12	Heb. 4:4-5:10	Prov. 17:6-12
12-Nov	Ezek. 13-14	Heb. 5:11-6:20	Prov. 17:13-22
13-Nov	Ezek. 15:1-16:43	Heb. 7:1-28	Prov. 17:23-28
14-Nov	Ezek. 16:44-17:24	Heb. 8:1-9:10	Prov. 18:1-7
15-Nov	Ezek. 18-19	Heb. 9:11-28	Prov. 18:8-17
16-Nov	Ezek. 20	Heb. 10:1-25	Prov. 18:18-24
17-Nov	Ezek. 21-22	Heb. 10:26-39	Prov. 19:1-8
18-Nov	Ezek. 23	Heb. 11:1-31	Prov. 19:9-14
19-Nov	Ezek. 24-26	Heb. 11:32-40	Prov. 19:15-21
20-Nov	Ezek. 27-28	Heb. 12:1-13	Prov. 19:22-29
21-Nov	Ezek. 29-30	Heb. 12:14-29	Prov. 20:1-18
22-Nov	Ezek. 31-32	Heb. 13	Prov. 20:19-24
23-Nov	Ezek. 33:1-34:10	Jas. 1	Prov. 20:25-30
24-Nov	Ezek. 34:11-36:15	Jas. 2	Prov. 21:1-8
25-Nov	Ezek. 36:16-37:28	Jas. 3	Prov. 21:9-18
26-Nov	Ezek. 38-39	Jas. 4:1-5:6	Prov. 21:19-24
27-Nov	Ezek. 40	Jas. 5:7-20	Prov. 21:25-31
28-Nov	Ezek. 41:1-43:12	1 Pet. 1:1-12	Prov. 22:1-9
29-Nov	Ezek. 43:13-44:31	1 Pet. 1:13-2:3	Prov. 22:10-23
30-Nov	Ezek. 45-46	1 Pet. 2:4-17	Prov. 22:24-29
1-Dec	Ezek. 47-48	1 Pet. 2:18-3:7	Prov. 23:1-9
2-Dec	Dan. 1:1-2:23	1 Pet. 3:8-4:19	Prov. 23:10-16
3-Dec	Dan. 2:24-3:30	1 Pet. 5	Prov. 23:17-25
4-Dec	Dan. 4	2 Pet. 1	Prov. 23:26-35
5-Dec	Dan. 5	2 Pet. 2	Prov. 24:1-18
6-Dec	Dan. 6:1-7:14	2 Pet. 3	Prov. 24:19-27
7-Dec	Dan. 7:15-8:27	1 John 1:1-2:17	Prov. 24:28-34
8-Dec	Dan. 9-10	1 John 2:18-29	Prov. 25:1-12
9-Dec	Dan. 11-12	1 John 3:1-12	Prov. 25:13-17
10-Dec	Hos. 1-3	1 John 3:13-4:16	Prov. 25:18-28
11-Dec	Hos. 4-6	1 John 4:17-5:21	Prov. 26:1-16
12-Dec	Hos. 7-10	2 John	Prov. 26:17-21
13-Dec	Hos. 11-14	3 John	Prov. 26:22-27:9
14-Dec	Joel 1:1-2:17	Jude	Prov. 27:10-17
15-Dec	Joel 2:18-3:21	Rev. 1:1-2:11	Prov. 27:18-27
16-Dec	Amos 1:1-4:5	Rev. 2:12-29	Prov. 28:1-8
17-Dec	Amos 4:6-6:14	Rev. 3	Prov. 28:9-16
18-Dec	Amos 7-9	Rev. 4:1-5:5	Prov. 28:17-24
19-Dec	Obad-Jonah	Rev. 5:6-14	Prov. 28:25-28
20-Dec	Mic. 1:1-4:5	Rev. 6:1-7:8	Prov. 29:1-8
21-Dec	Mic. 4:6-7:20	Rev. 7:9-8:13	Prov. 29:9-14
22-Dec	Nah. 1-3	Rev. 9-10	Prov. 29:15-23
23-Dec	Hab. 1-3	Rev. 11	Prov. 29:24-27
24-Dec	Zeph. 1-3	Rev. 12	Prov. 30:1-6
25-Dec	Hag. 1-2	Rev. 13:1-14:13	Prov. 30:7-16
26-Dec	Zech. 1-4	Rev. 14:14-16:3	Prov. 30:17-20
27-Dec	Zech. 5-8	Rev. 16:4-21	Prov. 30:21-28
28-Dec	Zech. 9-11	Rev. 17:1-18:8	Prov. 30:29-33
29-Dec	Zech. 12-14	Rev. 18:9-24	Prov. 31:1-9
30-Dec	Mal. 1-2	Rev. 19-20	Prov. 31:10-17
31-Dec	Mal. 3-4	Rev. 21-22	Prov. 31:18-31

SCRIPTURE INDEX